THE AMERICA'S CUP 1851~1987
SAILING FOR SUPREMACY

LESTER-TOWNSEND PUBLISHING, SYDNEY

THE AMERICA'S CUP
1851~1987
SAILING FOR SUPREMACY

By Gary Lester and Richard Sleeman
LESTER-TOWNSEND PUBLISHING, SYDNEY

Published in 1986 by LESTER-TOWNSEND PUBLISHING PTY. LTD.,
SYDNEY. P.O. Box 39, Broadway, Sydney. NSW. 2007.
Copyright c Gary Lester 1986
ISBN 0 949853 08 9

Typeset by Photoset Computer Services
Printed and bound by Tien Wah Press, Singapore
All rights reserved. No part of this publication may be reproduced, stored in a retrieval system, or transmitted, in any form or by any means, electronic, mechanical, photocopying, recording or otherwise, without the prior permission of the publisher.

Designed by JIM HATTERSLEY
Book Editor — JAMES MURRAY
Editorial consultant — DAVID HOOLEY
Artist sketches — TERRY WELSBY

National Panasonic (Australia) Pty Limited.
Official supplier of video and colour television
for the America's Cup Defence 1987

CONTENTS

Foreword — 8
1851 The One Hundred Guinea Cup — 10
America
1870 The First Challenge — 20
Magic — Cambria
1871 Two Defenders, One Victory — 30
Columbia/Sappho — Livonia
1876 Canada's First Bid For Cup — 38
Madeleine — Countess of Dufferin
1881 Iron Lady Sinks Challenge — 44
Mischief — Atalanta
1885 NYYC Welcomes British Return — 50
Puritan — Genesta
1886 Home Comforts Sink Galatea — 58
Mayflower — Galatea
1887 Cup Loses Veil of Cordiality — 66
Volunteer — Thistle
1893 Australia Considers The Cup — 72
Vigilant — Valkyrie II
1895 Accused Americans Win Again — 78
Defender — Valkyrie III
1899 The Lipton Era Begins — 86
Columbia — Shamrock
1901 Back With Another Shamrock — 94
Columbia — Shamrock II
1903 Superboat Retains Cup — 100
Reliance — Shamrock III
1920 Closest Challenge Yet — 108
Resolute — Shamrock IV

1930	**Lipton's Fabulous Era Over**	**116**
	Enterprise — Shamrock V	
1934	**Sopwith Almost Takes Cup**	**124**
	Rainbow — Endeavour	
1937	**End of the J Class**	**132**
	Ranger — Endeavour II	
1958	**New Columbia, Same Result**	**140**
	Columbia — Sceptre	
1962	**The First Aussie Challenge**	**146**
	Weatherly — Gretel	
1964	**No Sovereign Rule for British**	**156**
	Constellation — Sovereign	
1967	**Intrepid Destroys the Dame**	**162**
	Intrepid — Dame Pattie	
1970	**Faster Aussies Beaten Again**	**172**
	Intrepid — Gretel II	
1974	**Courageous Right to the End**	**182**
	Courageous — Southern Cross	
1977	**Cup Stays in New York**	**190**
	Courageous — Australia	
1980	**Freedom Wins, Loses a Race**	**200**
	Freedom — Australia	
1983	**They Said It Couldn't Be Done**	**210**
	Australia II — Liberty	
1987	**The Latest Challenge**	**225**

America's Cup Records — **237**

FOREWORD

THERE has been, perhaps, no greater moment in Australian sport than that historic day in Newport in 1983 when Australia II crossed the finish line ahead of Liberty.

That it had taken 132 years to wrest the Cup from the New York Yacht Club is in itself testimony to the significance of the moment.

It is therefore appropriate that two Australian authors should coincide the defence in Perth with a major publication on the Cup's history.

One might have felt that The America's Cup looked unattainable such was the consistency and thoroughness of the Americans.

Yet the yachtsmen of Australia did not allow such thinking to dampen their confidence.

We were in the forefront from the very first Australian challenge in 1962 when the Americans themselves acknowledged that Gretel was a faster boat than Weatherly.

Such were the performances of Australian yachtsmen in Newport that they never believed the Cup to be out of reach.

Of course, their confidence in their own ability was not mistaken. That historic day arrived and it will seem a little strange that the challenge is not being held in Newport, for so long the traditional venue, though no Australian is complaining I am sure.

What a history has been before us. In the 24 defences prior to 1983, the New York Yacht Club built up a wall of invincibility.

It did not appear to matter whether they were designing schooners and cutters from the early defences, the J-boats of the pre-Second World War era or the smaller, more streamlined 12-metre yachts of modern times, they were intense about their work.

This book, a marvellous compilation of facts, stories and famous photographs, recalls the fabulous history of The Cup.

The America's Cup has instilled a strong sense of pride and achievement in Australians, just as it must have meant so much to the British and others, particularly during the Sir Thomas Lipton era.

Sir Thomas, in five challenges with his Shamrocks, made The America's Cup immensely popular. The Cup enjoyed a significant growth during his challenges, just as they did when Australia first challenged in 1962.

The authors tell of the men who sailed for the Cup.......the famous helmsman and the owners who down through the ages made it all possible.

I was fortunate enough to have been a part of America's Cup history. It has in some ways been a part of my life — and still is.

This handsome and beautifully illustrated volume allows us to understand the full meaning of the Cup down through the ages to the present day.

I am honoured to have been asked to write this foreword. I am especially pleased that two professional writers such as Gary Lester and Richard Sleeman have taken so much time to research this most important part of sporting history.

This book will have a special place on my bookshelf. It is a well written documentation of America's Cup racing and I commend the authors and the publisher for their painstaking efforts.

Indeed, it is a book to be enjoyed by all.

Sir James Hardy K.T. O.B.E.

1851

The One Hundred Guinea Cup

America (New York Yacht Club) defeated fourteen English yachts around the Isle of Wight.

THE *America*, the 270 tons schooner described by the British as a "rakish, piratical-looking craft", was almost too fast for its own good. So overwhelmingly superior did it become against the British defenders in 1851 that the America's Cup, as we have come to know it, might have ended there and then on the waters of the Solent.

Britain at the time enjoyed the reign of a youthful Queen Victoria, and until the arrival of the *America*, the English yachtsmen enjoyed their reign on the ocean racing waves.

The British prided themselves on having the world's fastest pleasure vessels and they felt no threat in the invitation by English merchants to New York businessmen to send one of their famous New York harbour pilot-boats, renowned for their speed, across the Atlantic. The initial intention was to berth the pilot boat on the Thames and provide exhibitions of the boat's speed as part of the World Trade Exhibition, the first of the great expositions.

Back in New York, John C. Stevens, Commodore of the newly formed New York Yacht Club, decided against taking a pilot boat to England. Instead he formed a syndicate and built "the fastest yacht afloat." Stevens was even more convinced he had taken the right path when he received a further invitation from the Royal Yacht Squadron.

The Solent would be the destination and Commodore Stevens left no doubt in his reply that with his new yacht, *America*, he was more than interested in racing against Britain's best yachts.

Yachting had been an established sport in Britain for more than two centuries, most vessels owned and raced by the gentry, and a good deal of the racing conducted in the Solent, a treacherous piece of water yet the traditional sailing lane of English yachting. In America in 1850, yachting was comparatively new. Few men were rich enough to enjoy the sport. It was a time when the great West was unconquered and the people of America were looking for ways to make their fortunes. Sailing was the recreation of a select few.

The first attempt to form a sailing club was in 1835 when a few keen Boston merchants formed the Boston Yacht Club. It lasted just two years....until reformed many years later. The New York Yacht Club was six years old when the British invitation came. The club was formed on July 30, 1844 in the cabin of the *Gimcrack*, John C. Stevens' 25 ton schooner. The nine yacht owners present unanimously appointed Stevens the club's Commodore.

Twelve months later the club occupied its first club house, a modest building on Commodore Stevens' grounds, in Hoboken. The club's membership grew to 122 by 1846 and the yachts in its fleet numbered 12. By 1850, the club was established and its fleet had grown to include a number of sloops and schooners, many of them centreboarders, fast and manoeuvrable around the shoals of New York Harbour, but not fit for consistent ocean racing.

The British were aware that the club possessed several keel yachts, keel schooners, which were converted pilot-boats, and therefore reasonably fast ocean going vessels. The pilot boats were built for speed, after all, since success in business for their New York Harbour owners depended on how quickly they could get to an in-bound vessel waiting to be taken through the harbour shallows.

Stevens and his New York Yacht Club committee were not prepared to put America's yachting reputation, as new as it was, on the line with one of these converted yachts. The invitation demanded a new boat. The credit for the *America* goes to one man — George Steers, described as, "a genius who left a strong imprint on American shipping." Steers was already renowned for his ship designing capabilities, though he was not interested in designing the large commercial clippers

The America winning at Cowes. This lithograph by J. G. Dutton is taken from an on-the-spot sketch by artist Oswald W. Brierley.

and steamers. He felt more inspired designing and building smaller, faster vessels.

Stevens and George Schuyler, a foundation member of the New York Yacht Club and syndicate member of the new yacht, could not have found a more willing designer. The yacht was built at William H. Brown's New York shipbuilding yards and marked the dawning of a new era in ocean racing.

Steers' father, a shipwright, was born in Devon and went to the United States in 1819 where he worked in the Washington navy yard. George, the eldest of 13 children, was born one year later. By the age of 16, he had designed and built his first boat. However, in 1856, at the age of 36, just six years after building the *America*, George Steers died from injuries suffered when thrown from a carriage he was driving.

Stevens, the man most responsible for getting the *America* across the Atlantic, was from a family of some means. Along with his three brothers, and his father, Colonel John Stevens, he was deeply interested in inventions and the development of steam navigation.

With his brother Robert, John C. Stevens started the first day-line steamers between New York and Albany in 1827. Stevens introduced cricket to the United States and though a patron of art, he was no less interested in horse racing.

While the owners of the *America* believed they were getting the fastest boat afloat, her first trials were not encouraging. She was beaten by the *Maria*, owned by Commodore Stevens and designed by his brother, Robert Livingston Stevens. The *Maria* was almost unbeatable in calm waters. She was advanced for those times and it was claimed that she cost $100,000, more than three times the cost of the *Am-*

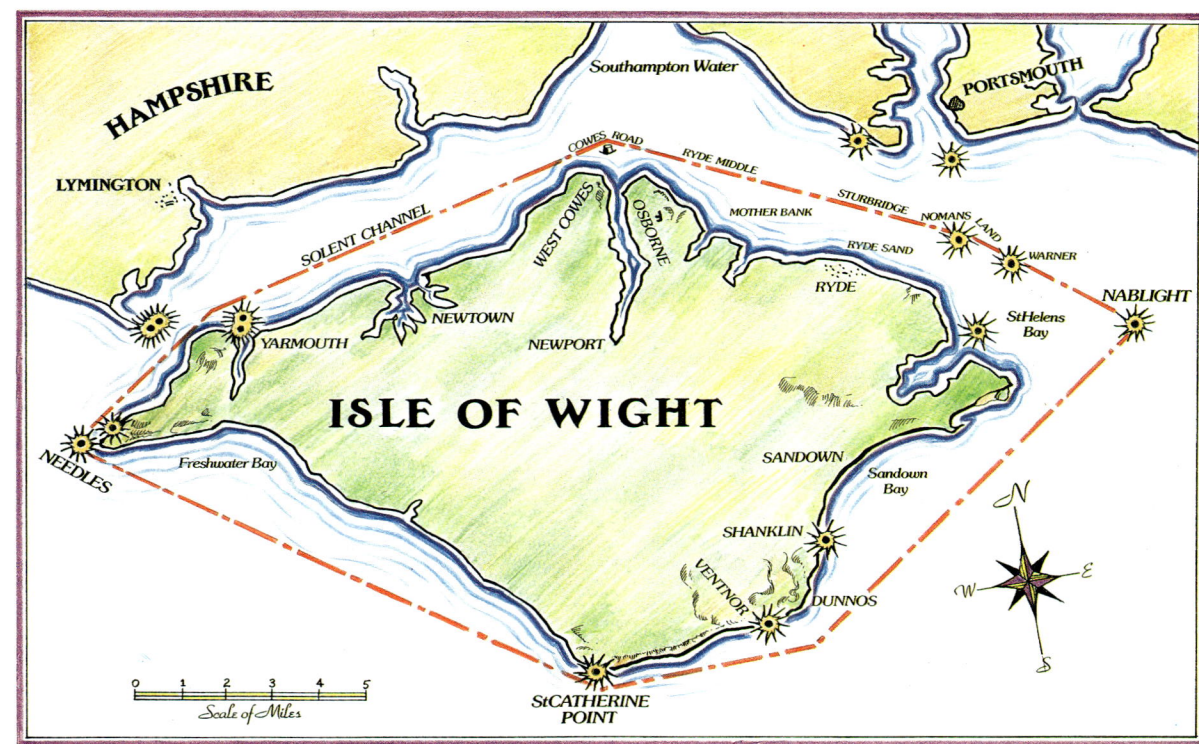
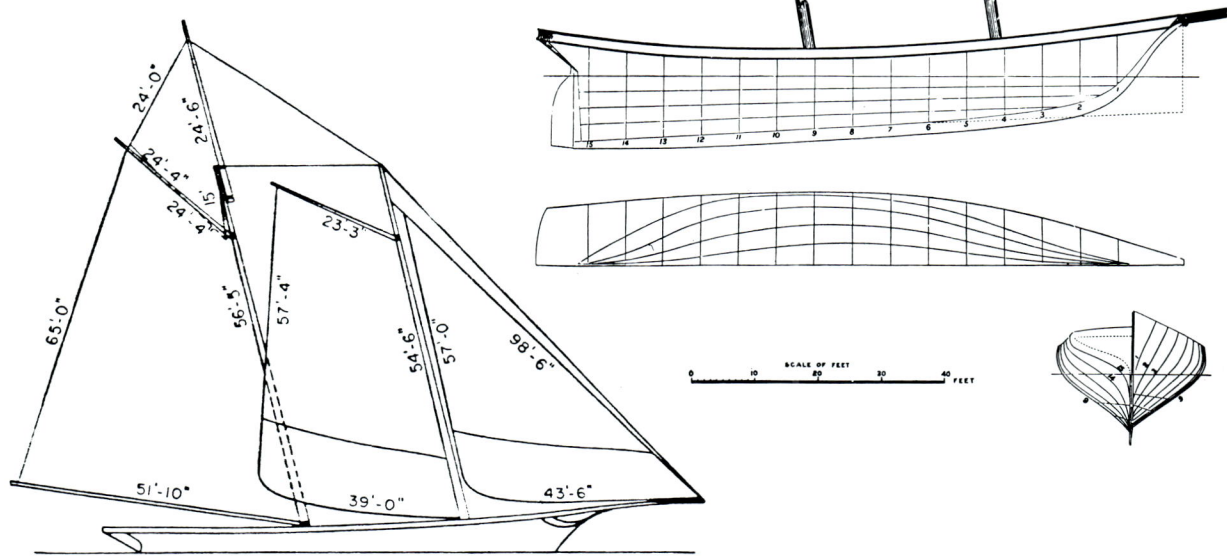

Left, Fred S. Cozzens' painting, The Early Races, Maria, America, Una Ray. Above (top), sketch of the course around the Isle of Wight; (bottom), scaled dimensions of America.

erica. Nevertheless, in heavy weather she was unlikely to beat the *America* or any of the other smart schooners of that time. She was lost at sea, with all hands in 1870, the year of the first challenge for what was to be The America's Cup.

The British were confident, even smug about the coming race, as can be seen in the invitation from the Earl of Wilton, Commodore of the Royal Yacht Squadron. Wilton wrote: "....I shall have great pleasure in extending to your countrymen any civility that lies in my power, and shall be very glad to avail myself of any improvements in shipbuilding that the industry and skill of your nation have enabled you to elaborate."

Stevens replied graciously, yet with a touch of gamesmanship, explaining that they expected, "the sound thrashing we are likely to get by venturing our longshore craft on your rough waters."

Like most yachts in history, the *America* was not ready on time. Instead she was delivered on June 18 — almost three months late — and sailed three days later for Le Havre on the other side of the Atlantic. She carried 13 on board — captain Dick Brown, Steers, the designer, and Nelson Comstock, as mate, among them. Stevens joined the crew in Le Havre, having crossed the Atlantic by steamer. The crossing of the *America* was made in seventeen and a half days — she would later become the first yacht to cross the Atlantic both ways.

Even as the *America* ventured across the Atlantic, Americans at home and abroad feared that American honour would be lost on the English seas. According to the *Lawson History of the America's Cup*, one American businessman in Le Havre told Commodore Stevens and fellow syndicate member, Colonel Hamilton: "The eyes of the world are on you; you

The America's Cup 1851-1987

will be beaten, and the country will be abused.......if you go and you are beaten, you had better not return to your country."

Stevens and Hamilton remained undaunted. They had no intention of turning back. The *America* sailed superbly across the Atlantic and gave the crew valuable time to sort out the teething troubles expected in any new yacht. After reaching Le Havre, the *America* was outfitted for racing. Her hull was painted black and she was fitted with new racing sails. The reason for rigging the yacht in a French port instead of in England was to deny the English too close a look at her before she began racing.

The secrecy about Ben Lexen's winged keel on *Australia II* can be seen to be part of a long tradition. So was betting among the yachting fraternity and the Americans were not keen to tip their hand. They considered there was money a-plenty to be made out of the trip and Commodore Stevens and his crew were determined, at least until this stage of the trip, not to show the British the speed of the *America* until the money was on.

The *America* left Le Havre for England on July 31, 1851, arriving in the Solent that night, becalmed some 10 kilometres off Cowes. With little wind to carry her and with fog moving in, she anchored to wait until morning. When the fog eventually lifted, Stevens and his crew found that an English cutter, *Laverock*, one of the latest and fastest of her class, had come out to greet them.

Laverock, it seemed, was anxious to test the *America*, and in taunting fashion, issued its own challenge. Stevens had the choice of "going slow" or taking up the unofficial challenge. Unable to contain himself, and prepared to cast aside his betting plans, he chose the latter.

Stevens described the scene of that morning later in a speech in New York: "The yachts and vessels in the harbour, the wharves and the windows of all the houses bordering on them were filled with spectators, watching with eager eyes the eventual trial. They saw we could not escape, for the *Laverock* stuck to us, sometimes lying-to and sometimes tacking round us, evidently showing that she had no intention of quitting us.......We got up our sails with heavy, heavy hearts; the wind had increased to a five-or six-knot breeze, and after waiting until we were ashamed to wait longer, we let her go about two hundred yards,

Left: The America after refurbishing "like a painted ship, upon a painted ocean." Above: The battered hull of America in dry dock ready for rebuilding.

and then started in her wake.

"......During the first five minutes not a sound was heard save, perhaps, the beating of our anxious hearts or the slight ripple upon her (the *America's*) swordlike stem. The captain was crouched down upon the floor of the cockpit, his seemingly unconscious hand upon the tiller, with his stern, unaltering gaze upon the vessel ahead. The men were motionless as statues, their eager eyes fastened upon the *Laverock* with a fixedness and intensity that seemed almost supernatural. The pencil of an artist might, perhaps, convey the expression, but no words can describe it. It could not and did not last long. We worked quickly and surely to windward of her wake. The crisis was past; and some deep-drawn sighs proved that the agony was over."

The *America* finished almost a kilometre ahead and news of her speed spread quickly through yachting circles. Yet not all contemporary writers were impressed, some finding weaknesses in her rakish look; others believed she should be carrying a fore-topmast to give her more speed; another claimed her hull was too low and yet another described her as a "big-boned skeleton."

The Times, London compared the consternation among British yachtsmen to "the appearance of a sparrowhawk on the horizon creates among a flock of woodpigeons and skylarks." Whatever the case, Stevens had not only lost his chance of making a considerable amount of money from side-bets, he had virtually scared off British yacht owners.

Stevens set about posting challenges, the first of these sent to the Royal Yacht Squadron after he and his crew had waited two days "for a proposal to race." He grew impatient at the delays. No apparent effort was made for a special race, nor did anyone appear to be prepared to offer a suitable trophy.

On August 8, the Royal Yacht Squadron invited Stevens to enter the *America* in a race "to be sailed for by vessels of all rigs and nations on the 13th instant." Although Stevens intended to enter the race, his reply did not reach the Royal Yacht Squadron in time.

Believing that a large stake would induce a number of offers, he challenged any British owner for any sum, "from one to ten thousand guineas", stipulating that the breeze should not be less than six-knots. While the British yachtsmen were staggered by the size of the offer, the Press looked unfavourably, and with some embarrassment on the fact that no local yachtsman had taken up the challenge of the American visitors.

According to *The Times*, London, "......the effect produced by her (the *America's*) apparition off West Cowes among yachtsmen seems to have been completely paralysing. She has flung down the gauntlet to England, Ireland and Scotland, and not one has been found there to take it up." *The Times* added in a later article, ".....if she be permitted to sail back to New York with her challenge unaccepted, and can nail up under it, as it is fastened on one of her beams, that no one dare touch it, then there will be some question as to the pith and courage of our men."

With British honour at stake, one yacht owner, Robert Stephenson found the courage to accept a match against the *America*, even though he knew full well that the *America* was superior to any local vessel. Stephenson agreed to race his 100 ton schooner *Titania* for 100 pounds, 20 miles from the Nab light and back. Although she was new, the *Titania* was not considered to be of champion class. Stephenson agreed to race the *America* more out of the need to uphold the reputation of British yachting than with any firm belief that he could beat the American yacht.

In the meantime, Stevens had entered the Royal Yacht Squadron Regatta to be sailed on August 22, six days before the match race with *Titania*. Stevens made it clear in his request to enter the Regatta that "should there be little or no wind on that day, this vessel will probably not sail."

The race was for boats of all sizes, sailed without time allowance around the Isle of Wight for a trophy valued at 100 guineas. The trophy became known as the One Hundred Guinea Cup, although its correct title was the Royal Squadron Cup, until it became more famously known as The America's Cup. Confusion continued in the following years where the trophy was consistently referred to as the Queen's Cup, which was a distinct and separate event to the Squadron Cup on the British racing calendar.

The trophy, itself, was an ornate silver pitcher, elaborately decorated with scrolls and shields, later to be filled with the dedication to the *America's* victory. Later winners were added after each defence. The Cup was made in London in 1851 and was 27 inches high and weighed 8½ pounds. It has no top or bottom, and to the chagrin of Stevens and his fellow

Below, the America under sail in the 1900s. Left, British yacht Volante, one of the smallest in the fleet to race America. She led early but was fouled and forced to withdraw.

owners — and the winners that followed — it is not fit for celebratory liquids.

Local knowledge of the winds and tidal conditions would be against the *America*. One report explained: "The course around the Isle of Wight is notoriously one of the most unfair to strangers......"

When the day dawned, a light north wind blew which later turned to the west, of sufficient strength to tempt Stevens to enter the race, which was to start from anchor with the cutters in the front line and schooners, including the *America*, in the second line.

The Royal Yacht Squadron waived a number of rules to allow the *America* to compete. They accepted that the *America* could withdraw if the wind did not exceed six knots, and they waived the condition that boats owned by more than one person were not eligible (the *America* had been barred from a previous regatta in England because of her syndicated ownership).

This was history in the making from the most humble of moments....just another race for the Royal Yacht Squadron Cup worth 100 guineas. The difference this time was the inclusion of an American visitor. Eighteen yachts entered, but three, the *Titania*, *Stella* and the *Fernande* did not start.

There was a certain eloquence about the reports of the day. The excitement generated by the race fairly radiated from the pages of *The Times*, London and the *Illustrated London News*. *The Times* correspondent recorded the moments leading to the start of the race; "A large portion of the peerage and gentry of the United Kingdom left their residences and fortook the sports of the moors to witness the struggle between

the yachtsmen of England, hitherto unmatched and unchallenged, and the Americans who had crossed the Atlantic to meet them. All the feelings of the vast population which swarms in our southern ports and firmly believes in 'Rule Britannia' as an article of national faith; all the prejudices of the wealthy aristocracy and gentry, who regarded the beautiful vessels in which they cruised about the Channel and visited the shores of the Mediterranean every summer as the perfection of naval architecture, were roused to the highest degree, and even the Queen of England did not deem the occasion unworthy of her presence.

"In memory of man, Cowes never presented such an appearance as upon last Friday. There must have been upwards of 100 yachts lying at anchor in the Roads; the beach was crowded from Egypt to the piers — and the esplanade in front of the club thronged with ladies and gentlemen, and with the people inland, who came over in shoals with wives, sons and daughters for the day.......Flags floated from the beautiful villas which stud the wooded coast.......The windows of the houses which command the harbour were filled from the parlour to the attic.....It was with the greatest difficulty the little town gave space enough to the multitudes that came from all quarters to witness an event so novel and so interesting, and the hotels were quite inadequate to meet the demands of their guests."

Cards containing the names and colours of the yachts, described the course as being "round the Isle of Wight." The printed program described it as being "round the Isle of Wight, inside No-man's buoy and Sandhead buoy, and outside the Nab."

The mist that hung over the fields and woods from sunrise lifted as start time neared and at 9.55 a.m. a preparatory gun was fired from the clubhouse battery. The day was decidedly warm and at 10 o'clock the starting gun was fired, the start described as being "effected splendidly, the yachts breaking away like a field of racehorses; the only laggard was the *America*."

The crew of the *America* were unable to raise the sails of their yacht because the wind had forced her to overrun her anchor. Unlike the other vessels, she had to wait until her anchor could be raised (at the sound of the starting gun) before her sails could be set.

Gipsey Queen, a 160 ton schooner, was the first away but by No-man's buoy, just an hour after the start, *Volante*, a 48 ton cutter, the second smallest yacht in the fleet, had, with the advantage of the light breezes, taken the lead. The *America* was in fifth place, exactly two minutes behind.

The patriotic and hopeful British rejoiced at the early news. They remained even more confident when not long after it was revealed that *Gipsey Queen* had regained the lead with the *America* still in her wake. However *The Times* yachting correspondent noted, "......but the nautical cognescenti shook their heads, and said the triumph would be shortlived......"

As the wind freshened, the *America* began to display her superiority, and the same correspondent recorded the scene on that historic day;

"....she (the *America*) 'walked along' past cutter and schooner, and, when off Brading had left every vessel in the squadron behind her — a mere ruck — with the exception of the *Volante*, which she overtook at 11.30, when she very quietly hauled down her jib, as much to say she would give her rivals every odds, and laid herself out for the race round the back of the island.......Now 'the Yankee' flew like the wind, leaping over, not against, the water, and increasing her distance from the *Gipsey Queen, Volante* and *Alarm* every instant. While the cutters were thrashing through the water, sending the spray over the bows, and the schooners were wet up to the foot of the foremast, the *America* was as dry as a bone. She had 21 persons on her deck, consisting of the owners, the crew, cook and steward, a Cowes pilot named Underwood, and some seamen who had been lent her from *Surprise*, a London-built schooner yacht."

Not all had gone smoothly for the *America*. Claims were made that three English yachts had fouled her as she endeavoured to pass them. Whenever the *America* attempted to pass, the yachts would cut in, or change course. The appointment of the pilot, Underwood was important, for the Americans had been warned to be wary of those offering their services. Underwood had been engaged by the American Consul in Southampton before the *America* arrived in Cowes and Commodore Stevens found him to be a man of integrity.

It was said of him, "too little credit has, as a rule, been accorded this pilot for his part in the famous race. He was, without knowing it, making history, for him to have done from motives of patriotism something less than his best would have been an easy matter."

From the moment the *America* rounded St Catherine Point, virtually south of Cowes on the other side of the island, the race was as good as over. The moderate south, south-west breeze carried her to the Needles on the west side with "the *Aurora* the last that kept her in sight, until, the weather thickening, even that small comfort was lost to her."

As the wind fell after passing the Needles, the *America* was passed by the royal yacht *Victoria and Albert* with Her Majesty on board. The *Aurora* was calculated as being "five or six miles astern." Yet Colonel Hamilton later gave this account of his anxiety;

"After we got round the Needles the wind died away and we were alarmed by the appearance of a small vessel, so light as to be pressed upon us by the gentle puffs which could hardly move the *America*, of 170 tons." Hamilton need not have worried for the small vessel was the royal yacht's tender, the *Fairy*, which was sent off to see which yachts were in sight while members of the royal party went ashore for a short break.

As evening fell, heavy clouds gathered in the northern sky and many of the thousands who had waited on the southern shoreline of West Cowes had gone. At 8.34 p.m., more than 10 hours after the race began, the *America* was greeted by the gun from the

Commodore John C. Stevens

flag-ship. According to the *Illustrated London News*, "*Aurora* was announced at 8h. 58m.; the *Bacchante* at 9h. 30.; the *Eclipse* at 9h. 45m.; the *Brilliant* at 1h. 20m. (Saturday morning). No account of the rest."

However *The Times*, gave the *America's* finishing time as 8.37 p.m. and *Aurora's* 8.54, just eight minutes behind. These times were later accepted as official, though many questioned *Aurora's* time since no one saw her finish and according to Commodore Stevens, "I could not learn correctly at what time, or in what order the others arrived."

The Times explained that *Aurora* "slipped up very rapidly after rounding the Needles in consequence of her light tonnage and breath of wind." Whatever the case, she was the best of the British, yet by some oversight, *Aurora's* name is the one that does not appear on the Cup.

The distance around the island was given as 53 nautical miles, although it was accepted that the yachts travelled 70 miles. Despite the ease of her victory, the *America* had to await the outcome of a protest before being awarded the race. Mr. G. H. Ackers, owner of *Brilliant*, the only three-masted schooner in the race, complained that the *America* had passed the Nab lightship on the inside and not on the outside as the English yachts had done.

Commodore Stevens argued that since he did not receive instructions on the manner of passing the lightship, and since he was not made aware of local rules, he had no way of knowing the correct procedure. The race committee accepted Stevens' explanation and awarded the Cup to the *America*.

One of the many stories that has lingered through the history of The America's Cup relates the conversation between Queen Victoria and her signalmaster, who, on peering across the watery expanse from the deck of the royal yacht, was asked by Her Majesty: "Which is first?"

"The *America*."

"Which is second?"

"Ah, your Majesty, there is no second."

The day after the victory, Queen Victoria went aboard the *America*, so impressed was she with the manner of the victory. That night a fireworks display lit up the foreshores of Cowes. Two days later, the *America* had been expected to enter the Queen's Cup, but Stevens did not start her because the breeze was less than six knots at race time. However, when the wind strengthened, the *America* went out an hour and a half after the yachts left Cowes and returned just minutes behind the winner, *Alarm*.

One wonders how yachting history would have been influenced had the *America* won two cups instead of one. Would it have lessened the significance of the Squadron Cup — later to become The America's Cup — and therefore rendered the trophy less important?

Less than a week later, Commodore Stevens kept his date with the *Titania* in a match race for 100 pounds on a course 20 miles to windward and return. Despite losing her fore gaff in the race, the *America* won by 52 minutes, her last race of the season.

The appearance of the *America* in English waters was a great cause for wonder by the locals and a good number of them believed the boat must have had a propeller. Colonel Hamilton related the story of the "sporting clergyman" who said: "I would not wager a guinea against the Yankee craft; but I would give a hundred to see her bottom." A remark which made the clergyman something of a prophet of the curiosity about *Australia II's* keel.

Hamilton also recalled the story of the Marquis of Anglesey, regarded as "the father of British yachting", who fought in the battle of Waterloo. Hamilton recalled: "......he came aboard the *America*; and after a salutation he went to the stern, leaned over so far that the commodore took hold of his leg to prevent him from going over — he was looking most eagerly for the propeller."

The race against the *Titania* was the last under the ownership of Stevens and his syndicate. They sold the *America* for 5000 pounds ($US25,000) to Lord John de Blaquiere, an officer in the Indian army. It was calculated that considering the cost of building her, the expense of racing and the amount of prize-money won, that Stevens and his co-owners would show a profit of $1,750.

The *America* had an immense impact on British yachting. The *America's* sails were made of cotton while the British used flax and it was pointed out that her foresail and mainsail were laced to the booms while the British set their sails loosely in the Dutch fashion.

Noted yachting expert, Captain A. J. Kenealy wrote: "The sailing of the *America* formed an important epoch in the yachting history of the world.......There is no doubt that the splendid American schooner did more to develop the art of yacht naval architecture than any other craft."

1870

The First Challenge

Magic (NYYC) defeated Cambria (Royal Thames Yacht Club) and 16 other yachts

COMMODORE John Stevens and his fellow owners felt immense pride in their achievement, even if they left the *America* behind. They had set off to face the might of British yachting with an untried boat, and returned unbeaten, and with the Royal Yacht Squadron Cup.

The syndicate owners took turns to look after the trophy, often displaying it on the dining room table during social gatherings, of which there were many among the wealthy, aristocratic classes of New York. Yachting then, as it is now, was a pastime of the rich. For six years the Cup played no further part in yachting history other than to be an object admired on social occasions.

Yachting was not exactly a day to day topic of conversation among the rank and file. According to *The New York Times* in 1851, "........the New York Yacht Club was looked upon, by the very few who were aware of its existence, as a drowsy, fossilized association of old fogies." Such a belief may have been born out of ignorance since the New York Yacht Club had only been formed in 1844 and was the exclusive domain of a rich minority. The extravagances of wealthy yachtsmen were of little importance to a populace increasingly interested in the search for gold, and for a country whose cry was "Go West, young man."

By the time of the first challenge for The America's Cup — 1870 — the transcontinental railroad would link the Atlantic and Pacific oceans for American travellers. The British were in no hurry for revenge. They accepted that Americans now ruled the ocean racing waves and so conclusive had the victory been that they were more intent on recasting and reviewing their yacht designs than on a re-match. Besides, to them, The Squadron Cup (some erroneously called it The Queen's Cup) was gone forever. No consideration was given at the time to offering the trophy for an international challenge.

History does not record exactly why the surviving owners of the trophy offered it to the New York Yacht Club as a perpetual challenge trophy open to all foreign nations. It is accepted, however, that one of the members, George L. Schuyler was responsible for implanting the idea in the minds of his co-owners.

Some of the original owners had died and Schuyler sensed that once all syndicate members had died, the Cup might eventually become a relic of the past, and placed, as sacrilegious as it may be to suggest, on the scrapheap. Perpetuation was better than a dusty attic. Their decision was to be one of, if not, the most significant gesture in yachting history.

On July 8, 1857 — almost six years after the victory over the British — the cup was placed in the keeping of the New York Yacht Club. Along with it, went certain conditions, significant, as much for the historic part they played in yachting as for their looseness of terms. These conditions, known as The Original Deed of Gift are recorded here:

"Any organized yacht club of any foreign country shall always be entitled through any one or more of its members, to claim the right of sailing a match for this cup with any yacht or other vessel of not less than thirty or more than three hundred tons, measured by the custom-house rule of the country to which the vessel belongs.

"The parties desiring to sail for the Cup may make any match with the yacht club in possession of the same that may be determined upon by mutual consent; but, in case of disagreement as to terms, the match shall be sailed over the usual course for the annual regatta of the yacht club in possession of the Cup, and subject to its rules and sailing regulations — the challenging party being bound to give six months' notice in writing, fixing the day they wish to start. This notice to embrace the

This famous Currier & Ives print captures Magic, the winner of the first America's Cup race.

The First America's Cup Race — 1870

NAME OF YACHT	ARRIVAL AT HOME STAKEBOAT			ACTUAL TIME OF MAKING RACE			CORRECTED TIME BY ALLOWANCE		
	H.	M.	S.	H.	M.	S.	H.	M.	S.
1. Magic	3	33	54	4	07	54	3	58	21.2
2. Idler	3	37	23	4	11	23	4	00	35.1
3. Silvie	3	55	12	4	29	12	4	23	45.3
4. America	3	47	54	4	21	51	4	23	51.4
5. Dauntless	3	35	23.5	4	09	23.5	4	29	19.2
6. Madgie	3	55	07	4	29	07	4	29	57.1
7. Phantom	3	55	05	4	29	05	4	30	44.5
8. Alice	4	18	27.5	4	52	27.5	4	34	15.2
9. Halcyon	4	03	08	4	37	08	4	35	00.9
10. Cambria	4	00	57	4	34	57	4	37	38.9
11. Calypso	4	15	29	4	49	29	4	40	21.3
12. Fleetwing	4	02	09.5	4	36	09.5	4	41	20.5
13. Madeleine	4	14	46	4	48	46	4	42	35.4
14. Tarolinta	4	10	23	4	44	23	4	47	29.2
15. Rambler	4	17	35.5	4	51	35.5	4	48	33.5

Tidal Wave, Widgeon and Alarm failed to complete the course.

Lithograph by T. G. Dutton published in London in 1870 showing British challenger Cambria on the crest of a wave during her cross-Atlantic race against Dauntless.

length, custom-house measurement, rig and name of vessel.

"It is to be distinctly understood that the Cup is to be the property of the club, and not of the members thereof, or owners of the vessel winning it in the match; and that the conditions of keeping it open to be sailed for by yacht clubs of all foreign countries upon the terms above laid down, shall forever attach to it, thus making it perpetually a challenge cup for friendly competition between foreign countries."

The letter was signed by: J.C. Stevens, Edwin A. Stevens, J. B. Finley, Hamilton Wilkes and George L. Schuyler.

The New York Yacht Club wasted no time in accepting the Cup and the conditions. On July 21, the committee sent notices to all foreign clubs, inviting "spirited contest for the championship" and promising "a liberal, hearty welcome and strictest fair play." Yet no foreign club appeared interested in an international challenge trophy and New York Yacht Club members felt that the trophy was destined to finish on the club shelves to gather dust.

The United States had its own problems, though — the Civil War which began in 1860 and lasted until 1865. The war forced the cancellation of major yachting regattas and little consideration was given to racing for any cup, let alone The America's Cup. Twelve months after the war had ended, a race across the Atlantic, in the winter of 1866, was to have a significant effect on the interest of British yachtsmen.

Three schooners, *Henrietta*, owned by James Gordon Bennett, Commodore of the New York Yacht Club, *Fleetwing* and *Vesta*, started from the Sandy Hook lighthouse on December 11. The stake was $90,000 and the winner, *Henrietta* took 13 days, 21 hours 55 minutes, nine hours ahead of *Fleetwing* with *Vesta* just 40 minutes further astern. *Fleetwing* was hit by a large wave during the voyage. Six men were swept overboard and drowned.

The race revived interest in American ocean racing and trans-Atlantic crossings by American clipper yachts became more frequent. In the summer of 1868, the American schooner, *Sappho* sailed into English waters, hoping to emulate the feat of the *America* 17 years earlier. She was regarded as the largest and fastest in the New York Yacht Club fleet.

In a race around the Isle of Wight, following the same course as the *America*, the *Sappho* was beaten by four British schooners, including *Cambria*, owned by Mr. James Ashbury. The defeat of Sappho was all the encouragement the English required.

Ashbury was inspired to seek a challenge with the New York Yacht Club. According to reports of the time, Ashbury was motivated by reasons other than patriotism. He was an aspiring Member of Parliament, and was keen to improve his social standing. He saw his attempts to win back the Cup as the best vehicle for his ambitions.

The son of a wheelwright, who invented a new railway carriage, thus laying the foundation for the family fortune, Ashbury did not rank highly on the social register. He struck two problems with his challenge.

Firstly, Ashbury's proposal to the New York Yacht Club was from an individual. The Original Deed of Gift stipulated that the challenge must come from a club. Secondly, many yachtsmen, believing Ashbury's challenge to be prompted only by his social climbing, did not treat the challenge seriously.

Ashbury's proposal was presumptuous to say the least. He either ignored the very principles of the Deed of Gift, or did not take them seriously. He suggested that the Americans send their best schooner across the Atlantic to race in English waters.

He wrote: "The vessel referred to I would desire to see arrive in England in ample time to take part in the matches of the Royal Yacht Squadron at Cowes." Ashbury went on to suggest he would then race the selected American yacht across the Atlantic "for a cup or service of silver, value 250 pounds" and at its conclusion race a single American yacht in a best of three series around Long Island, "to decide the championship and final possession of the *America's* Queen's Cup of 1851."

Ashbury concluded that if he lost the best out of three series, he would present to the New York Yacht Club, or the owner of the vessel, a cup valued at 100 guineas. He also stipulated that if he won, he would keep the cup for himself.

Not surprisingly, the New York Yacht Club, ever mindful of the conditions of the Deed of Gift — when it suited them — refused to accept Ashbury's invitation, informing him, however, that they would accept only a challenge for The America's Cup. They also informed him that a challenge must come from "a regularly organized foreign yacht club."

Ashbury was far from deterred, explaining that he would obtain consent from one of several royal yacht clubs. Ashbury was also under the impression that he would race just one American yacht. The New York Yacht Club evaded the issue of a match race in all their correspondence, assuring Ashbury that he would be "heartily welcome" and the club was prepared to "maintain their claim according to the conditions upon which they accepted the Cup."

Yet the New York Yacht Club did not uphold every condition. They refused to abide by the match race stipulation, believing that since the *America* raced against a fleet in 1851, Ashbury's yacht should meet with the same treatment.

The haggling over terms and conditions had been counter-productive and the summer of 1869 passed without the proposed challenge taking place. Ashbury was undeterred and held tenaciously to his ambitions. He proposed again, to sail for the Cup on May 16, 1870 over a triangular course "from Staten Island 40 miles out to sea and back."

He added: "The Cup having been won at Cowes, under the rules of the R.Y.S., it thereby follows that no centreboard vessel can compete against *Cambria* in this particular race, but in all other respects I must conform to the stipulations and rules of the N.Y.Y.C.

Ashbury's objection to the centreboarders was regarded as reasonable by historians since the Americans specialised in centreboard yachts because of

Magic on the final reach, and victory.

their maneouvrability around the shoals of New York harbour. Ashbury's yacht, *Cambria*, out of necessity, since she would have to sail across the Atlantic, had to be a well built ocean going keel yacht.

In view of the number of objections it would not have surprised anyone had Ashbury refused to come. Yet as talks continued, the New York Yacht Club suggested that Ashbury bring *Cambria* anyway and the two parties debate their differences when he reached New York.

Ashbury planned to race the American yacht *Dauntless*, a fast keel schooner which had been sailing in English waters, across the Atlantic. Betting on such races was quite acceptable and one sailing enthusiast was so sure of *Dauntless'* invincibility he wagered $100 to $40 about the crack American yacht winning the race. He was to lose his money.

After 23 days at sea, and although considered the slower yacht, *Cambria* finished one hour, 43 minutes ahead, a cause for consternation among the optimistic members of the New York Yacht Club. *Dauntless* was considered unbeatable in ocean racing. What hadn't been known initially was that the angry sea, and the fickleness of the wind, the bane of all sailors, conspired to slow the *Dauntless*.

On the third morning of the race, *Dauntless*, caught in a rising sea, lost two men overboard, one, Charles Scott, an outstanding sailor and a strong swimmer, and Albert Demar, a German baron who couldn't swim. *Dauntless* spent almost two hours looking for the two men. Scott was last seen floating face down, the theory being that he had struck his head as he fell and lost consciousness.

Cambria was given a rousing welcome on her arrival at Sandy Hook, her chances in the challenge

The schooner, Dauntless, seen here in later years. She was on stand by as defender during the 1870 series.

race ahead greatly enhanced. *The Lawson History of the America's Cup* described *Cambria* as, "a keel schooner, built of oak, with teak topsides. Her interior fittings are remarkably rich and beautiful, and in good taste. She has 21 tons of ballast, smeltered and run into her timbers, and has also four tons of lead bolted to her keel. Under sail, she spreads a vast area of canvas, and works in the wind with the ease and facility of a weather vane."

While Ashbury was involved in the Atlantic race, the New York Yacht Club was firm in its endeavours to ensure that *Cambria* sailed against a fleet of American yachts. As *Dauntless* and *Cambria* entered the latter stages of the race, the New York Yacht Club met to adopt a resolution that the *America* be admitted "one of the fleet to compete for The Queen's Cup." Here again is a reference to The Queen's Cup. The original cup was that of the Royal Yacht Squadron and not The Queen's Cup.

The *America* in 1870 was owned by the United States Government and served as a training ship for midshipmen at the United States Academy. Few gave it any chance of winning. Ashbury's argument that he race against a single vessel and not a fleet appeared to dissipate among the Atlantic seas, for he accepted, although with some reluctance, the terms of the New York Yacht Club.

The club had voted 18 to one that each and everyone of the N.Y.Y.C's fleet could enter. They also decided there would be one race and if Ashbury did not accept the terms there would be no race. Ashbury, having come so far, and buoyant after his victory over *Dauntless*, conceded that the terms of the New York Yacht Club were better than no race at all.

The New York Yacht Club's claim that the conditions were the same as the *America* experienced in its race round the Isle of Wight against an English fleet was hardly acceptable. Each yacht in 1851 was after personal gain. In 1870, each of the 17 American vessels raced with a singular goal — to stop the Cup leaving the United States. Also among the American fleet were centreboarders such as *Idler, Magic, Halcyon, Phantom* and *Madeleine*, some of the finest yachts on America's east coast.

Ashbury felt disadvantaged. *Cambria's* sails, *The New York Times* correspondent noted, were "quite unfit for match sailing, consequent on two seasons of severe work and the recent Atlantic race. In order to give her a better chance on Monday week, her owner has ordered a new stay sail, foresail and mainsail from Mr. Wilson, the well known sailmaker of this city."

Although New York Yacht Club members feared the *Cambria*, by virtue of her defeat of *Dauntless*, *The*

New York Times had a differing view: "His (Mr. Ashbury's) only hope of winning the Cup, it is said, lies in the chance of a stiff breeze on the day of the race."

Among American yachtsmen, betting favoured the *America* and *Dauntless*, sentiment playing no small part in their predictions. Entries for the race were accepted until Saturday morning August 6, two days before the race was set. In all, 18 yachts were at the start. American yachting pride, not to mention a trophy, were at stake; a challenger had arrived, hellbent on retrieving British supremacy on the open seas.

The New York Times reported on that Monday morning, August 8, 1870:

"The great yacht race for the possession for the celebrated Queen's Cup which has been looked forward to with intense interest for several weeks took place in the lower bay....and was probably the most exciting and splendid nautical spectacle that has ever been witnessed here, exceeding as it did the most sanguine expectations of yachtsmen. The contest was probably attended by more public and widespread enthusiasm than any American sporting event that has ever occurred, either on land or on water. As early as eight o'clock in the morning the streets in the vicinity of the East and North rivers and along the Battery betokened that something unusual was about to happen. Large crowds of people were seen hurrying to the docks for the purpose of embarking on vessels which were to convey them to the scene of the race.

"Women and children were especially numerous, and appeared to be as eager to see the yachts as their male relatives and friends. The majority of them presented a very respectable and genteel appearance and it seemed as if the greater part of the middle and wealthy classes had, moved by a simultaneous impulse, turned out on the occasion, and had suddenly become warm patrons of the noble pastime yachting.....

"The excitement even invaded the most aristocratic portions of the city, and private carriages, filled with fair and gaily dressed inmates, were seen in large numbers on Fifth and Madison Avenues carrying their owners toward the river side. Wall Street was also stirred by the same enthusiasm, and was comparatively silent and deserted in the afternoon. Gold and stocks were almost forgotten for the nonce and bets on the yachts and on the result were the principal events on Change."

No doubt was left by the eloquent writer that The America's Cup had captured public imagination. Little has changed over more than a century, and 24 subsequent defences. The sentimental favourite, the *America*, at 178.6 tons, was one of the largest yachts in the race.

The medium sized pleasure sloop, *Imogene*, served as the stake boat and anchored just below Vanderbilt's Landing, near the Long Island shore. At 8 a.m., the yachts began taking their positions. *Cambria* was one of the first to go into line since she was given first choice of position. Ashbury selected the side closest to Staten Island since at the time a stiff

breeze was blowing from the west, allowing him to make a swift and favourable start.

Unfortunately for Ashbury the wind shifted by race time and the *Cambria* was immediately at a disadvantage and had to make a port tack soon after getting underway. These were the days of anchor starts whereby yachts could remain in position for hours on end.

The line of 18 yachts at the start extended almost across the bay, each vessel 100 feet apart, their bows pointed towards the Battery and lying so still that one writer noted: "They each looked, with their naked masts and long hulls sitting low in the water, as idle as a painted ship upon a painted ocean."

Pleasure craft gathered, among them more than 30 steamers, gaily decorated and some five or six of them, each with a band; the shoreline was alive with the masses, many of them never before witness to

The finish of the first America's Cup race off Staten Island. According to the artist, the five distinguishable yachts are (from left) Cambria, Dauntless, America, Idler and the winner, Magic. Cambria, the British yacht, actually finished tenth on corrected times.

yacht races, yet caught up in the emotion and fervour of the day. The crowd was estimated at 50,000 and it was reported that, "old mariners and harbor boatmen declared that such a sight and such a multitude had never been seen in New York Bay before."

The course was from the flag-boat abreast of Clifton House, Clifton, Staten Island, to the buoy at South-west Spit, passing it to the west and south, then to the lightship off Sandy Hook, rounding to the northward and eastward, and returning over the same course. The total distance was approximately 35 miles.

From the very start, it was apparent that *Cambria* would have little chance of winning the race. *Magic* was the first out of the Narrows, with *Silvie* second, followed by a number of other American yachts. *Cambria* was left far behind, "under Fort Richmond and pointing for Coney Island."

Cambria, 12th early, moved to eighth and appeared to be going well as it rounded the lighthouse. As the yachts turned for home, the wind blew strongly, *Magic* making about 12 knots and every inch of canvas stretching and straining, testing the very strength of each mast. It was here that *Cambria* struck disaster. While gybing, a necessary manoeuvre that would help the boat make up some leeway, a sudden and even stronger puff of wind struck her and took the fore-topmast over the side.

The loss of sail and tangled rigging left her even further behind. A small spare staysail was quickly rigged between the two masts. *Magic* which had led throughout, finished the course less than two minutes ahead of *Dauntless*, and less than four minutes ahead of *Idler*. The *America* was fourth, and *Cambria* eighth. On corrected times, *Cambria* dropped to tenth.

Magic's victory was gloriously captured by Lt. J.D. Jerrold Kelley, ".....the strength and beauty of the struggle was soon consummated by a glorious victory, for as the *Magic* rushed across the line it was not only in the fastest time ever made over the course, but, all things considered, with the greatest victory to her record ever won by a yacht since the world was young......the stately *Dauntless* passed by the mark, carrying the reverberations of the nations's delight into a further and a greater echo....for the *America*, fourth in the race, flew by the finish line, showing that as the sons were worthy of the sire, so were the brain and skill of old greater than story had told........"

Magic was originally known as *Madgie*, the name of another yacht in the race. She was built in 1857 by T. Byerly & Son, of Philadelphia, and was rigged as a sloop. Two years later, she was rigged as a schooner and won her first race in June 1865 in a New York Yacht Club regatta. In 1869, she was rebuilt at City Island.

The *America's* performance was quite remarkable for a yacht that had not raced for 10 years and had been sunk at one time in Florida. Claims were made after the race, although Ashbury did not protest, that *Cambria* had been fouled early in the race by *Tarolinta* who forced her about when *Cambria* was on a starboard tack. She was also baulked by *Fleetwing*.

Ashbury took his defeat in good spirit. Before returning to England he raced in Newport and New York, ever ready to race all comers and prepared to offer trophies for the races. Ashbury's sportsmanship and determination endeared him to Americans and he was socially accepted on his return home. A dinner was given in his honour in Manchester and in Brighton, his countrymen proud of his achievements.

Ashbury had made history. His persistence provided the first challenge for The America's Cup and he left New York determined to return.

The America's Cup 1851-1987

1871

Two Defenders, One Victory

**Columbia (NYYC) and Sappho (NYYC) 4 defeated
Livonia (Royal Harwich YC) one.**

JAMES Ashbury's second attempt to win the Cup was not so easily handled by the New York Yacht Club. Ashbury made it clear on his return to England that he had scant regard for the Deed of Gift as interpreted by the club and sought legal aid to force the New York Yacht Club to accept the definition of the word, "match" as it was originally intended.

Ashbury knew, as almost everyone did, even most Americans, that the odds were stacked against him, and any other challenger for that matter. It was quite useless for him to return to New York unless he had the opportunity of facing one American yacht rather than a fleet. Competition on unfamiliar waters on the other side of the Atlantic in a keel yacht against centreboarders was hard enough without facing further barriers.

Ashbury found an ally in one of the original owners of the *America*, George Schuyler, for when the New York Yacht Club sought Schuyler's opinion on the issue, he sided so strongly with Ashbury that the embarrassed club committee agreed to face the challenger one-on-one. The reply from Schuyler was blunt and damaging to the reputation of the New York Yacht Club. "....It seems to me that the present ruling of the club renders the *America's* trophy useless as a challenge cup."

While the club accepted Schuyler's view, they did so with a proviso. They reserved the right to choose any yacht at their disposal for each race. This gave them the chance to consider the weather conditions of the day before selecting the yacht to represent them, a healthy start in anyone's language.

Ashbury was determined to compete and to grab any concessions he could. Even before he returned from the previous challenge he sent orders to Michael Ratsey at Cowes to design and build a new boat.

The result was *Livonia*, so named after a province in Russia where Ashbury made considerable money from railroad building contracts. Immediately, the British claimed *Livonia* to be the finest sailing ship of its kind. Yet in trials, she showed few of the characteristics of a yacht fit to take the Cup away from the Americans.

What pleased Ashbury, however, was her likeness to an American schooner, a fact that influenced him to ignore her ordinary trials and take her to New York for the next challenge.

Livonia was heavily sparred, with sails of American cotton; she had a full, rounded mid-section and the greatest sail spread carried by any challenger for the Cup. Her sail area was 18,153 square feet. Despite her immense sail area her main mast was only 68 feet long, much of her sail carried aft on a long boom that projected beyond the stern. *Livonia's* timbers were of oak, and she registered 264 tons.

Ashbury's legal battle to ensure the next challenge was in the form of a match race was taken up even before *Livonia* was launched in April, 1871. Ashbury was determined to hit the New York Yacht Club where they were "weakest." Ashbury also persisted with another plan. He notified the New York Yacht Club that he would represent not only the Royal Harwich Yacht Club but several other clubs. With the authority of each club and with *Livonia* as their representative, he would race for The America's Cup as many times as the number of clubs he represented, perhaps as many as 20 clubs.

If he won just one of those races, the Cup would return to Britain with him. Ashbury was Commodore of the Royal Harwich Yacht Club, as well as a member of several others. In the end, he proposed challenging through 12 clubs.

Sappho, a keel boat, replaced Columbia in the 4th and 5th races.

Fred S. Cozzens print depicting Columbia, sails billowing, leading defence contenders, Sappho and Palmer.

Ashbury's sudden proposal caught the New York Yacht Club unaware, for he made it appear in his letter that his conditions would be accepted without dispute.

The New York Yacht Club was not prepared for a long, drawn out war of words and since *Livonia* was about to sail from England, they allowed Ashbury to leave without voting formally on his proposal. On October 4, after *Livonia* arrived in New York, the New York Yacht Club voted to sail the 12 races, all of them against *Livonia*, but as representative of the Royal Harwich Yacht Club only.

The event would be a best-of-12 race event. The New York Yacht Club cited a point of racing ethics which required a challenge from "one party" to be exercised before dealing with another.

Ashbury was incensed with the New York Yacht Club's attitude, claiming that "seeing that the masts of *Livonia* were reduced to cross the Atlantic, as yet the sails are unbent, the trim of the vessel as a consequence requires to be found, and it will take at least four or five races to get the *Livonia's* exact time." Ashbury added, "A decision to reduce the 12 races will result in the *Livonia's* at once returning to England without any race, either public or private."

In seeking 12 races, Ashbury forced the New York Yacht Club to agree to a series. The 1871 defence would be a best-of-seven series. Thus The America's Cup as we know it today began to evolve.

His objections laid the foundation for two important conditions — match racing and a best-of-seven series. Ashbury had two other grievances; one, that it was unfair for *Livonia*, a keel boat, to race against a centreboarder, and, two, that the races should be sailed on an ocean course outside Sandy Hook instead of on the difficult waters of New York Harbour.

Ashbury reasoned that victory on the inside course was determined more by local knowledge of the waters than by the respective merits of the boats and crews. Although the first objection was thrown out by the club, they compromised on the second. Races would be sailed alternately on the inside course, the regular New York Harbour course, and outside, a course 20 miles to windward from Sandy Hook lightvessel and back.

According to the *Lawson History of the America's Cup*, three of the races were to be sailed over the club course, and four, including the sixth and seventh races, over the course from the "light-vessel 20 miles and back."

Despite the concessions, the New York Yacht Club still held the upper hand — they were in their home waters; they had the use of the centreboarders and they had the choice of any one of four yachts.

The four yachts chosen were the centreboarders, *Columbia* and *Palmer*, and the keel boats, *Dauntless* and *Sappho*. *Columbia* and *Palmer* were each adaptable in light and moderate winds while *Dauntless* and *Sappho* were better suited in heavier weather. The obvious advantage was that the New York Yacht Club had the yachts to cover conditions on both the inside and outside courses.

Columbia was the latest of the four boats. She was built by J.B. Van Deusen in 1871. Owned by Frank Osgood, she was 107.11 feet overall and 96 feet on the waterline.

By comparison, *Livonia* was 127 feet long overall and 106 feet 6 inches on the water line. Although she had shown herself to be an able seagoing schooner during her 29 day voyage across the Atlantic, *Livonia* never really had a chance. She left Cowes on September 2 and ran into a hurricane. Forced to heave to and ride out the storm, she lost sails, broke her fore boom and lost her bowsprit. She arrived in New York Harbour, hardly fit to take on the best of American racing yachts.

The first race, scheduled for the morning of October 16, brought New Yorkers to the harbour by the thousands, many of them anxious to see the new English challenger. The wind was light to moderate and from the northwest. The race was over the inside course, and not surprisingly the New York Yacht Club selected a centreboarder, *Columbia*.

Only two American yachts waited at the starting point, *Columbia*, and *Sappho*, which was more suited in a breeze, particularly on the outside course. *The New York Times* reported the committee's decision: "The committee were not long in deciding which boat was to represent America on this eventful day, and steaming up alongside of the *Columbia*, Mr. Minton hailed Rear-Commodore Osgood and briefly announced the honour in store for him."

Columbia and *Livonia* were similar in appearance, according to reports, both were painted black with "a gold line round the deck line." At the shrill of the starting whistle, both yachts slipped their mooring cables, set their headsails and moved with the breeze.

Columbia moved away more quickly. As a centreboarder she was more manoeuvrable in light breezes. The heavier keel boats, such as *Livonia*, needed more wind.

The wind had died away considerably at the start.

Above: The idleness of Livonia's decks before racing. Left: Livonia's owner, James Ashbury, who challenged the rules of the America's Cup and left New York under protest. Right: Livonia, a 264-ton schooner, built along American lines. She was the first challenger to win a race.

According to *The New York Times*, "....there was only enough to keep all canvas well filled." By the time they reached the Narrows, *Columbia* was three minutes ahead and at the light vessel, she was 15 minutes ahead.

"As the *Columbia* came up close to the buoy, it was pleasant to watch the discipline on board.....the Rear-Commodore (Frank Osgood) was all alive, and, heedless of the cheers with which his boat was saluted, attended to business, and gave his orders relative to the staysail. She presented a beautiful picture."

With so little wind about, the heavier *Livonia* struggled to make headway; *Columbia* increased her margin and at the finish of the race, was 25 minutes 18 seconds ahead — 27 mins four secs on corrected time. As New Yorkers rejoiced, *Livonia* crossed the finish line to a "warm welcome." It was cold comfort.

Ashbury saw his chances in the second race considerably enhanced since it was on the outside course. Yet the course as laid out was 15 miles to windward, and back. Ashbury did not appear concerned at the discrepancy.

What ultimately concerned him was what he saw as a breach of the sailing rules by *Columbia* and it led him to protest. *Columbia's* selection ahead of the keel

yachts *Dauntless* and *Sappho* surprised onlookers, since not only was the race on the outside course, but a fresh westerly had sprung up before the committee made their choice.

According to one correspondent, the wind, "was blowing a 10-knot hummer from the west north-west, quite sufficient to test the sailing qualities of any yacht, and as the *Dauntless* was in readiness, everybody supposed she would go."

Columbia won the race but it was far from clear cut. *Livonia* led to the outer mark, the point on which Ashbury focused his protest. Before the race began each captain received his instructions. When *Columbia*'s skipper Nelson Comstock read them, he noted that there were no directions as to the manner of rounding the outer mark.

"How shall I turn it?" he asked. *Columbia*'s owner Frank Osgood went back to the committee boat to seek clarification. He returned with the instruction, "Turn as you please." The English, however, did not query the point. According to reports, they accepted the custom of their own waters which stated that in the advent of no instructions, the mark should be left to starboard.

On a course east north-east and in a lively and fresh 10-knot breeze, *Livonia* proved her worth and headed for the controversial outer mark a minute in front of *Columbia*. Those who challenged the decision to use *Columbia* had no doubt that the race committee had selected the wrong boat.

But from the time *Livonia* gybed round the mark to leave it to starboard — a difficult exercise with the topsail, or jackyarder, aloft — the race was lost. *Columbia* cut in between the marker-boat and *Livonia*'s stern, and left the mark to port.

The New York Times eyewitness account was straight to the point, "It was a magnificent sight as they both came round the stake-boat. The *Livonia* was first at 1.20, and jibed her main boom, while the *Columbia* came shooting in between her and the stake-boat at 1.21.40, and tacking, took the windward position."

Columbia won by 5 mins 11 secs, and on corrected time, 10 mins $33\frac{1}{4}$ secs, establishing a race record for

The America's Cup 1851-1987

30 miles in Cup matches. Ashbury sent his protest to the Cup committee immediately the race was over.

Part of his protest read: "It is with great reluctance that I make such a protest, especially as I never made a protest in my life before this one......but I am confident that you will admit that I am, under the circumstances, justified in claiming the race."

Ashbury erred on one account — he had protested once before....in a match race with *Sappho* in 1868. Ashbury's protest was thrown out immediately, the race committee explaining that: "Sailing regulations for the outside course ....leaves the matter of turning the stake optional."

The New York Times, unaware of the drama, wrote: "The victory was nobly won." Ashbury disagreed, as did the correspondent for *The Spirit of the Times* who made it clear that Ashbury had every right to protest. He wrote: "Mr. Ashbury was perfectly justified in asking for another race, the committee was at fault in not acceding to him......That the course was not fully 40 miles, is shown by the time, 3h. 1m. 10s., and while this was an added reason for another race, the fact that it was not a race to windward for half of the course, was a third reason."

J. D. Jerrold Kelly, writing in his book, *American Yachts*, agreed. "Mr. Ashbury did not claim the victory then, but asked for another race, and, messieurs, you should have given it to him." The race committee stood firm. Ashbury didn't get the race re-run and sailed the rest of the series under protest.

One of the amazing aspects of the 1871 challenge was that while the two selected yachts raced for the Cup, the other three American "defenders", and any number of other American yachts, were allowed to join in the race from behind. Even race descriptions in the local New York press included references to the unofficial entrants.

While the chance to race, even if only unofficially, allowed the owners of the non-selected boats to keep their vessels in good racing trim, it also denied them the chance of sailing officially in the third race. *Columbia* had become slightly disabled during the second race, and her owner, Rear-Commodore Osgood sent word that she would not be able to start. *Sappho* was on the ways which left the choice between *Palmer* and *Dauntless*.

At 9.40 a.m. the owner of *Palmer* informed the race committee that she had been disabled in the race the previous day and could not be sailed. The committee then went to *Dauntless* and was told that she could not go because she had split her mainsail. As spectators waiting for the start of the race began to grumble, sailmakers were sent for and began to patch the torn sail.

With the sail mended, *Dauntless* was being taken in tow to the starting line when her rigging became entangled in the towing hawser. *Magic*, the winner of the 1870 race, was on hand, and Ashbury, having already agreed to a delayed start, agreed to race her, "or any other American schooner."

The race committee ruled out *Magic*, feeling that it would be too much of an injustice to Ashbury, and

Columbia leading Livonia in the second race, October 18.

were prepared to concede the race when Osgood arrived with his disabled *Columbia*. Her foremast had sprung at the hounds; she was hastily rigged; crew from *Dauntless* was sent aboard to help sail her while *Magic's* skipper, Andrew Comstock, brother of Nelson, was the new skipper.

Even in these early days when the Americans were so demanding in their preparations, it is staggering that they should blunder so badly. What's more, *Columbia* was still in tow when the order was given to start. The American boat was 100 metres behind — and never recovered.

Livonia won, though many saw it as justice after the previous day's protest. As the boats prepared for the fourth race, Ashbury, still peeved at the race committee's decision to dismiss his protest, notified the committee that he sailed the rest of the series, "without prejudice to my confirmed claim." Ashbury believed the score was 2-1 in his favour.

Sappho, with its crew fresh and eager for a race, was chosen as the defending yacht, the first chance *Livonia* had of beating a keel boat. It was no contest, and *Livonia*, behind by two minutes at the start, lost by 30 minutes, 21 seconds. *Sappho* was chosen for the fifth race — over the inside course — and won again, this time by 25 minutes, 27 seconds. It was her last race in The America's Cup. She was sold to an Italian nobleman and raced in Europe.

The result according to The America's Cup race committee was a resounding 4-1 to the New York Yacht Club. A defiant Ashbury refused to accept that the series was over and notified the New York Yacht Club that *Livonia* would be ready to race again the next day. He opened his letter to the race committee: "Gentlemen, assuming that I am right as to the ultimate validity of my protest as regards race No. 2, I now claim the continuation of the series for the possibility of winning two more, in which case I should claim the Cup, as already intimated."

Ashbury was at the start the next day, not only to race for The America's Cup but also to race *Dauntless* for a 50-guinea cup. Beaten by *Dauntless*, he arranged another race, the "seventh America's Cup race", and since no official boat was at the start to greet him again, he therefore, declared that he had won the Cup, four races to three.

On his return to England — without the Cup — Ashbury accused the New York Yacht Club of "unfair and unsportsmanlike proceedings". Before Ashbury returned home, however, he left three cups with the New York Yacht Club to be sailed for by the club's yachtsmen.

The club, in view of Ashbury's statements, refused to accept them and returned them to Ashbury in England. Future challengers were indebted to Ashbury for he paved the way for more equitable challengers, ridding the Cup of a number of injustices. Ashbury, however did not return. It was left to another country to challenge next.

Madeleine winning second and deciding race of 1876.

1876

Canada's First Bid for Cup

Madeleine (NYYC) 2 defeated Countess of Dufferin (Royal Canadian YC) nil.

THE Canadian challenge was doomed from the start. Their challenger, *Countess of Dufferin*, was hastily constructed, poorly rigged and given the thumbs down by American yachtsmen on her arrival in New York Harbour on July 18, 1876.

That's not to say that the challenge was without meaning. In many ways there was a sense of relief in New York that a challenge did come, and it is conceded that the Canadians kept alive interest in The America's Cup.

Relations between the British and American yachtsmen had cooled somewhat following James Ashbury's unsuccessful attempt in 1871. The British had little regard for the ethics of the New York Yacht Club and, conversely, the Americans felt Ashbury had been petulant and ungentlemanly. If the future of The America's Cup had been left to the yachtsmen of both countries, the trophy might not have been an object of competition again.

Thankfully, the Canadians were spirited and competitive enough to try their hand. Apart from providing a link in The America's Cup chain, they managed to achieve a number of important concessions, not the least, an agreement from the New York Yacht Club that they would select only one yacht for their defence.

It wasn't that the New York Yacht Club was immediately forthcoming in its decision to select one yacht. In correspondence with the Canadians, they left open their options, stating, "a yacht would be at the starting point on the morning of each race to sail the match."

The club, fearing another drawn out wrangle similar to those faced with Ashbury, agreed to sail only one defending boat. Such a decision must have brought a wry smile to the face of Ashbury, who fought so hard to obtain the same concession in his two challenges.

It appeared that since Asbury's controversial second challenge, the New York Yacht Club committee had broadened its outlook and were prepared to contest the Cup on more equitable grounds.

The Canadians happened along at the right time even if they were no match for the skilled and highly efficient American yachtsmen. It is generally conceded that the two Canadian challenges, 1876 and 1881, were the weakest of the early races for the Cup.

The *Countess of Dufferin* was the last of the challenging schooners. She was designed and built by Alexander Cuthbert, although Americans claimed she was hardly an original design. According to the *Lawson History of the America's Cup*, she was modelled on the American line and from a design by a New Jersey boatbuilder P. McGiehan, who years earlier had built a sloop called *Cora* for a Canadian yachtsman.

Cuthbert set out to design a yacht to beat *Cora* and did so with a sloop, *Annie Cuthbert*. Yet when asked to design a schooner to beat the Americans, he simply built an enlarged replica of the *Annie Cuthbert*. The Canadians had considerable faith in his ability, particularly after his success with the *Annie Cuthbert*.

Some American yachting people were scornful of the challenge since it came from the Royal Canadian Yacht Club of Toronto, which was based inland and was not of salt water origin. According to one report: "She (the *Countess*) had fresh water written all over her, and this, in the eyes of the salts, was a crime."

The dates for the challenge had originally been set for July 10, 12 and 14, but were later changed to August, the first race on the 11th. The *Countess of Dufferin*, named in honour of the Canadian Governor-General's wife, left Lake Ontario in June. After some important adjustments to its rig in

Quebec, Captain Cuthbert and his crew, sailed the schooner down the St. Lawrence and around the coast of Nova Scotia, and south to New York.

While the journey gave Cuthbert time to evaluate his vessel, he could in no way have been expected to modify the faults in her. Yet the Americans were expecting a racing yacht of some style. Messages had been received in New York from eyewitness accounts of the *Countess*, that she was a merchant of speed....a worthy challenger.

The moment the schooner sailed into New York Harbour, the expectant New Yorkers saw only a schooner "as rough as a nutmeg grater", and lacking the appearance expected of a Cup challenger. According to the *Lawson History*, "here was a schooner built in a hurry, on limited means, rigged and fitted out in a rush, and brought from fresh water to salt, which was expected by the men of the coast to present as good an appearance as the perfectly finished craft owned by millionaire club men, manned by experienced sailors, and tried, remodelled, and fixed over until they were absolutely as good as they could be made."

The *Countess of Dufferin* would be the first yacht to

A Currier & Ives print of Royal Canadian Yacht Club's Countess of Dufferin.

race over a best-of-three race series, another concession of the New York Yacht Club, such a decision made long before the arrival of the Canadian challenger in the New York waters. The *Countess* was classed no better than an average centreboard schooner, although she was regarded, in one report, as "fairly fast" in light breezes. Her sails were so poorly cut that they had to be taken off and recut by the renowned American sailmaker, Wilson.

Later, four feet were added to her main boom to give her more mainsail. Her displacement was 138 tons, her length 107 feet, with a beam of 24 feet and her draft, with centreboard up, of six feet six inches. The Canadian challenge which had been made by Major Charles Gifford, vice-commodore of the Royal Canadian Yacht Club, was conditional on the six months notice clause in the Deed of Gift being waived. The clause was inserted to give the defending club time to prepare, particularly if it was necessary to build a new yacht for the challenge.

The New York Yacht Club did not feel inclined to build a new yacht, such was the abundance of good, class schooners at their disposal, and therefore, had no objection to Major Gifford's demand.

The club's defender was *Madeleine*, one of the smartest schooners in the club's fleet. She had been built in 1868, at Rye, New York, originally as a 70 ton sloop, but later she was lengthened and rigged as a schooner. She was 106 feet in length, 95 feet on the waterline, with a 24 feet beam and a seven feet four inch draft, with a centreboard.

Madeleine wasn't the only candidate. The New York Yacht Club had a number of fast and adequate centreboarders in the fleet, among them *Idler*, *Palmer* and *Columbia*. When elimination races were run only two yachts turned up for the start, *Idler*, and *Madeleine*. The latter won and subsequently earned the right to defend the Cup.

Owned by John S. Dickerson and skippered by Josephus Williams, *Madeleine* was one of the finest looking schooners in New York; she had proven herself in racing and just before the challenge began, she was placed in dry dock, where the copper on her bottom was burnished until, as one report claimed, "it shone like gold."

Madeleine made a striking appearance on the waters of New York, as *The New York Times* correspondent remarked, in comparing her with the *Countess of Dufferin*. "The *Madeleine*, saucy, rakish and smart, with her tall, graceful masts, seemed fit to sail for a kingdom, at least in such halcyon weather, while her rival looked squat and heavy, and while she seemed fit for some rough knocks, never suggested the idea of speed."

For the *Countess of Dufferin*, it was a desperate case of work and more work. Major Gifford entered the yacht in the Brenton Reef Cup, an international trophy presented to the New York Yacht Club by Commodore James Gordon Bennett in 1871. The course was from the Sandy Hook light-vessel to Brenton Reef, off Newport, and back, an ocean racing event that would give the crew of the Canadian schooner valuable experience under race conditions.

While four American yachts, the *America*, *Tidal Wave*, *Idler* and *Wanderer* entered the race the *Countess of Dufferin* was only in the event as an unofficial entry. Although the *Countess* did lead the *America* in the run to Brenton Reef, she eventually fell well behind the four American yachts, and finished many hours behind the winner *Idler*.

After the race, the Canadians asked for a postponement of the Cup races, advising the New York Yacht Club that they wanted a new set of sails. The New York Yacht Club refused their request since it would

The America's Cup 1851-1987

Madeleine running from the Canadian challenger, Countess of Dufferin in choppy seas. It was a familiar sight since Madeleine completely outclassed the challenger, leading all the way in both races, winning the first by ten minutes and the second by 27 minutes.

interfere with their already busy racing schedule. However, it was disclosed later that the *Countess of Dufferin* did get a number of new sails, including mainsail and foresail.

The first race, on Friday, August 11, was sailed on the regular New York Yacht Club inside course, "from the clubhouse at Stapleton, round the southwest Spit Buoy, round the Sandy Hook lightship and return, finishing off the West Bank."

The start was marred by the interference of a small sloop, and the *Countess of Dufferin*, being forced to clear a brig anchored to leeward of her course. It meant that the Canadian schooner was blanketed by the *Madeleine* and was almost half a minute behind at the start.

Again heading its story, The Queen's Cup Race, *The New York Times* reported: "The first tack was a very brief one, but short as it was, the *Madeleine* began to manifest. She went buoyantly through the water, but movements of the *Countess* were sluggish and she seemed to drag heavily astern."

As the two schooners worked their way through the Narrows, the *Madeleine* held a commanding, although be no means winning, lead of two minutes. On reaching open water, the *Madeleine* made a long reach into Gravesend Bay to avoid the flowing floodtide. The *Countess of Dufferin* for some unaccountable reason, kept to the West Bank, toward, as one account had it, "Dix's and Hoffman's Islands, where she experienced the full force of the tide."

When the *Countess* changed course and followed the *Madeleine* she was a mile to leeward. It was the end of the Canadians' chances. At the lightship, the *Madeleine* led by almost five minutes.

The run home was uneventful. *Madeleine* increased her lead steadily at every buoy before crossing the finishing line nine minutes, 58 seconds ahead (ten minutes, 59 seconds on corrected time). Despite the apparent ease of *Madeleine's* win, the *Countess of Dufferin* attracted more admirers than at any time since she arrived in New York.

The New York Times reported, "Everybody thinks better of the Canadian yacht, beaten though she be, and a good many people held that under certain conditions of wind and seaway a victory for the

Madeleine is not at all so assured today (the day of the second race) as it was yesterday."

The *America* raced as one of the unofficial yachts, an accepted practice still, as long as such entrants did not interfere with the participating vessels. For the second race, sailed on the outside course, the Canadians made an unusual decision — they engaged the services of Joseph Ellsworth, an experienced New York Harbour skipper from Bayonne, New Jersey, as pilot.

Some reports had him on board during the first race, but most references to Ellsworth dealt more specifically with the second race. In official records, J. E. Ellsworth is shown as skipper of the Canadian yacht. The *Countess of Dufferin's* crew was also supplemented by a number of New York sailors.

Thick fog blanketed New York and its surrounds as the yachts prepared for the second race. Not a breath of wind disturbed the sea, and it wasn't until the *Madeleine* and the *Countess of Dufferin* reached the starting line that a start seemed possible.

One newspaper reported: "Just outside the Hook they were cast off from the steam-boat, and their sails were run up with all possible despatch. There was some promise in the day, but it inclined altogether in favour of the *Madeleine*. A pleasant sailing breeze was the heaviest weather that could possibly be anticipated, and for the conditions of the water there was not the faintest suggestion of a whitecap."

While it had been hoped that the race would be to windward and return, the wind shifted too much to the south to be a dead beat. The *Madeleine* again crossed the starting line ahead of the *Countess*, this time by 34 seconds. The *America* and *Wanderer* entered the race, unofficially again, five minutes later.

As this description from *The New York Times* reveals, it was a perfect summer's day, though not necessarily for sailing; ".....it was only a soft breeze, with the warm breath of the summer in it. Then, the surface of the broad ocean was barely rippled, the waters had just motion enough to glance and sparkle in the sunlight and it was, in truth, summer from verge to verge. There was not a speck in the zenith, but all along the horizon, except in open space to the south, the bright fleecy clouds were spread like an irregular fringe. The ocean steamers went by, driving through the calm waters with strong, vigourous pulsations, and saluting the yachts as they passed."

The *Madeleine* was never in danger of losing the race and by the turn for home she held a commanding lead of almost 13 minutes. The Canadian yacht wasn't even second round the buoy. The *America* had overtaken the *Countess* and was just three minutes and one second behind the *Madeleine*.

The run home was uneventful. The *Countess of Dufferin* was outclassed in the light breezes and finished in the growing darkness some 27 minutes and 14 seconds behind the *Madeleine*. On corrected time, the *Madeleine* won by 28 minutes, 46 seconds.

One of the more remarkable aspects of the challenge was the performance of that grand lady, the *America*. Twenty five years old, a keel boat at that, she beat the *Countess of Dufferin*, a centreboarder, in light airs by some 19 minutes. It was further proof of the mastery of designer George Steers who most assuredly created a masterpiece.

Few challenges were as straightforward or as uninteresting. Yet the Canadians could feel satisfied that they also helped change the course of The America's Cup conditions, paving the way for more equitable future challenges. For the first time also, the race yachts were started under sail, and not from anchor.

The New York press and some American yachtsmen were rather flattering in their summaries. One writer suggested after the first race defeat by more than 10 minutes that the *Countess* stood a chance of squaring accounts if given stronger breezes. Such a patronising attitude was not lost on the Canadians back home, who were understandably embarrassed by the condescending offerings of their neighbours.

The Canadian people were not prepared to accept that the Royal Canadian Yacht Club's challenge represented a bid on behalf of Canada, and therefore saw it as a misguided attempt by a few optimistic sailors.

It was clear that the challenge was doomed from the start because of lack of money. As subsequent, and more particularly, contemporary America's Cup races have shown, where money is lacking, the challenge has no chance.

Cuthbert consoled himself by claiming he had made, "as good a showing as *Livonia*, anyway." Few, if anyone, shared his view, although it was obvious that *Livonia* was a better prepared boat, and, at the least, if Cuthbert had been in charge of the English yacht he might have fared no worse than Ashbury.

Like Ashbury, Cuthbert was no quitter. As soon as the second race was over, he looked for support from Canadian sportsmen for a second challenge. He argued that with certain changes, he could improve the boat enough to return the following year and make a more worthy challenge. Cuthbert's idea was to gain complete control of the boat, rebuild its stern, thereby reducing the overhang, restep her masts and change her sails.

Not surprisingly the syndicate became entangled in financial problems and the yacht was barred from racing again in New York. While the wrangle over money continued, Cuthbert sailed the schooner back to Canada where, to satisfy creditors, the *Countess of Dufferin* was sold to a Chicago businessman, a member of the Chicago Yacht Club. She finished her racing days on Lake Michigan.

With the third challenge completed, the Americans' hold on the ornate trophy was even tighter. Nothing in the art of pleasure and racing boat design in any foreign land indicated they would be challenged seriously.

Even though the British maintained their stand-off position, they did not altogether believe that the Cup was unattainable in the future. However, it was left to Alexander Cuthbert, a resourceful, abundantly optimistic yachtsman, to make another bid.

Mischief leads Atalanta at start of first race.

1881

Iron Lady Sinks Challenge

Mischief (NYYC) 2 defeated Atalanta (Bay of Quinte YC) nil.

THE second Canadian challenge helped New Yorkers to cast side the gloom of 1881. In the November, the nation still mourned the death of their 20th President, James Abram Garfield, who was gunned down on July 2 at the Washington Railroad station.

He died on September 19, less than two months before the Cup was to start. Garfield was President for four months; he was succeeded by Vice-President, Chester Alan Arthur.

The fair breezes brought not only a challenger from neighbouring Canada, but a more relaxed and buoyant atmosphere for New Yorkers anxious to forget their mourning.

When Alexander Cuthbert sailed home, thrashed so comprehensively in the previous challenge, New Yorkers felt they had seen the last of him. But five years of persistence brought him back, though, as with most Cup challenges, there were ulterior motives. It was claimed that Cuthbert was using The America's Cup to advertise his boat building business.

Such motives were not out of order, for no one had to explain or qualify their reasons for challenging and the Americans were only too happy to accept his challenge again.

The British had shown no indication that they were prepared to cross the Atlantic, so why not Cuthbert? This time Cuthbert represented the Bay of Quinte Yacht Club, Belleville, Ontario, hardly a heavyweight in yachting and not heard from again in America's Cup yachting. The formal proposal for the challenge was made on May 16, 1881. Cuthbert had not learnt by the mistakes of his previous challenge. His new boat, *Atalanta*, was as hastily built as his first yacht, the *Countess of Dufferin*, and his syndicate had even less money.

Yachting experts considered her hull rough, her general design poor, and her sails badly set. Her crew was composed mainly of amateurs from the Bay of Quinte Yacht Club. Launched at Belleville in September, she arrived in New York on October 30, via the Erie Canal, towed through 14 kilometres of the canal by mules.

Such an unsophisicated entry led to changes in the Deed of Gift the following year which stipulated that all challengers must travel to the Cup destination under sail. The *Atalanta* enjoyed one distinction — she was the first sloop to challenge for the Cup. All previous challengers had been schooners.

Despite the New York Yacht Club's agreement to select one defending yacht for the previous challenge, they did not accept as a matter of course that the 1881 challenge should follow the same pattern. Only after the flag officers of the New York Yacht Club, to whom the committee had gone for advice, made their stand plain, did the Cup committee accept the fact that they could sail only one defender. The yardstick, confirmed in 1881, was established for all future Cup defences.

The Americans established a number of firsts in the 1881 challenge. For the first time they sought to have a boat built specifically for the purpose of defending the Cup. The New York Yacht Club, after reviewing all possible contenders, selected the sloop, *Arrow* as the defender.

However, she was owned by a non-member of the New York Yacht Club, and, therefore, was unacceptable. While the club considered buying the yacht, David Kirby, her designer, agreed to design and build a new boat, promising the club that she would be faster than *Arrow*.

The result was the *Pocahontas*, a centreboard sloop; 72 feet 6 inches in length; 65 feet on the waterline, beam of 21 feet 6 inches, with a six feet 7 inches draft, according to one report, "a typical, old-fashioned single-sticker, built from a model whittled out, and scaled by the eye."

The *Pocahontas* was a failure; she performed badly in the trials, although she still retained the dis-

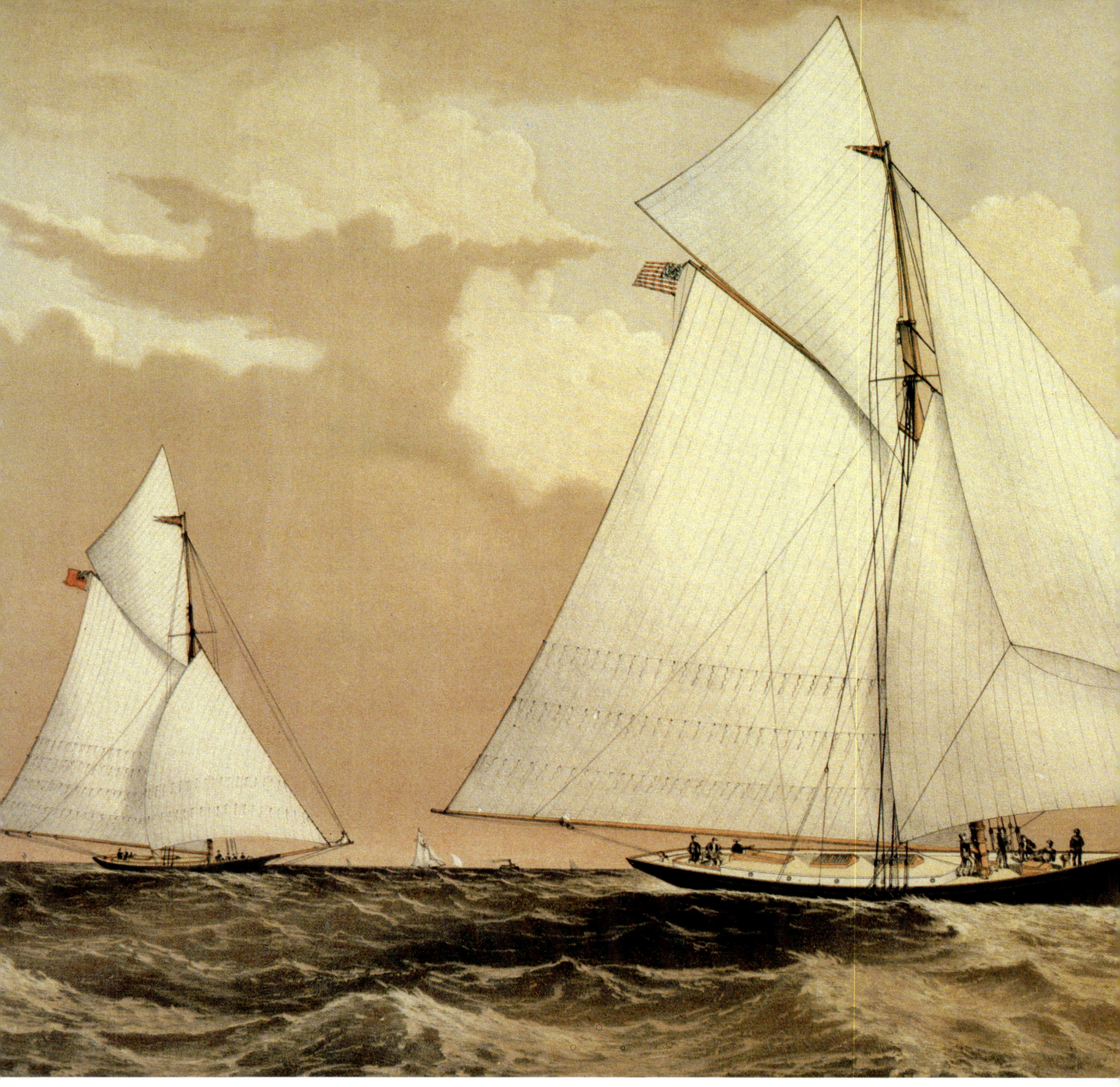

tinction of being the first yacht built specifically to defend the Cup. Three trials were held to determine the defending yacht, the first on October 13. The competing yachts were *Gracie, Mischief, Hildegard* and *Pocahontas*.

Mischief won two trials, the second by a mere 14 seconds; *Gracie* won the other convincingly; *Hildegarde* lasted just one trial after losing her topmast and *Pocahontas* could beat neither *Gracie* nor *Mischief*.

Pocahontas did not race again, spending the rest of her years as a cruiser. Great rivalry had developed between the owners of *Mischief* and *Gracie*, each believing their sloops to be the more suitable defender.

According to *The New York Times*, the general opinion among yachtsmen was that *Gracie* was the faster boat. "Among the New York members outside of the Regatta Committee, the preference seems to be decidedly for the *Gracie*.....Last spring, immediately after the race of the New York Yacht Club, her rigging was altered and her ballast rearranged. Since then she has had nine different races with the *Mischief*, and has won seven by from 5 to 50 minutes, while the *Mischief* has won only two. In one of the races won by *Mischief*, the *Gracie* carried away her topmast, and in the other was stopped by a passing tow within a mile of the finish and delayed between two and three minutes, but the *Mischief* won by only 14 seconds."

Notwithstanding the general concensus that the

Left: Artist Charles R. Parsons' historic painting of Mischief and Atalanta during the second race. Above: Gracie, many expected her to be the defender instead of Mischief.

Gracie was the fastest sloop in the New York Yacht Club fleet, *The New York Times* correspondent appeared to have a soft spot for her.

The Cup committee were evenly divided on the merits of *Gracie* and *Mischief*, and according to reports, the committee did not make their decision until the morning of the first race.

When race day, November 8, arrived both *Gracie* and *Mischief* were taken to the starting point. There the committee announced that *Mischief* would defend the Cup. The decision caused a minor uproar among the New York Yacht Club members, for *Mischief* was owned by an Englishman, J. R. Busk.

Although Busk was a member of the club, members felt it only right that the Cup be defended by an American-owned yacht. According to *The New York Times*, "This declaration did not give general satisfaction to yachtsmen, and when it was announced later to Capt. Cuthbert, of the *Atalanta*, he expressed relief by saying that he felt that the selection gave him a chance of winning, as he was satisfied that the *Gracie* could beat him."

Cuthbert had first hand knowledge of *Gracie's* speed. The day before, *Gracie* ran up along side the *Atalanta* and, although she went about on her lee, she went right by the Canadian yacht.

The New York Yacht Club's decision to select *Mischief* was influenced by the time allowance factor. *Atalanta* allowed *Mischief* two minutes 44 seconds

The America's Cup 1851-1987

while the Gracie had to concede the Canadian sloop 7 minutes, 40 seconds.

Mischief was unusual in that she was made of iron, earning her the title of "The Iron Pot". Designed by A. Cary Smith, of New York, she was the second metal yacht built in the country, and was two years old when she defended the Cup.

Despite the general opinion that *Gracie* was the faster boat, *Mischief* was by no means a laggard as this description of her, and her influence on the future of American yacht building, in the *Lawson History of the America's Cup*, reveals;

"She was as fine a sloop as could be found, and a departure from the old type of 'skimming dish', having less beam, a straighter sheer, higher freeboard, and a shorter, fuller overhand after. Her ballast was lead, stowed low in her iron hull. Her lines slightly suggested the cutter, and her rig was a compromise between sloop and cutter. She was the first scientifically-designed yacht employed for Cup defence, all the others having been built from models

Mischief and Atalanta, a mis-match again, the Canadian boat losing the second race by more than 38 minutes.

cut in wood. She was a designer's, rather than a builder's creation, and as such led the way to new methods in the creation of cup-defending vessels. She marked a very important point, therefore, in the evolution of American yacht building, and also she indicated strongly the steps we were to take a little later toward the English type of boat, though she was by no means revolutionary, as the *America* had been among racing schooners."

Mischief's dimensions were, 67 feet 5 inches overall, 61 feet on the waterline, 19 feet 10 inches and with a 5 feet 6 inches draft.

Thick fog hung over the harbour on that first day; light showers of rain fell and there was little wind as the yachts were towed to the race starting position off Stapleton, Staten Island at 10 o'clock. The fears of both crews were confirmed not long after, and with no change in the weather the race was postponed, the first such postponement in the Cup's history.

Fog greeted the yachts again the next day, but lifted before 10 o'clock. According to reports, "a strong, steady, south west wind blowing all doubts of the race being sailed were removed." Few yachts ventured out with the competing vessels; wind and intermittent rain squalls unsettled *Mischief* and *Atalanta*, each taking to sheltered waters as they prepared to start.

Atalanta was knocked down by "a heavy gust off the land until immersed to the house." *Mischief* crossed the starting line on a starboard tack a minute ahead of the slow moving *Atalanta* which was under reefed mainsail and jib.

According to the *Lawson History*: "She heeled so far in the puffs which swept viciously up the channel that the judges ordered the captain of their tug to keep near her, fearing she might be knocked flat and need help."

The owners of *Gracie*, anxious to prove that they had the fastest yacht, were given permission to start the sloop, and she began her chase 10 minutes after the *Atalanta*. By the time the yachts had gone but a quarter of the journey, the only interest in the race was whether *Gracie* would beat *Mischief* home. *Atalanta*, as most feared, was no match and her crew were much to slow in their handling of the sails.

Mischief rounded the light-ship 13 minutes ahead of *Atalanta* and went on to win by 28 minutes 20.25 seconds. Yet *Mischief* wasn't the first home. Unofficially that honour went to *Gracie*, finishing more than a minute ahead of *Mischief* although she had started 11 minutes after her.

Although *Gracie* had to keep to leeward of the competing yachts to avoid interfering with them, she sailed the journey in four hours, five minutes, 46 seconds, beating *Mischief* by six minutes 27 seconds and *Atalanta* by almost 40 minutes. *Gracie's* time was the fastest recorded for the distance.

The second race, the next day, was on the outside course, 16 miles to leeward of Buoy Five, off Sandy Hook and back. The wind was brisk from the west, the day fine, but the result inevitably the same. *Atalanta* was beaten by 38 minutes 54 seconds, which remains the biggest defeat in the history of the cup.

If nothing else, one might consider that the vanquished *Atalanta* crew were the best fed losers. When the tug, the *E. Luckenbrach* drew alongside *Atalanta* to tow her out to the Hook for the start of the race, the skipper was informed that Captain Cuthbert and several of his crew were ashore having breakfast.

Cuthbert and *Atalanta* finally arrived at the start an hour late. Again *Gracie* entered the race and again the only interest centred on which of the American yachts would finish first.

Although *Gracie* took eight seconds less to cover the journey, *Mischief* beat her by four minutes 38 seconds on corrected time. *Atalanta* was eight kilometres astern of *Mischief*.

Debate over the New York Yacht Club's choice of *Mischief* continued after the series had ended. *The New York Times* correspondent, ever ready to fuel the argument, wrote: "One old yachtsman remarked yesterday that, as the real owner of the *Mischief* is an Englishman, he could see no reason for the selection of the *Mischief*, except, perhaps, that her nominal owner, Mr. William Krebs, is chairman of The America's Cup committee."

The record books will show the *Mischief* as the fourth American defender of the Cup. The owners of *Gracie* can be consoled that they had the fastest boat.

The final summary belongs to *The Spirit of the Times*: "..... *Mischief*, a tried and proven sloop, confessedly one of the fastest in the world, thoroughly fitted out and equipped, fully manned and magnificently handled, distanced the *Atalanta*, a new yacht, hastily built, totally untried, and miserably equipped, with sails that misfitted like a Chatham Street suit of clothes, and bungled around the course by an alleged crew, who would have been overmatched in trying to handle a canal boat anchored in a fog."

Captain Cuthbert was in many ways "captain undaunted". He announced at the conclusion of the race that he would leave the *Atalanta* in New York and challenge the following spring.

The America's Cup committee, fearful that the Cup would lose its appeal because of another one-sided event against the Canadian, requested a new Deed of Gift.

A clause in the Deed of Gift barred a beaten vessel from challenging a second time, "Until after the expiration of two years from the time such contest has taken place." *Atalanta* was taken back to Lake Ontario where it remained and raced with success for some 15 years.

It is believed to have outlasted the Bay of Quinte Yacht Club which had ceased to exist by the turn of the century. The challenge of 1881 may not have provided The America's Cup with the greatest races in its history, but Cuthbert, whatever the motives that drove him, maintained the link in the chain and he has the honour of being the only challenger or defender who wore the mantle of owner, designer, builder and skipper.

His two challenges were the only ones by Canada to reach a defence series.

1885

NYYC Welcomes British Return

Puritan (NYYC) 2 defeated Genesta (Royal Yacht Squadron) nil.

THE challenge of 1885 promised much ... a new era in America's Cup racing; the English had returned after a lapse of 14 years and the Americans, seemingly unbeatable in Cup races, had to rethink their boat design principles.

The English yachtsmen and designers had not been idle. They had developed fast and able cutters, the prime example as far as the American yachtsmen were concerned, was a Scottish-built vessel, the *Madge*. The *Madge* arrived in New York in the August of 1881, three months before *Atalanta's* challenge, crossing the Atlantic on the deck of the steamer, *Devonia*. According to the *Lawson History*, she was "as wet as a half-tide ledge in a sea way, but speedy and handy, and she made a deep impression here.

"....we had no sloop on this side of the water fast enough to defend the Cup against a large, powerful, and fast English cutter. These circumstances led to a renaissance in yacht-building in the United States that year. Old traditions were jettisoned, radical steps were taken, and American yachting was benefitted by a new type of yacht, the forerunner of the deep, fast boats of the present day."

The *Madge* was raced with outstanding success in American waters, winning seven of her eight races. It was clear that the American designers needed to abandon their traditional thinking and look at ways, through experimentation, of developing even faster vessels.

While American yachting had much to think about after the appearance of the *Madge*, The America's Cup committee looked at a more specific and updated Deed of Gift. The club felt the original deed was no longer adequate and, prompted by Captain Cuthbert's plan to leave the *Atalanta* in New York in preparation for another challenge the following year, sent the deed to George Schuyler, the only surviving member of the original donors of the Cup.

One significant new clause was that the challenging club must hold its regattas on an ocean course, thereby prohibiting future challenges from Canadian clubs based, for instance, on the Great Lakes. Another demand was that a beaten vessel could not challenge again until another series had passed, or after a period of two years.

Both clauses angered the Canadians, for it not only directly ended Captain Cuthbert's plans to race *Atalanta* in 1882, but also virtually ended any further participation by a Canadian club, at least for almost a century. Cuthbert's plan to leave his yacht in New York and challenge again had obviously worried the Americans who felt that not only would time and money be wasted in such a venture but that the status of The America's Cup would be lowered.

The Deed of Gift also made it clear, once and for all, that the challenger would have to meet only one defending vessel during a series of races.

Americans had become patriotic, even sentimental, towards the Cup. While few showed any interest at all in the first challenge in 1870, four successful challenges in their own waters instilled in them a firm national pride. In 1882, after the conditions of the Deed of Gift had been accepted, the New York Yacht Club issued circulars to yacht clubs of repute around the world, inviting them to challenge for the Cup. The club enclosed a copy of the new Deed with each invitation.

The British, who had given up all hope of challenging again with a schooner, viewed with interest the disastrous Canadian attempts. While the ease of the New York Yacht Club's victories did not dampen their ambitions, it did convince the English yachtsmen that their only chance of success was with a cutter, the best British yacht of that period.

Puritan winning the second and final race. From a painting by Franklyn Bassford.

Four years after the *Madge* first raced in American waters, the British made their move. Mr. J. Beavor-Webb, a successful English designer, challenged on behalf of Sir Richard Sutton, representing the Royal Yacht Squadron, and on behalf of Lieutenant William Henn, who represented the Royal Northern Yacht Club. The dual challenge surprised the Americans, particularly the New York Yacht Club committee.

Beavor-Webb designed both *Genesta* and *Galatea*, the former owned by Sir Richard Sutton, the latter owned by Henn. The challenging clubs proposed that races with *Genesta* be sailed between August 20 and September 1, and should *Genesta* be unsuccessful, those with *Galatea* sailed before September 17, each challenge over the required best-of-three series. The Cup, they decreed, would return to England should *Galatea* be successful.

The British also requested that the New York Yacht Club's defending yacht be named prior to the day of the race and that the races be conducted over an ocean course, "free from tides and shallow water."

With due courtesy, the New York Yacht Club accepted both challenges. However, they informed the British that the second challenge, that of *Galatea*, would have to be met the following year should *Genesta* be unsuccessful. The club also agreed to name the defender a week before the races, but reserved the right to substitute another yacht should the chosen yacht be disabled.

Genesta was classed as being typical of the British cutter of that period. She was not unalike the *Madge*, which had such a profound impact on the Americans in 1881; she had a large sail area, was narrow-gutted, long and very different to typical American cutters and schooners.

The New York Yacht Club refused the request that all three races should be sailed on the ocean course. It was proposed, and later accepted by the challenging syndicate, that the first race should be over the inside course, of 38 miles; the second, over a triangular course, of 40 miles, and the third, 20 miles to windward or leeward, off Sandy Hook — the time limit to be seven hours. Of greatest concern to the New York Yacht Club, however, was in finding a yacht fast enough to match the obvious improvement in British design and yacht-building.

It was a factor they had not been forced to consider so seriously in previous challenges. Recognising the very real danger, the club appealed to all yacht clubs of the United States, a significant step, and indicative of their concern.

Clubs were invited to enter "single-masted vessels of not less than 60 feet in length on the water-line" for trials in late June or early July.

Although the invitation may have at first suggested that another club would be given the chance to defend the Cup, the circular made it clear that "any vessel taking part therein shall be subject to selection by the committee in charge as the representative of the New York Yacht Club ...."

The response was remarkable, though it was not surprising that a syndicate from Boston, the original nursery of saltwater sailing in the United States, should feel inclined to build a boat with the sole purpose of earning the right to defend the Cup.

It brought together two men who were to play a prominent part in The America's Cup over the next three challenges — designer Edward Burgess and part owner (manager of the syndicate) General Charles J. Paine.

Burgess, virtually unheard of in New York yachting circles, designed what was to be regarded as a pioneering vessel, called *Puritan*. The *Lawson History* describes her;

" *Puritan* was a radical departure from the old-time American sloop, and a type in herself, combining the beam, power and centreboard of a sloop with some of the depth and the outside lead of an English cutter. In this respect she was the first vessel of her kind, the pioneer in the combination of American and English ideas which has resulted in the wonderfully fast yachts of the present. She was far removed from the 'skimming dish' types that preceded her as the racers of the present period are removed from her. She was at that time undoubtedly the fastest American yacht ever built, and events in the racing season of 1885 justified the belief that had she not been built, the Cup would have gone back to England that year."

Puritan was 94 ft long ; 81 ft. 1½ in. on the waterline; beam of 22 ft 7 in; draft 8 ft 8 in. Her interior was furnished in mahogany and pine and classed as luxurious with every convenience, including a ladies cabin, two state-rooms and accommodation for 18 men.

Several of the *Puritan* syndicate were either members of the Eastern Yacht Club of Marblehead, or at least associated with the club. *Puritan* was, therefore, enrolled among the club's fleet under the name of Edward Burgess and later qualified as the Cup defender, although Burgess was not a member of the New York Yacht Club.

General Paine was a member of the club, and this enalbed *Puritan* to qualify as the defender.

While the Bostonians were producing their vessel, the New York Yacht Club was deeply involved in its own building project. They took scant interest in other candidates since they were of the belief that they would eventually provide the defender.

A. Cary Smith, considered the finest of all American yacht designers of that time, was chosen as designer. He produced a conventional centreboarder with an iron hull and, according to reports, she was "designed as an improved *Mischief*". When the first trial race was sailed, August 21 — later than anticipated — only four yachts were at the start, *Puritan*, *Priscilla*, *Bedouin* and *Gracie*.

Bedouin, a cutter, was very English in design. She was considered an able craft, having won a number of races in the preceeding two years. She was 83 ft overall and 70 ft 8 in above the waterline. *Gracie* was well known to the yachting fraternity, having been a triallist — an unlucky one at that — in the 1881 defence.

An artist's view of Puritan fouling Genesta. The British defender's bowsprit catches the luff of Puritan's mainsail.

Neither *Bedouin* nor *Gracie* were a match for the two newly constructed yachts. *Puritan* won the first trial by 11 minutes, 12 seconds on corrected time; *Priscilla* won the second trial by 5 minutes, 14 seconds. However, *Puritan* won the third by just one minute 52 seconds from *Priscilla*, qualifying the Boston built boat as the defender.

There was little doubt that *Genesta* was one of Britain's finest racing cutters. She won seven and was placed second ten times in 34 races. Of composite build, her frame was made of steel and she was planked with oak.

Despite the Americans' high regard for *Genesta*, many New Yorkers were anxious to lay heavy bets on *Puritan*.

It is a curious aspect of yachting that even in those times men saw sidewagers as a product of the sport, so much so that *The New York Times* headed a front page story; BETTING ON THE PURITAN.

"Bets are freely offered on the *Puritan*, but, except in insignificant sums, they (Americans) find no takers. One Wall-street man has had $5,000 in his

hands for at least a week to bet on the Yankee sloop, but up to last evening had not been able to place it."

The matter of betting reached the ridiculous the next day when the same paper reported that Englishmen would only bet in hats! "As a rule, when a *Puritan* man makes overtures to a *Genesta* man, the latter replies, in substance, as follows: 'Well, I won't bet any money, but as a matter of sentiment I will bet you a hat'."

There is a familiar ring to the *Genesta* syndicate's attempts to deny access to the yacht while it was in

Puritan to windward of Genesta in running seas. Genesta proved herself a worthy challenger in the second race.

dock to anyone other than those closely associated with the challenger.

A guard was placed at the gate of the dock, allowing only those who presented a card to enter. Such secrecy irked the curious New Yorkers, who gathered each day determined to view the new vessel. After all, *Genesta* was seen as a new phase in yacht designing and the Americans were anxious to discover whether

Above (left): Owner of Puritan, General Charles Paine and (right) Edward Burgess, designer of the 1885 defender. The two Bostonians shared three Cup defence victories.

the English had indeed produced a "superboat".

Beavor-Webb, finding some humour in the Americans' irritation, explained that the reason for the secrecy was that *Genesta* had been outfitted with an electric motor in her keel. Some members of the Press actually took him seriously! Beavor-Webb eventually relented, after a threatening mob, reported to be in its hundreds, gathered at the gate leading to the dock.

According to a report: "General astonishment was expressed at the full fullness of the cutter's sides. Her characteristic lines may be pretty clearly indicated by saying that she differs from other cutters in being U-shaped instead of V-shaped."

Considerable argument raged over the style of the defender. While Americans claimed she was a sloop, Beavor-Webb argued that she was a modified cutter. It was assessed that Beavor-Webb had made the statement to ensure that the new British cutter would remain popular should *Genesta* be beaten.

Yet the *Puritan* was in some ways a tribute to English designing since, as the *Lawson History* states, *Puritan* was a "combination of American and English ideas."

As race time neared, the Americans received an unexpected bonus. Most accepted that *Puritan* would have to give a time allowance of some two to three minutes to *Genesta*. Such deductions were made from the measurements given by Beavor-Webb and because *Genesta's* top mast had been shortened by some two and a half feet. To the Americans' surprise, *Puritan* had to allow the Genesta only 31 seconds.

The first race was set for September 7, but was called off because of lack of wind. *Puritan*, not yet at the outer buoy when the race was abandoned after five hours, was two miles ahead of *Genesta*. Neither boat had a chance of finishing the event within the seven hour time limit.

The race showed, however, that *Puritan* was by far the faster boat in light airs. It also showed that interest in the Cup had never been higher. Park-Row was impassable after five o'clock because of the multitude waiting outside newspaper offices for the latest bulletin. *The New York Times* devoted four complete columns on the front page — to a race that was called off!

The next day, both yachts met at the start in a freshening south to south east wind, as one report had it, "perfect sloop weather". New York yachtsmen were convinced that *Puritan* could not be beaten.

For the second time, the race had to be postponed. While both yachts were manoeuvring for the start, *Puritan* attempted to cross *Genesta's* bow, thereby fouling the challenger, and causing damage to both boats. The *Puritan* skipper miscalculated the speed of the yachts and failed to clear *Genesta*, whose bowsprit shot through *Puritan's* mainsail, "making a wide triangular rent."

Genesta's bowsprit broke off and fell into the water, carrying the jib with it. There was little doubt among American observers that *Puritan* had been at fault since *Genesta* was on a starboard tack and had right of way.

It took the race committee little time to confirm that the blame lay squarely with the *Puritan*. Here was the stroke of fortune the English could well have used. Yet to the surprise of the Americans, Sir Richard Sutton refused to accept the race under such circumstances.

To qualify as the winner, *Genesta* had only to make some running repairs and cover the journey within the time allowance. Sir Richard queried the race committee, asking them could he have time to rig a spinnaker-boom to replace the bowsprit.

While the committee deliberated on his request, Sir Richard informed them that he did not want to win a race that way. "We want a race; we don't want a boilover," he said.

Genesta, on the right, leading during a race before she went to New York. She was one of Britain's top racing cutters and proved a worthy America's Cup challenger, losing the second race by just one minute 38 seconds.

His gesture ensured a popularity few foreigners earned in New York, for no previous challenge involved such a magnanimous decision.

The New York Times reported one New Yorker as declaring, "Sir Richard Sutton is the most popular man just now in America," adding that he was "the talk of the town" and "praised on every hand."

Even when the owners of *Puritan* offered to meet the expenses of repairs to *Genesta*, Sir Richard again declined.

Repairs took just two days and by Friday September 11, both yachts were ready to complete the twice postponed race. Yet the race would be postponed twice more, each time because of lack of wind. On the third attempt, the yachts were becalmed after six hours of sailing. Significantly, *Puritan* was ahead by one and a half miles. As New Yorkers began to wonder if a curse had been placed on the series, the day arrived, September 14 — a full week after the first attempt to race had been made.

Genesta won the start, though only by a few seconds, and although she was to cause some moments of worry during the outward journey, she lost the lead after the first few minutes of the race and did not regain it. *Puritan* won by 16 minutes and 47 seconds. American anxiety had built up over the postponed starts, as *The New York Times* testified. "The wind was falling light and hearts on the tugboat were falling heavy."

They had little need for concern. *Puritan* and *Genesta* made good time on their homeward journey, *Puritan* taking six hours, six minutes, five seconds overall, almost an hour within the required time.

The second race — and the last as it turned out — was the closest and hardest fought to date. Just one minute 38 seconds separated the two yachts at the finish.

The sea was classed as lumpy and the wind rose to gale proportions — "cutter weather". Observers were high in their praise of *Genesta*, particularly her crew, rated in the *Lawson History* as, "as fine a lot of seamen as ever crossed the ocean to race for the cup." No boat, it was said, was ever handled with greater skill.

Genesta led at the start and held a two minute advantage at the halfway mark. At one stage on the homeward journey the wind blew at 30 knots. "Both yachts were sailing with their lee rails under water and their decks awash."

Confidence rose among the cuttermen. *The New York Times* explained: "This is the weather they have been yearning for; this is the tune to make the Yankee Doodle sick; here is the dance at which sloops must pay the piper."

Sadly for *Genesta*, it was not to be. Gradually, *Puritan* made up the leeway, the *Lawson History* explaining, "The *Puritan* then had the advantage of heading up a trifle higher, while still maintaining a pace equal to that of the cutter; and thus the boats, bow to bow, rushed bravely through the water. It was a most exciting struggle, and the anxiety of the spectators, as the yachts approached the finish line, was intense."

Despite the high praise for *Genesta*, it was pointed out that the captain, John Carter had erred on the beat home by carrying too much sail. The challenger maintained a topsail which flapped about in the strong, gusting breeze, while *Puritan's* topsail was hauled down.

Genesta had shown itself to be a worthy challenger and one of the finest boats of her type. Her second race performance helped to restore credibility to The America's Cup, and Sir Richard Sutton's sportsmanship created an atmosphere of goodwill, the like that had not been seen between the British and American yachting fraternities since The America's Cup began.

Sir Richard remained in New York with *Genesta* and won three cups before returning home.

The America's Cup 1851-1987

Mayflower saluted by the spectator fleet in first race.

1886

Home Comforts Sink Galatea

Mayflower (NYYC) 2 defeated Galatea (Royal Northern YC) nil.

IF the result of the 1886 challenge followed a familiar path, the manner of the challenge was unlike any before it. At different times, The America's Cup has been intense, controversial, even bitter.

Lieutenant William Henn, an Irish-born sailor, brought a new dimension. He exuded such casual airs, and a seeming lack of urgency, that New Yorkers initially believed he was attempting to deceive them into thinking his Beavor-Webb designed cutter, *Galatea*, was a creaking old sea bucket.

Enforcing those feelings amongst the Americans was also the fact that Henn brought with him his wife, the first woman to cross the Atlantic in a racing yacht, several dogs and a pet monkey. Below decks, *Galatea* was a virtual floating Victorian Mansion, with its expensive rugs, heavy tables, mementoes, paintings, lounges, lace in every living room and, as time wore on, many gifts from admiring New Yorkers.

The star attraction, however, was Peggy, the pet monkey, which as one report explained, was as adept at pulling on a halyard as a professional sailor.

Whenever racing began she would run excitedly to the bowsprit and jump up and down. Peggy died before the Henns returned to England. She was given a full sailor's burial, with pall bearers and lowered into the sea wrapped in a Union Jack.

The Henns proved to be highly popular figures around New York. Relationships between the competing British and American yachting fraternities had been warm and cordial following the impressions left by Sir Richard Sutton the previous year.

The Henns frequented theatres and clubs in New York, helping to support claims that their visit was more social than business. The couple seemed little inclined to correct the impression. On the Sunday before the first race — two days before in fact — neither Lieutenant Henn nor his wife went near *Galatea*, preferring the company of yachting friends at Larchmont Manor.

Lieutenant Henn joined the Royal Navy when he was 13 and retired, at his own request, 15 years later. He served in Africa and in 1872 was second in command in the mission to locate the missionary, Dr. David Livingstone.

Mrs. Henn enjoyed her husband's passion for sailing, and, indeed, helped to buy *Galatea*. She and her husband lived on board a yawl, the *Gertrude*, for seven years before deciding to try their hand at racing yachts, although their initial intention was to buy a larger boat, rather than indulge in racing.

Henn made no apologies for his preference for the pleasures of cruising. According to historians it was this apparent casual attitude of the cruising sailor that planted so much suspicion in the minds of the New Yorkers. Henn was simply being himself, a fact that later added to his popularity in America. No one doubted his enthusiasm for sailing or his knowledge of the seas.

Mrs. Henn's popularity among the women of New York was to become somewhat of a burden for *Galatea*. She was visited regularly by admiring women bearing gifts, many of them potted plants, unnecessary extras in a racing yacht already weighed down by so many lavish extras. While the plants may have added to the appearance of *Galatea*, they detracted from the vessel's speed.

The Henns enjoyed the admiration of their yacht. According to *The New York Times*: "Lovely women, with faultlessly dressed escorts, carefully picked their way down Pike-street and across the dust of South-street, and went into ecstasies over the graceful contour of the craft..."

Little mention is made of the dogs, though one assumes they remained on board and returned

Above: The luxurious interior of the British defender Galatea with its chaise lounges and antiques. Right: The graceful Galatea with an intrepid forehand on the bowsprit. Inset: Galatea's owner, Lt. William Henn.

home with their owners.

The *Galatea*, for obvious reasons, was regarded by the Americans as a cruiser rather than a racer and was felt to be far less formidable than *Genesta*. Built in Glasgow by John Reid and Sons, *Galatea* was launched on May 1, 1885 and failed to win any of her 15 races in the first year. Though overhauled the following year, she could only manage two second placings, hardly the record of a potential America's Cup winner!

Interest in the Cup ran high in America and the New York Yacht Club wasted no time in accepting Henn's challenge. It was felt that after *Puritan's* victories Boston might again provide the challenger.

General Paine, his appetite for competition whetted after the previous year's series, assumed the responsibilities of owner and asked Edward Burgess, by now the most talked about yacht designer on the East Coast, to build an improved *Puritan*.

Burgess, who had been a sailor since his youth, was criticised initially when yachting experts saw *Puritan's* line. It was said that he did not have the technical training for yacht designing and New Yorkers doubted his ability to produce an America's Cup yacht. After all, Burgess was a naturalist, having graduated from Harvard in 1874. He was forced into designing to support himself when his father's business crashed. His vision of future yachts was honed, however, from a summer spent on the Isle of Wight. There he watched and studied the local cutter and led to his "compromise", a cross between the British and American yachts.

General Paine, from an old Bostonian family, was 53 and he, too, graduated from Harvard with a law degree, but he did not practise. A shy man, he inherited a considerable fortune and invested in railroads in the west and in Texas. He volunteered for duty in the Civil War and commanded troops, where he won his rank. However, Paine remained close to his first love, sailing, and when the opportunity came to enter The America's Cup stakes, he was not only a man with the wealth to achieve his dreams, but a yachtsman of immense talent, known for his skill and ability to extract even the slightest improvements from his boats.

Paine and Burgess were an awesome combination — Burgess on the drawing board and Paine on the deck of a Burgess designed vessel. Burgess' second attempt was *Mayflower*. According to the *Lawson History*; "In general appearance she was much like *Puritan*, having the same straight stem and handsome

overhanging stern. Her bow, however, was longer and finer, and where *Puritan's* was hollow, *Mayflower's* was fuller. Most of the changes made were the fruit of General Paine's ideas, skilfully adapted by Mr. Burgess. *Mayflower* was built chiefly of wood, her length overall being 100 feet. She had the same feature of outside ballast and weighted centre-board as her predecessor."

Mayflower did not meet with instant success. She lost each of her first three races against *Puritan* and the Press and public immediately classed her as inadequate as a defender and gave her little or no chance in the trials.

General Paine had other ideas and gave the New York critics an insight into his thoroughness. Paine spent many tedious hours readjusting her, some of the changes only slight but when combined, made her a faster boat.

Although adept in the art of fine tuning, Paine still understood the value of a professional skipper in match racing. He hired Martin Stone, an experienced captain, who had sailed the schooner *Halcyon* for General Paine, to skipper *Mayflower* in its races.

Mayflower's three trial opponents were *Puritan*, *Priscilla* and *Atlantic*, a new boat built for the Cup defence by a syndicate from the Atlantic Yacht Club. *Atlantic* was made of wood and was not as fast as *Mayflower*; nor were *Puritan* and *Priscilla*. Paine and Burgess had done their homework well. *Mayflower* won both trials.

In keeping with the camaraderie that developed between the British and American crews, it was not uncommon for the crew of one of the yachts to visit "the enemy" — before the races began.

Two days before the first race, while *Galatea* lay in dock, members of the British crew visited the *Mayflower*. When they arrived they found a large crowd watching from the shore. According to one report: "There was one little fellow who looked almost too puny to be an able seaman. His quickness, however, was astonishing. He went up the rigging, over the topmast, and down again in less than a minute, and then gravely saluted the people on the shore who clapped their hands and shouted, 'well done'."

As the day of the first race neared, it was easy to understand the continued suspicion with which New Yorkers viewed Henn and his yacht. Henn trialed *Galatea* while towing a dinghy and rarely worked with a racing trim. Critics wondered right up until race time whether he was hiding some marvellous superboat with hidden qualities. What they didn't understand was that while Henn was competitive, he was not the type to be bothered with the pains of subtefuge and mystery, and as the Americans were about to find out, *Galatea* was virtually as they had seen her.

So concerned were the English that *Galatea's* designer, Beavor-Webb took command as the first race neared, endeavouring to extract every second of speed from her. One reason for her sluggishness early in her racing career was that the lead for her keel had not been poured properly. The keel was riddled with

Mayflower captured so majestically by artist, William F Halsall.

holes which filled with water. Though the mistake was corrected, she still lacked the speed expected of her.

The mystery built around *Galatea* by the Press brought out "the greatest fleet of yachts and steamboats ever seen in American waters" for the first race. As betting on the outcome became more brisk — one American laid $1000 to $750 on the *Mayflower* — the yachts prepared for the start in a light southerly breeze.

Galatea won the start by a mere second. It was clear not long after that she had not been hiding any super powers. *Mayflower* sailed better to windward and although the challenger appeared to tack quicker, within 15 minutes of the start, *Mayflower's* lead was one minute. It was here that both yachts found a large schooner, anchored close to shore, in their way.

Mayflower luffed round it, but *Galatea* was forced to leeward, losing even more time. Captain Stone remained at *Mayflower's* wheel throughout the race while Paine and Burgess stayed near, occasionally offering advice. The race, anxiously awaited by expectant New Yorkers, lost its lustre after *Mayflower's* early lead. The American boat won by 12 minutes and two seconds. The dominance of American yachts now left a questionmark on the Cup, even in *The New York Times* which had devoted reams of gushing prose to each race.

"There is such a thing as a success that loses value by too-muchness: such was the victory of the *Mayflower* over the *Galatea* yesterday morning." If *The New York Times* correspondent harboured doubts of the event's merits, he did not allow it to affect his colourful pen! He wrote of the day: "The delicate veils of vapor that wrapped the mutilated torso of Liberty on Bedloe's Island, and made the Brooklyn Bridge look like a spider's web thrown by a gigantic camera on rain clouds, melted away from the upper harbor..... The horizon frowned with wicked-looking clouds, over which appeared the characteristic American thunderheads, crisp, dazzling white, crinkled yet sharp in outline against the bluest blue...... Out of the smoky north appeared the huge white bulks, black-bordered, hurrying their thousands to the meet; from the Kill Van Kull issued a fleet of oyster smacks, most picturesque of all our craft...... the mass of first arrivals.... Boats of every build.... Everybody

Galatea and Mayflower during the first race. Mayflower is to windward. She proved herself the faster of the two yachts and sailed away to win the race by 15 minutes.

had on his best bib and tucker, his best smile and best sea-talk ....and many-body (sic) brought their wife or sweethearts to prevent too broad a smile. So the hurly-burly glided, skipped, slid, bobbed, dashed, forged, rolled, crept and spurted down the Narrows...." Such a day of expectation. Such a flop!

The second race, two days later was abandoned because of heavy fog. The race started in a good breeze but ended with *Galatea* and the Committee's boat lost. The only excitement was provided by *Galatea* as it sailed toward the starting mark at the Scotland lightship. Two pigeons sent from the official race tug, the *E. Luckenbach* to New York City bearing news of the weather, instead headed straight for *Galatea*, one resting as the report had it, on "*Galatea's* spreader and the other on one of her forward stays."

When Beavor-Webb saw that the two birds were apparently not prepared to leave their perches, he sent a crewman aloft to scare them away. Superstitious sailors exclaimed; "That breaks their luck! They can't win now." They were right, but then *Galatea* was not without its luck. It was at least two miles astern when the race was postponed.

As the two yachts reached the start for the re-run, Henn sent a message to the committee tug requesting that the race to be over 30 miles and not 40. Henn had taken ill on board and was anxious to return to shore to see a doctor. However, in the true spirit of yachting he did not want to miss the race.

The race committee claimed they did not have the power to change the distance and ordered the race to start over the selected distance, 20 miles out and 20 miles back. Henn not only remained on board and suffered physically, he suffered his second defeat. The America's Cup once again remained at the New York Yacht Club.

Although Henn had not found success on the waters, he was liked and respected as a good sailor by the Americans. He also believed that the Royal Yacht Squadron would not challenge again since the weather "is so calm" and that few British owners were keen to miss a whole season while challenging for a cup in foreign waters. But it did not stop the challengers arriving. The next was just 12 months away.

The America's Cup 1851-1987

Volunteer, the 1887 winner, running before the wind. From a painting by James G. Tyler.

1887

Cup Loses Veil of Cordiality

Volunteer (NYYC) 2 defeated Thistle (Royal Clyde YC) nil.

WHILE cordiality had been trademarks of the two previous challenges, the 1887 event only served as a reminder that rancour and mistrust were just beneath the surface in events of international significance.

Lieutenant Henn hadn't completed his challenge when the next was being conceived, though, as Henn made clear, it would not come from the Royal Yacht Squadron. This time the challenger would be from Scotland. Although no challenger had even come close to wresting the ornate silver trophy from its place of rest in the New York Yacht Club, the Royal Clyde Yacht Club's members lacked no confidence in their endeavour.

They set upon a course that antagonised and distanced the New York Yacht Club. They had faith in their designer, the highly qualified Scotsman, G.L. Watson, who went to New York to study the designs of the American sloops. Strangely, he did not synchronise his trip with the *Mayflower-Galatea* races, arriving after they had finished. Watson later admitted that he may have erred in not watching the races for they would have given him first hand impressions of the difference between the English cutter and the American sloop.

In New York, Watson studied American yacht building techniques and was surprised at the eagerness of the locals to help him. Perhaps the cordiality of the previous two challenges influenced them, or perhaps they felt pity toward any challenger.

Watson was also considered a highly skilled yacht designer, his workmanship obvious in the brilliant little cutter the *Madge*, which opened up American eyes to the advances of British design in 1881. Later when the Scottish challenge was cloaked in secrecy, several American yachtsmen expressed their regret that they had accorded so free a hand in friendship. They felt they had been duped, particularly after the Royal Clyde Yacht Club refused to divulge boat dimensions despite repeated requests from the New York Yacht Club. Friendships were strained and the New York Yacht Club doubted the challenging club's honourable intentions.

The head of the syndicate was James Bell, a keen supporter of yachting and a prominent Glasgow businessman. He was a Vice-Commodore of the Royal Clyde Yacht Club and appeared to have no other motive for challenging than to satisfy his passion for sailing.

The Royal Clyde Club's challenge letter to the New York Yacht Club stated simply that the name of their yacht was *Thistle* and that its waterline length was 85 feet.

The *Thistle* had been built in secret, and the challenging syndicate felt no obligation to reveal any dimension other than that required by the Deed of Gift. Requests from the New York Yacht Club for more information on the *Thistle's* lines met with stony silence.

Even when *Thistle* was launched it was covered in canvas. Watson, who had also designed the royal racing cutter *Britannia*, was a clever, clear thinking designer. He noted from his American studies that *Thistle* would need "acres of sail". *Thistle* was credited as having 9,000 square feet of sail, though it was some time before anyone outside the *Thistle* syndicate was allowed to see it.

Watson was also wary at being branded a "traitor" by British yachtsmen for he ignored the areas that would make her competitive in domestic conditions. This was a yacht built specifically for the America's Cup, American waters and the lighter American airs.

Livonia was built for the 1871 challenge, but with a view to racing in British waters, and with British lines. Watson was fortunate that the tonnage rating system used in British yachting had been abolished. Designers were no longer dependent on the beam of a vessel for determining a rating

The America's Cup 1851-1987

and could make their vessels as wide as they wanted.

Further conjecture over *Thistle's* secret design was fuelled by the publication in American newspapers of what were said to be the yacht's plans. Americans suspected that Watson had "planted" the plans to aid and abet his game of hide and seek.

Of course, the challengers could not keep *Thistle* under cover forever and the wraps were taken off for the British season. She was all her syndicate expected of her. In her first 15 races, she won 11, including a victory over the *Irex* regarded as the fastest yacht in England.

Anxious Americans waited to see her, desperately keen to learn not only her secrets, but the exact dimensions of her length at the waterline for it would determine which of the Cup yachts was to concede an allowance.

Not surprising when *Thistle* sailed into New York Harbour on August 16 she resembled the American defender, *Volunteer*. After all, Watson was a creative designer; he had spent his time in New York wisely.

Thistle arrived in New York after a run across the Atlantic lasting 22 days. Her overall power surprised American yachting enthusiasts and as this impression from the *Lawson History of the America's Cup*, reveals

"*Thistle* was well built and showed great power.

Homes and hotels of upper Fifth Avenue in 1887 as New York catches America's Cup fever. Below, the course off Sandy Hook followed by the yachts in the second and deciding race.

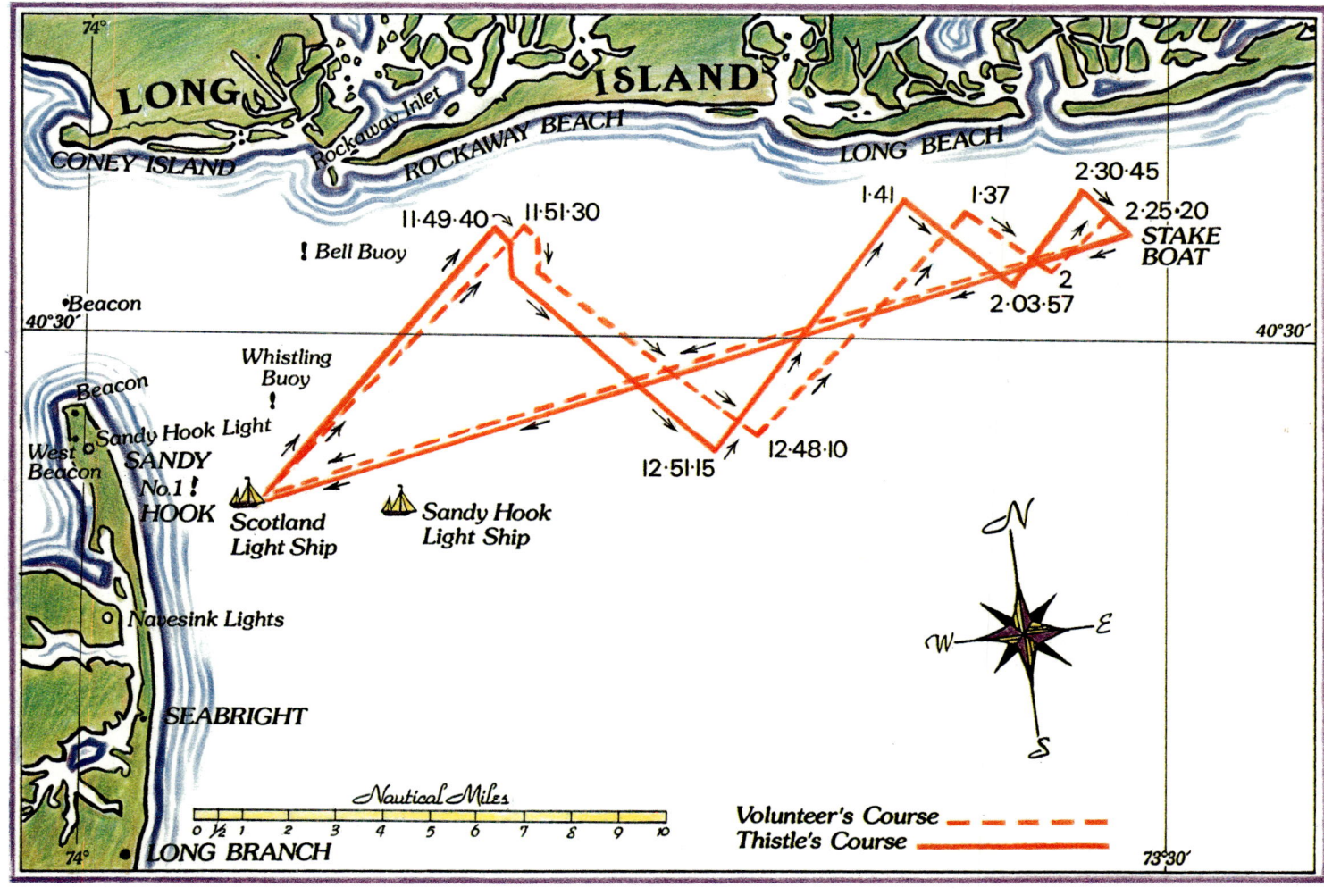

68

The America's Cup 1851–1987

The challenger Thistle as captured by artist Barlow Moore in a race in British waters in May 1887, four months before the first defence race.

Her dimensions were as follows; Length overall 108.50 feet; water-line 86.46 feet; beam 20.35 feet; draft 13.80 feet; mast from deck to hounds 62 feet; topmast 45 feet; boom 80 feet; gaff 50 feet; bowsprit outboard 38 feet; spinnaker-boom 70 feet; ballast 70 tons; displacement 138 tons; sail area 8968 square feet; racing measurement 89.20 feet. *Thistle's* hull was plated with Siemens-Martin steel, the lower plates being 3/8 and the upper 5/16-inch thick. The three lower strakes were lap-seamed, but the top body was plated flush. The frames were of unusual strength, and were tied by steel diagonal stringers, keelsons and floorings forming a network of the most secure description. Partial bulkheads gave still further strength, and there was also forward a collision bulkhead. The keel was of lead. It weighed about 70 tons, and was placed about three foot lower than *Volunteer's*. The yacht's channels and chainplates were placed outside, as was usual on British vessels. The sternpost showed considerable rake, and the clipper bow was considered handsome. She had a reefing bowsprit which could be shortened six feet."

Although two yachts came from the same school of yacht design, there were important and obvious differences. *Volunteer* was a centreboarder and had a

The America's Cup 1851-1987

Volunteer and Thistle in the first race, September 27. This was the last Cup race over the New York Yacht Club's inside course. Volunteer won by almost 20 minutes.

wheel for its skipper, Henry Haff while *Thistle* had a deep keel and possessed a tiller.

Thistle was no less handsome, and according to noted critics, the best challenger to that time. Yet as events would have it, Burgess and General Paine were one step ahead.

As testimony to their prowess and the awe in which they were held, when it was learned that the two Bostonians were attempting their third defence, no other American was prepared to build a yacht to challenge them. And just as well! *Volunteer* was another classic yacht, fulfilling Burgess' promise that he would build a vessel faster than *Mayflower*.

Volunteer was late in being designed since Burgess waited, along with the rest of eastern America, to learn of the dimensions of *Thistle*. In past challenges, the Americans were aware of the challenging yachts lines and could, therefore, design their defender accordingly. But this time the challenging club allowed only the smallest detail to be known. For that reason *Volunteer* was launched two months after *Thistle*. Built in great haste, *Volunteer's* finish was rough. She was made of steel and was bigger than any other yacht Burgess had attempted.

Compared with *Mayflower*, *Volunteer* had less beam and because her ballast could be stowed two feet lower in her hull, she was more stable. Haff, her skipper, was a veteran boatman from Islip, Long Island and had been on board *Mischief* when she beat *Atalanta* in 1881.

Volunteer was fast, no doubt about it, and because of her dominance the defender trials were seen as a waste of time and money. She had beaten *Mayflower*, *Puritan*, *Priscilla* and *Atlantic* in a number of races and when the trials were held, only *Mayflower* was prepared to face her. After a postponement because of lack of wind, *Volunteer* beat *Mayflower* so conclusively, that the cup committee considered a further trial unnecessary, and announced the same day that *Volunteer* was the defender.

Such a decision was not lost on *The New York Times*: "It is the *Volunteer*. It took only one good race to settle it. A scared dog, a defaulter, a streak of lightning, or anything else that is supposed to change its location with the celerity of a telegram humming along a wire, would have grown tired of following the *Volunteer* yesterday.

"Hyperbole is pardonable when the British Lion and the American Eagle are glaring at each other across a cup which means a feather in the cap of one or other of two distinctly maritime nations."

Of considerable interest among New York's yachting fraternity were the official dimensions of both yachts. The New York Yacht Club had been assured that the length of *Thistle* at its waterline was 85 feet.

Yet when the two vessels were officially measured on September 22, just four days before the first race, *Thistle's* waterline length was 86.46 feet.

The New York Yacht Club reacted with some anger to the discrepancy, their feelings heightened by the fact that the *Thistle* had been built in secrecy. They concluded that the challengers had deliberately lied about the dimension. The Cup committee deemed the "error" so serious they suggested that *Thistle* be barred from racing and the match cancelled.

In retrospect, historians concede that the Americans were making a mountain out of a mole hill. Yet in view of the significance attached to the match races, it is easy to understand how easily either side could magnify the dimensions of a problem. At the very heart of the issue was the credibility of the Cup itself and not insignificant to them, the wounded pride of the New York Yacht Club.

As other challenges have shown, where nations are drawn together in sporting conflicts such as The America's Cup, emotions, seemingly kept well in check, can run deep.

The America's Cup committee referred the question of *Thistle's* eligibility to the grand man of The America's Cup, an ageing George Schuyler, not the first time he had been called on as adjudicator.

The committee explained to Schuyler that a "great discrepancy was seen to exist ...." Watson saw, the differences in waterline length as an "overlook". Bell explained that the original measurement had been made "with the most perfect good faith." He further stated that "the extra length is penalised more heavily under your rule than under ours, and is not an advantage."

Since *Thistle's* waterline length was shown to be longer and not shorter than originally stated, the British vessel's allowance would be reduced, to the point where *Volunteer* had to concede six seconds to the British vessel, far less than the American's had anticipated.

Another factor pointed out to the Cup committee by Bell was the lack of necessity to supply the exact waterline length since the vessel had to be measured eventually by the New York Yacht Club.

Bell wrote: "Under the New York Yacht Club's rules, which were mutually accepted, competitors are at liberty to shift ballast up to 9 p.m. of the day prior to the race...."

"Were *Thistle* claiming to race at a water-line length of 85 feet, having 86.46, there would be grave reason for complaint, but *Thistle* is tendered for measurement of length and sail area as per New York Yacht Club rules....."

The question of allowances, however, was not the overriding issue with the Cup committee. They saw their authority and credibility under challenge. Schuyler, in his reply to the Cup committee, stated that despite the "remarkably inaccurate information" the variation was not sufficient reason to disqualify *Thistle*.

The Scots, however, were popular and all animosity between the two sides had disappeared. Again the betting was dull. According to *The New York Times* correspondent, "The visiting Scotchmen are not betting men and do not talk money."

Thistle was manned by a crew of 40 and skippered by Captain John Barr, considered one of the finest sailors in the world, and no stranger to American waters. A strict Presbyterian, he would allow no profanities on board. *The New York Times* recorded: "... if he could not win a race or handle a crew without swearing (he) would decline to win it."

Thistle was as light as her crew could make her. All her carpets were taken out; extra doors taken off and all unnecessary deck fittings removed. While there is no mention of it, one assumes they sailed without their bagpipers and without the liberal supply of Scotch whisky carried across the Atlantic.

The challenge syndicate declared that they intended to drink from The America's Cup after their success. They would remain thirsty men — the cup is bottomless. They were never to get even close to attempting a celebratory drink. Though *Thistle* promised much, and yachtsmen of the day proclaimed her the fastest vessel to challenge for the Cup, she failed.

The first race, on September 27, the last to be sailed over the New York Yacht Club's inside course, resulted in a 19 minute and 23 seconds victory to *Volunteer*. There was even more gloom three days later when *Thistle* lost the second race by 11 minutes, 48 seconds.

To signify the very end, *The New York Times* reported: "Take the cup back to the safe. Treasure it carefully for the children and the grand children and the great-grand-children to look at. It is America's Cup, and it always will be America's Cup till the stars and stripes grow lurid in the sunset lights of time. There is gloom among the children of Clyde. The bagpipe has the diphtheria. The red lion's tail has been twisted.......the Scotch Whiskey has lost its cheer........Sandy stares aghast at Colin, and Colin gazes gloom unto Sandy.........The Scotch can beat the English at it, but the Americans? Never! Westward the star of yacht building takes its way."

The British press reports basically rued the fact that they had not raced in home waters, suggesting that the results might have been different.

General Paine and Edward Burgess returned to Boston to a civic reception. They would never again be involved with The America's Cup; nor was *Volunteer*. Unlike *Puritan* and *Mayflower*, she was not used as a trial yacht for future challengers, spending the rest of her sailing years as a cruiser.

Captain Barr and his crew did not escape criticism, one report stating: "A gentleman who was aboard (*Thistle*) during the race expressed surprise at the lack of discipline among the Scotchmen. He said that Captain Barr appeared to be captain only in that his voice was the loudest in the crew."

Thistle left New York on October 4, less than a week after the second race. It would be some six years before the next challenge.

The Nathaniel Herreshoff designed Vigilant won all three races against Valkyrie II.

1893

Australia Considers the Cup

Vigilant (NYYC) 3 defeated Valkyrie II (Royal Yacht Squadron) nil

As the New York Yacht Club took steps to create a more rigid and standardised Deed of Gift, far away in Australian waters, yachtsmen were taking their first serious look at a challenge. Sydney yachtsmen waited keenly for the outcome of the *Thistle-Volunteer* races, though many of them were not surprised at *Volunteer's* victory. *Volunteer's* win so inspired a group of yachtsmen that they joined together to build their own yacht called *Volunteer*.

According to *Sydney Sails*, a book published in 1962 to mark the Royal Sydney Yacht Squadron's centenary, the designer of Sydney's *Volunteer*, Walter Reeks visited New York in October 1888, his object, "the building of an Australian yacht with which to challenge for The America's Cup."

Reeks inspected *Volunteer* in New York and spoke to officials of the New York Yacht Club about the Deed of Gift and other aspects of a challenge. When Reeks went to London soon after, he told yachtsmen, "I shall build a sloop yacht and will challenge under the new deed of gift when I send my boat, which will be in 1890."

On Reeks' return to Sydney, however, he could not persuade Sydney's yachtsmen, nor the city's financiers to back him. The Australian challenge died there.

The America's Cup went on in all its controversial glory. After rejecting a challenge from a Scottish businessman, Charles Sweet, the club appointed a committee of five to prepare a new Deed of Gift to be signed by George Schuyler. It was accepted officially on October 27, 1887, just one month after *Volunteer's* victory.

Unlike the previous two Deeds, this one was more in the line of a legal document, covering more than a thousand words and was a good many times longer than the previous deeds.

Significant changes were made. The challenging club was required to give in writing 10 months notice between the time of challenging and the first race. At the same time, the challenger would have to supply more comprehensive dimensions, such as load waterline length, beam at load waterline, the extreme beam and draught, "which dimensions shall not be exceeded."

The deed also stipulated that centreboard yachts should always be allowed to compete in future matches, without restrictions and that all races should be conducted on ocean course, free of headlands. The keenness to permit centreboarders to challenge was an obvious cover for the New York Yacht Club should they ever lose the Cup. They could challenge with a centreboarder in English waters without protest.

The ocean courses would be alternatively to windward or leeward, 15 miles, and a triangular course, the first leg to windward if possible.

The deed did not meet with universal approval. In fact, howls of protest came from across the Atlantic, and even in some American sectors, over the clause demanding more specific dimensions at the point of challenge.

It meant that the Americans would know at once the kind of yacht they were to face, and could build their defender accordingly. As if they didn't have enough of an advantage as it was!

The Press of the time challenged the New York Yacht Club's sense of fair play. According to the *Lawson History*, "No instrument set up in the world of sport has ever received more general condemnation than this Deed of Gift." Forest and Stream, considered the most conservative and fairminded of American yachting magazines, called the deed "an act to prevent yacht racing."

In the face of the growing storm, the New York Yacht Club relented and agreed to modify the terms of the deed, claiming that it would be prepared to run future challenges under the same

An artist's dramatic account of Valkyrie II's torn spinnaker, ripped to pieces in seconds during the third and final race.

conditions as those of 1885, 1886 and 1887 providing that should the challenging yacht win the event, it would hold to the new deed, dated October 1887.

Twelve months later the New York Yacht Club received its next challenge — from the Royal Yacht Squadron, on behalf of the Earl of Dunraven. However, Lord Dunraven assumed that he would not be forced to comply with the new deed if he won. The New York Yacht Club informed him that he would have to comply. After considerable correspondence, Lord Dunraven withdrew his challenge.

As the British began another apparent stand-off, frustrated and angry at the unfavourable terms of the New York Yacht Club, George Schuyler died. He was 79 and the last member of the original donors of the America's Cup. Schuyler died of heart trouble on board the yacht *Electra*.

On the other side of the Atlantic, Lord Dunraven remained silent, his decision to withdraw his 1890 challenge seemingly the last American yachtsmen were to hear of him. On November 25, 1892 however, Dunraven, through the Royal Yacht Squadron, made a second challenge. Again he sought amendments to the new Deed of Gift, including a request that he need supply only the waterline length and no other dimension.

Although Dunraven had come to understand that the New York Yacht Club would stand steadfastly by their rules, he still ventured into the lion's den with renewed optimism and requests for change. Whether it was his sheer persistence or the result of the earlier prolonged criticisms, the New York Yacht Club bowed to his request. Only the waterline length would be necessary with the challenge details.

The New York Yacht Club also agreed to a best-of-five race series and quite surprisingly, in view of their early demands, the Club agreed that any further challenge would be conducted under the same terms as the impending event. In many eyes the deed of 1887 was in tatters.

Lord Dunraven's challenger, *Valkyrie II*, was another G.L. Watson design. Built by D. & W. Henderson's on the Clyde, she was considered to be "a demon in light airs and a very devil in a blow."

Like *Thistle*, stories of *Valkyrie II's* sailing performances preceded her to New York. American yachtsmen never ceased to be wary of the possibility of a British "superboat", that in itself a measure of respect for designers such as Watson. Historians also make it clear that the reasons for some of the changes to the Deed of Gift were prompted by a fear that one day the Americans might lose the Cup. For instance, the reason for including a clause that allowed a future challenger to use a centreboard vessel was in case the Cup ever went to England. There was never any chance of the English challenging with a centreboard yacht. The Americans felt that in the event of the English becoming the defending nation, unless it was stipulated in the Deed of Gift, they would not allow a centreboard yacht to challenge.

The America's Cup was a major sporting event. Constant references were made in newspapers and magazines of the time to the many thousands — 50 thousand and over — who watched the races. Interest in the event was intense and there appeared to be an exaggerated feeling of expectancy. Problems became magnified, not least because the British were sending the type of vessel that might wrest the Cup away.

Valkyrie II was of composite build, steel and wood, and was seen as a powerful, though somewhat heavy boat when she arrived in New York on September 22.

The *Lawson History* describes her, "Her forefoot was cut away even more than *Vigilant's*, and her underbody was more graceful, though her coppered bottom did not present the glassy smoothness of the defender's bronze plates, she appeared heavier in hull and rig than the American boat, though smaller in beam, length and spars."

What the British had not been aware of was the great leap forward in American yachting. The 1887 defender *Volunteer* was already a relic of a past era in yacht designing technology.

A new, smaller keel vessel heralded in a new era, the most significant of the early designs was a yacht called *Gloriana*, built in 1891 and owned by E.D. Morgan who later owned The America's Cup defender, *Columbia*. *Gloriana* was narrower and deeper than the sloops and there was great disparity in her actual length and load waterline length, an advantage in time allowance considerations. For instance, *Gloriana* was 70 feet overall, yet only 45 feet 3 inches on the waterline.

The irony of *Gloriana* and the new American designs was that they were direct descendents of British yachts, the much talked about being *Madge*, which sailed impressively in American waters many years before, and two other yachts, *Clara* and *Minerva*. It was said that *Gloriana* was "as distinctive among American boats as the *America* or *Puritan*....".

While American yachting was undergoing such dramatic change, their great designer, Edward Burgess died. The son of a Boston sugar importer, Burgess designed three successful defenders and was honoured in various ways for his contribution to ship designing. After the 1887 challenge subscription funds from New England yachtsmen, and the New York Yacht Club, provided him with more than $20,000. Success brought him more work, too much for one man, and overworked and tired he contracted typhoid and died at home on July 12, 1891, at the age of 42. His son W. Starling Burgess later continued his designing business.

A new star arose among many excellent designers. His name was Nathaniel Greene Herreshoff, who not only designed six America's Cup defenders, but in partnership with his blind brother John, built eight defenders under the company name, Herreshoff Manufacturing Company.

Nathaniel was the fifth of nine children and was 45 when the 1893 challenge began. He had been successful in designing from the early 1870s. John, who had been blind since youth was an inventor of engines and boilers. New York yachtsmen went to Herreshoff for orders for two defence boats, *Vigilant*, a centreboarder, and *Colonia*, a keel boat.

At the same time, Boston provided its two defence boats, *Jubilee* and *Pilgrim*, the former designed by General Paine and his son, John B. Paine. Both yachts were of radical style with fin keels, a fact that surprised yachtsmen because of the size of both craft — *Pilgrim* was 124 feet long and *Jubilee*, 123 feet long.

But it was *Vigilant* which was selected as defender after winning the three trial races against *Colonia*, *Pilgrim* and *Jubilee*. The latter three never raced again.

Vigilant was owned by a syndicate managed by a wealthy banker C. Oliver Iselin. For the first time since anchor starts, the Cup committee agreed to a one-gun start which meant that each yacht's time, as it is today, was taken from the gun. It was, therefore, vital for each captain that he be first across. In the first race, sailed in calm, light conditions, *Vigilant* crossed 28 seconds ahead. Yet when the race was abandoned because of lack of wind, the *Valkyrie II* was 26 minutes and 20 seconds ahead of the defender.

The Americans were shocked. Here was the first significant evidence of a British "superboat", or so they thought. Many began to question the merits in the new look American designed yachts, some claiming they were too hard to handle. There was also a questionmark on the *Vigilant's* sails.

When *Valkyrie II* opened its spinnaker at the start, it was described as "a sail of the most filmy lightness.... thought at first to be silk ..." The next two attempts produced finishes, both races won by *Vigilant*, although *Valkyrie* had shown itself to be a most able yacht in light weather.

The third race, a 15-mile beat to windward and back, produced what was then declared the finest race in America's Cup history. The day was overcast and a strong easterly wind blew in off Sandy Hook. Both boats suffered damage at the start and the race was delayed.

When the race began both yachts headed into a stiff 25 knot wind. *Valkyrie* though nine seconds behind at the start, did better, pointing higher and after 40 minutes was some 200 yards ahead of *Vigilant*.

The *Lawson History* recorded: "The yachts were sailing with lee rails buried. The performance of *Valkyrie* was now by far the finest of any challenger, and though Americans did not realise it, she was driving home an argument for her type that was to lead to the abandonment of the centreboard in American cup yachts."

At the end of two hours sailing, *Valkyrie* was two minutes ahead. But as they rounded the mark and

headed for home, the seamanship of the *Vigilant's* crew was seen to advantage. With all haste and precision, according to the *Lawson History*, " *Vigilant* was under a pyramid of rounded and hardened canvas. Such sail-carrying is rarely witnessed in a Cup race."

It was later surmised that if the crew of *Valkyrie* had run up its sails in stops, they might have won the race. They might still have been successful anyway had *Valkyrie's* spinnaker not been ripped to pieces on the run home.

As it was *Valkyrie* lost by a mere 40 seconds, although as this report indicates, few knew who had won; "The finish was spectacular, and the crowds on the excursion steamers cheered themselves hoarse, without knowing which was the victor, for the Yankee boat won by only 40 seconds on corrected time."

The America's Cup had confirmed its status on the American sporting calendar. Lord Dunraven went home empty-handed but with excuses for defeat. He lived in the knowledge that he had given the Americans the toughest challenge yet. He added: "... I do not consider that the merits of the two boats have been determined." While the record books won't agree with him, there were many sympathetic Americans at the time who did. Many, too, did not like the look and style of *Vigilant*. They were sceptical of the future of its design. Thompson in the *Lawson History* wrote: "........she (*Vigilant*) was the prototype of a vicious kind of yacht, whose existence has been more a curse than a blessing to the sport of yacht-racing."

If the design of their defending yacht was the cause for their greatest problem in the next challenge, the New York Yacht Club would have been well satisfied. But such was not to be the case. Resentment and rancour were not far away.

Above: The start of the exciting third race. Valkyrie is closest to the starting boat. Below (left): Nat Herreshoff pointing out the finer points of yacht design. Right: Lord Dunraven, Valkyrie II's owner.

The America's Cup 1851-1987

1895

Accused Americans Win Again

Defender (NYYC) 3 defeated Valkyrie III (Royal Yacht Squadron) nil.

LORD Dunraven was in many ways an adventurer, an unusually creative man who loved writing and music. Born Windham Thomas Wyndham-Quin, fourth Earl of Dunraven, he was war correspondent for *The Daily Telegraph* and covered the Franco-Prussian War in 1870. He was an expert violinist and had only given up music when he discovered a love for sailing. His disregard for convention was often noted during his parliamentary career in the House of Lords.

His adventurous nature took him to the U.S. several times where he hunted deer and eventually bought acres of property in Colorado. He wrote a number of books and his autobiography is contained in two large volumes.

This then was the man who had returned to New York in 1895, his belly full of fire and his ambition unswerving. Lord Dunraven had been busy since his first challenge, returning to his sailing origins by racing small vessels in England. He had primarily become a small-boat owner and racer. *Valkyrie* was his first venture into the more expensive racing cutters.

George Watson, who had designed the previous two challengers, promised Dunraven a special yacht this time, although each of Watson's previous creations had, at one time, been regarded as "special" and even good enough to wrest The Cup from the New York Yacht Club.

Dunraven's challenge carried a number of requests for changes in the terms. Not the least of these requests, which later sparked one of the most controversial moments in America's Cup history, was the wish that races be sailed off Marblehead because of the congestion of spectator craft over the New York course off Sandy Hook.

He also asked for the yachts to be measured with all weights on board and their waterlines marked; all races to be started to windward and that he have the right to challenge with the fastest British boat available, if it were found that his yacht was not the fastest.

The America's Cup committee acceded to two requests — that the vessels be measured with weights on board and that he could substitute a second challenger if his first yacht was not considered fast enough.

On that basis, Dunraven challenged, listing his challenger as *Valkyrie III*, with a water-line length of 89 feet.

Watson had gone to the other extreme in designing *Valkyrie III* with a beam almost three feet wider than the American yacht *Defender*, and according to the *Lawson History*, "the greatest beam ever seen on either challenger or defender."

When *Valkyrie* was floated she was found to be unstable and 12 tons of lead were added to her ballast to correct the problem. Dunraven was forced to make several minor alterations and it meant that he, and his co-owners, had little time to trial the yacht before taking it to America.

Valkyrie showed in three races that Lord Dunraven would not need to seek a substitute yacht. She was indeed the fastest in England. In the meantime across the Atlantic, Nat Herreshoff was asked by a consortium that included Iselin, E.D. Morgan and William Vanderbilt to design a new boat for them.

Just as when Edward Burgess was the accepted master of American designers in the 1880s, word that Herreshoff was creating a boat for the 1895 challenge scared off all other intending syndicates. The new Herreshoff boat, called *Defender*, was the only one built for the challenge.

She was an extraordinary yacht in that she was the first keel boat to defend The Cup and the first American yacht built with aluminium. Expense was of no consideration. Herreshoff endeavoured to

The flying Defender, captured by James G Tyler.

make her as light as possible though many worried that she would never be sound enough structurally to withstand a strong blow. The opinion was that before her first season was over her mast would, under severe strain, put a hole through her bottom.

According to the *Lawson History*, *Defender* was carefully handled and had the shortest lifespan of any cup defender of her time. It wasn't the strain of racing, however, that caused an early end to her racing, but the corrosion of her hull because of the mixed use of metals. Electrolysis, not an English, nor an Irish boat, was to be her nemesis!

Commanded by captain "Hank" Haff, *Defender* was the first American defender to be crewed by a fully American crew. In the past, crews had been a combination of Americans, Swedes and Norwegians. According to the *Lawson History*, "The Deer Isle men were superior to Scandanavians in racing work chiefly because of their higher order of intelligence."

But for the generosity of the new owner of the *Vigilant*, Mr. A. E. Willard, *Defender* might not have raced in The Cup challenge.

No love was lost between either Iselin or Willard, and in a practice race off Sandy Hook, *Vigilant* flew a protest flag. The protest had not been heard when, in a later trial race, Willard, on board *Vigilant*, complained again that *Defender* had fouled his yacht. However, Willard refrained from protesting since a

Right, Valkryie III and Defender manoeuvre toward the start just 30 seconds before the foul. Above, five seconds after the foul. Note the trailing boat, Defender's badly bent topmast, caused by the starboard topmast-shroud springing out of the spreader.

yacht found guilty twice after a protest could not sail again in races under the jurisdiction of that club. Had Willard's protests been upheld, the New York Yacht Club would have had to look for a new defender. The Cup races between *Defender* and the *Valkyrie III* have been variously referred to as "a miserable fiasco."

Lord Dunraven was ever suspicious of American tactics, and in the end only one race was completed. Yachting historians believe that the true merits of the two yachts were never truly tested, though Defender did handle the light airs of the first race better than *Valkyrie*, winning by more than eight minutes.

Many Americans, depending on which newspaper they read, thought that the British yacht had triumphed.

In a heading which said GAVE THE WRONG NEWS, *The New York Times* told of how certain newspapers around the United States carried a story that *Valkyrie*, and not *Defender*, had won the first race.

"All Washington today is laughing over the ludicrous position in which the once discreet and careful

Washington Star yesterday placed itself by accepting and indorsing (sic) with ready gullibility The Associated Press faked story of the yacht race."

Much time was spent in explaining that the United Press International account was accurate and the only one to be taken seriously. Lord Dunraven, too, had to be taken seriously. When the race was over, he questioned American ethics, believing that the waterline length of *Defender* had been changed.

He suspected that, *Defender* had sailed the race immersed "three or four feet beyond her length as measured on September 6".

Dunraven had been suspicious for some time since he had heard the rumours circulated freely in New York that Iselin had once illegally added to the ballast of another yacht. Dunraven asked for a remeasurement and the two yachts were towed to the Erie Basin where it was shown that the waterline in *Defender* differed by only one-eighth of an inch, and one-sixteenth in *Valkyrie*.

Few New Yorkers knew of the drama, nor was there a hint that Lord Dunraven would later be expelled from the New York Yacht Club over the issue, which in essence amounted to an accusation of fraud.

The day of the second race, September 10, dawned warm and hazy and expectant New Yorkers rushed to the harbour prepared for another gala day of racing.

Lord Dunraven was joined on board *Valkyrie III* by his two daughters Lady Rachel and Lady Eileen Wyndham-Quin. He was soured by the doubts that persisted in his mind over the waterline length of *Defender*, and over the presence of a large spectator fleet, an incursion he complained about several times, as recent as the previous race.

The disregard with which some steamer captains had for the race yachts was seen in one newspaper report which stated, "that certain steamers intended to make trials of speed in following the international yacht-race." They were stopped by United States Government officials who warned they could be prosecuted.

But it didn't stop a large steamer *City of Yorktown* blundering between *Defender* and *Valkyrie III* as they manoeuvred toward the starting line.

Defender went astern and to leeward; *Valkyrie* went by her bow. After they cleared the steamer they converged, "*Valkyrie* to windward, and nearer the line though *Defender* was sailing the faster.... *Defender* being to leeward had the right of way, and held an undeviating course for the line..... *Valkyrie* in danger of crossing before the gun, bore off toward *Defender*."

As their tall topsails almost touched, it appeared that *Valykrie's* helmsman, Edward Sycamore tried to luff. It was not enough. A "loud twank" was reported as the end of *Valkyrie's* main boom caught in *Defender's* topmast-shroud, springing it out of the spreader "with her top-mast bending like a whipstock..."

Noted yachtsmen immediately cried "foul". To the surprise of everyone *Valkyrie* sailed on — crossing the line just 13 seconds after the starting gun as Haff raised the protest flag.

Defender leads Valkyrie III clearly on the first leg of the first race, September 7. Defender won by 8 mins 49 secs.

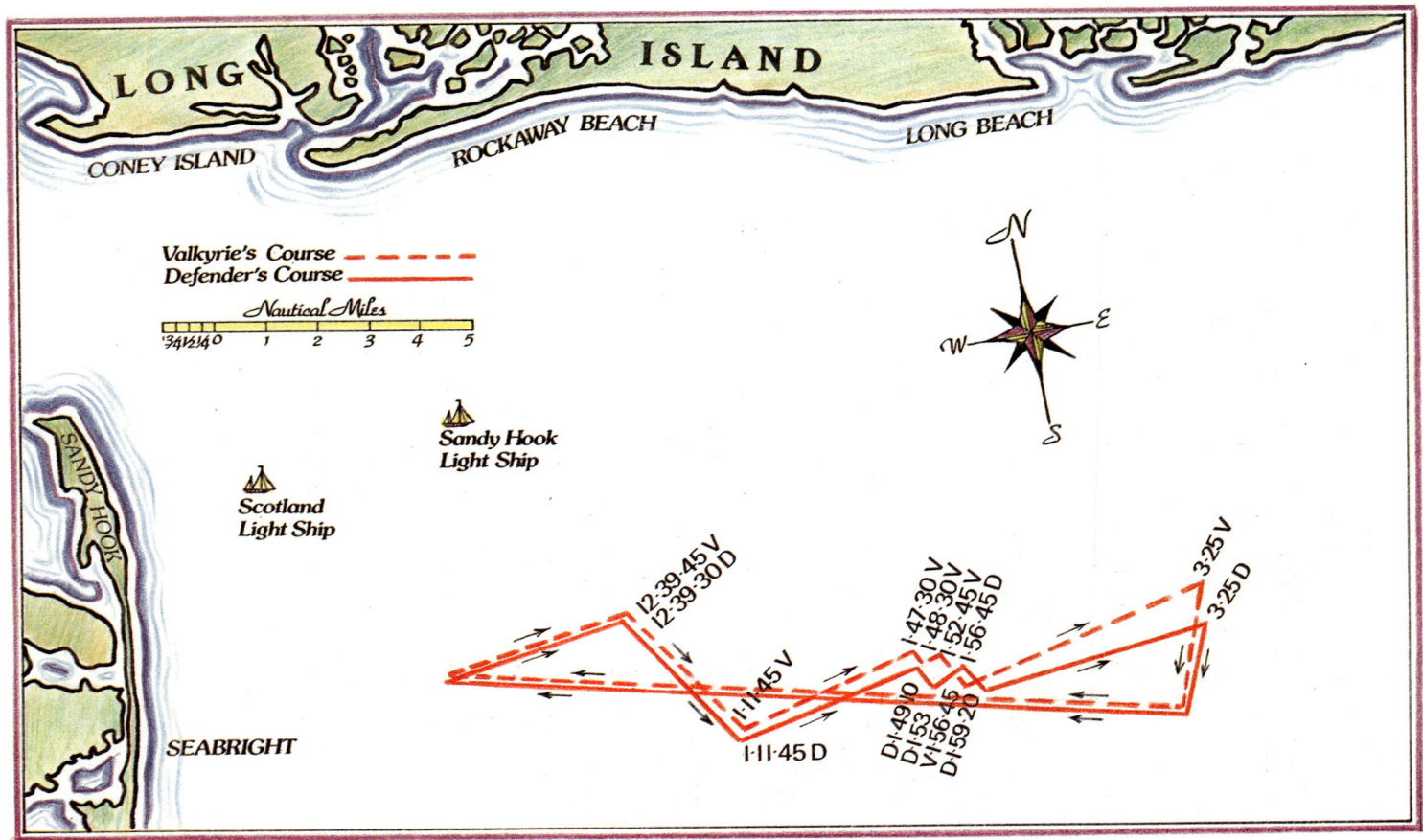

Map of course taken by Defender and Valkyrie III in the first race, September 7.

According to the *Lawson History*, "....the scarlet protest-flag fluttered on her deck, while the answering pennant flew from the committee boat."

Noting that *Valkyrie* intended to finish the race, Haff sent some men aloft to survey the damage and then set his partly disabled vessel after the British yacht. Courageously, *Defender* failed by just 47 seconds to catch her.

Historians are confused as to what steps followed. *The New York Times*, among others, claimed that the race committee tried to induce Iselin to withdraw his protest so that the race could be re-sailed. Iselin, however, stood firm, no doubt still peeved by Lord Dunraven's suspicions of him over the waterline length of his yacht.

The *Lawson History* states that Iselin did agree to resail the race, but Lord Dunraven, in a fit of pique, refused, believing he had not fouled *Defender* and should, therefore, have been awarded the race.

The race committee, after looking at photographic evidence that conflicted with Lord Dunraven's account of the mishap, awarded the race to *Defender*.

Not surprisingly, the British Press were angered by the decision not to resail the race. *The Daily News*, London, said the decision was "rather sharp practice", though other papers were not as harsh in their editorials.

More drama was to follow. Lord Dunraven, on September 10 informed The Cup committee that unless he could have a clear course on September 12, the day of the third race, he would not sail.

Dunraven felt that the whole of New York was against him. Not only was he angered by the protest, but also that a steamer should have wandered into the middle of the course as the two yachts faced the starting line.

His letter was stern and to the point. He felt he had been seriously hampered in both races and prior to the challenge had requested a new course for the races because of the spectator fleet. Also in his mind, no doubt, was the loss of *Valkyrie II*, his 1893 challenger, in a mishap in England. She was hit midships by another yacht at the start of a race because of a wayward spectator craft.

The New York Yacht Club sent a special committee to reason with Lord Dunraven. He agreed to race, only on the condition that the Cup committee declare the race void if the yachts are interfered with by the steamers.

The committee claimed it did not have the power to make such decisions and were left to wait the next day to see if Lord Dunraven would carry out his threat. He was indeed true to his word. The hordes of New Yorkers who went out in the decorated steamers unaware of the threat by the British owner had their first inkling near start time when *Valkyrie* arrived unprepared for racing.

When the preparatory gun was fired, *Valkyrie* was some distance from the line, and still under mainsail and jib only. Ten minutes later when the starting gun was fired, *Defender* moved into position, passing the line 24 seconds later. *Valkyrie* moved slowly over the line a minute behind and, to the astonishment of the Americans, headed for port. The large headline in the following day's *New York Times* rang out: LORD DUNRAVEN GIVES UP THE CONTEST.

The crew of Defender.

Lord Dunraven claimed that he had hoped the committee would postpone the race. He said; "I crossed the line because I thought the agreement demanded it; because I thought it the most courteous thing to do..."

Dunraven raised the flag of the New York Yacht Club as he returned, explaining later that it was "a sign of friendship and courtesy. It appears to have had the opposite effect."

The withdrawal met with mixed reaction in Britain, some yachtsmen believing Dunraven had acted in an unsportsmanlike manner. *The Daily Chronicle*, however, supported him, at the same time questioning whether they had witnessed the last of Anglo-American yacht races;

".... *Valkyrie* was right in not risking herself and her crew among the pitiless swarm of boats in Lower New-York Bay...... So we suppose there is an end to the rather ghastly farce called the international yacht race of 1895, and probably of all Anglo-American yacht racing...... He (Lord Dunraven) will have the sympathy of every Englishman."

Perhaps the sympathy of Englishmen, but of few Americans, particularly after his continuing accusations and criticisms on his return to England.

Lord Dunraven opened old wounds when he returned, going as far as to accuse Iselin again of adding ballast.

Back in his home country, Dunraven opened old wounds. He accused Iselin of cheating once again. Iselin reacted as one would have expected — he asked the club to clear his name, a request that was followed immediately since the accusation also attacked American honor. A select committee investigated the claims that *Defender* was at least one foot longer at waterline during the first race. Yet it was disclosed at the time that to change the waterline length by that much would have taken 13 tons of additional lead.

If that was the case, the crew of *Defender* had less than a day to take out the 13 tons of lead and then put it back after the yacht had been measured. Not possible!

Iselin was cleared and Lord Dunraven lost further credibility. What's more he was stripped of his honorary membership of the New York Yacht Club.

It could only have been seen as ironic, though sad as it was, that James Ashbury, the last English challenger to ruffle the feathers of the American Eagle, should pass away the day before Lord Dunraven's refusal to race.

Lord Dunraven gave up active racing after this series. Iselin and Herreshoff went back to the drawing boards to design and build a new defender. It would be four years before the Atlantic would be crossed again by a British challenger.

Columbia leading Shamrock off Sandy Hook during the 1899 series. From a painting by Chevalier Eduardo de Martino.

1899

The Lipton Era Begins

Columbia (NYYC) 3 defeated Shamrock I (Royal Ulster YC) nil.

SIR Thomas Lipton's love for the sea was well documented; he lived in Glasgow where, as his biographer explains, "the ends of its streets are masts, funnels.....It would have been strange if young Lipton had not learned to love it."

Lipton's parents were poor. His mother, an Irish-born working-woman, and his father were forced to migrate to Scotland during the Potato Famine of the 1840s. In Glasgow, the family saved and eventually opened a small general store.

Tommy Lipton was big for his age, and strong. He had no trouble handling the local bullies and not surprisingly he was head of his street gang. The same gang formed a yacht club and in a local pond sailed small wooden boats they had cut out of the lids of boxes. Tommy was "appointed" commodore and he named his boat *Shamrock*.

Enthusiastic and adventurous, Tommy left school at the age of 11 (there were no school inspectors in those days and no school leaving age) and took a job in a stationer's office. He spent his spare time on the docks watching the steamers and merchant vessels come and go and two years later accepted a job as cabin boy on one of the Burns steamers that sailed nightly between Glasgow and Belfast. His weekly pay was eight shillings! He was no spendthrift. When he was wrongfully dismissed from his job because of a misdemeanour by another boy, Lipton decided to go to New York, paying his own way. He arrived with just eight dollars to his name.

There he came to understand the operations of big grocery and department stores. He worked his way to the top in his four years in New York. Homesick, mainly for his mother, he returned to Scotland. With enthusiasm, diligence and a cheerful manner he opened his first grocery store. It was the start of an empire, a chain of shops that would not only make Lipton very rich, but give him the chance to challenge for The America's Cup.

It was said of Lipton that, "Hereditary offers no explanation for the phenomenon of Thomas Lipton," and that, "he was without literary or artistic interests."

He was brilliant at promoting and advertising his products and his stores. No doubt he saw the benefits of the publicity to his growing business empire, but few more timely entries into America's Cup yachting have been made. Lipton was right for that moment.

Lipton challenged officially through the Royal Ulster Yacht Club in August 1898, though he wasn't the first after the Dunraven challenge in 1895. While it was thought that the British would no longer challenge, Charles D. Rose, through the Royal Victoria Yacht Club, waited only two weeks after Lord Dunraven's "no race" before notifying the New York Yacht Club that he intended to challenge with a cutter, *Distant Shore*, in 1896. British criticism that their challenge was seen as giving support to the Americans over the Dunraven affair forced Rose to withdraw.

There were rumours of other possible challengers, but all of them were disregarded when Lipton made his official challenge. Appropriately the man of pork and tea fame, named his yacht *Shamrock*, just as he had done as "commodore" of his backstreet yacht club when he was a boy. But he was now commanding real yachts, real money in the big, wide world. The *Lawson History* said of Lipton: "Sir Thomas Lipton asked little and conceded much, and therefore was considered an ideal challenger.....The guarded attitude maintained by both sides in the Dunraven negotiations had given way to superlatively friendly discourse."

Obviously Lipton had not the slightest intention of inciting further animosity between the Americans and the British. He was a firm friend of Edward, Prince of Wales, a man who loved

Shamrock crossing the finish line at the end of the first race on October 16, ten minutes behind Columbia.

Sir Thomas Lipton

Oliver Iselin

William Fife, Jun.

yachting and one wonders how much an influence he might have been on Lipton at the time. He did not prompt the first inclination to challenge. Sir Thomas had hoped to finance a yacht capable of beating the Americans 10 years earlier. It fell through because there appeared no one capable of designing a potential challenger.

Knighted for his financial assistance to charities, Lipton was to challenge five times for The Cup.

The richest of tycoons were now involved with the America's Cup. J. Pierpont Morgan and partowners of America's defending yacht, *Columbia*, Edward Morgan and C. Oliver Iselin were extremely wealthy men. J. Pierpont Morgan was a banker, perhaps the richest in the world at that time.

It is accepted that the cost of building and racing *Columbia* in the challenge was $250,000, while Lipton would have spent between $400,000 and $500,000 by the time the summer was over. Never before had such money been thrown to the wind in America's Cup racing.

Part of the reason for the huge outlay was that boat construction was now of expensive metals. *Columbia* was plated entirely of tobin bronze, while *Shamrock* was a mixture of manganese bronze and aluminium alloy. Secrecy had surrounded the building of America's Cup yachts before 1899, but rarely had such care been taken to hide a defending yacht, as the builders, the Herreshoffs did with *Columbia*.

Shamrock, too, was given the same treatment by its designer. Sceptical yachtsmen on both sides of the Atlantic were caustic in their criticism of the practice since there seemed no reason why it was so important to hide the construction of yachts, each being built on different sides of the Atlantic at about the same time.

When *Columbia* was produced, it was obvious that Nat Herreshoff had improved on *Defender*. According to the *Lawson History*, "She was indeed a larger and finer *Defender*, with more beam and draft, a shallower body, finer overhangs and a thinner fin, with lead placed lower.....She was a beautiful boat, the handsomest yacht ever produced, all critics agreed, and from the first she showed great speed." Lipton's wish for an all-Irish challenger was quashed from the start. His designer, William Fife Junior, was Scottish, and his proposed Irish boat builders, upon seeing Fife's design, declined to build the yacht, claiming that they did not have the experience.

Instead *Shamrock* was built in London on the Thames. Nor did Lipton get his all-Irish crew. Most were Scottish with a few Englishmen drawn from Southampton. His captain, Archie Hogarth, was also Scottish.

Newspapers of the day carried constant reports of wars around the world. The British were confronted on several fronts in Africa fighting the Boers, and America was involved in the war against Spain. Only days before the first Cup race, Admiral George Dewey returned home to victory parades in New York and Washington.

When he sailed into New York Harbour, both Sir Thomas Lipton and C. Oliver Iselin saluted him from their respective luxury cruisers, *Erin* and *Corsair*.

In view of the world's problems, The America's Cup was something of a diversion, though a tedious one, as it turned out. Over the first 13 days, seven races had to be abandoned because of poor weather and lack of wind. Reams and reams of newspaper space was given to uncompleted races, further testimony to the significance attached to The Cup even in those days, until eventually *The New York Times* was forced to take the event off the front page.

Two large cameras were placed on the committee boat and for the first time, navy patrol boats, at the

Above: Guests aboard Sir Thomas Lipton's boat, the Erin. Thomas Edison is fourth from left. Above (right): Sir Thomas skipping in tandem on board the Erin. Below: On board Shamrock. The boom appears to go one forever.

direction of the United States Congress, were commanded to stop spectator craft from encroaching on the sailing area.

These were immensely rewarding times for inventors, and Marconi personally supervised testing of his wireless telegraphy system under the sponsorship of *The New York Herald*.

From a steamship in the harbour, *Herald* reporters sent stories back via Navesink on the harbour shores and via the Postal Telegraphy Company to the *Herald* office at 15 words a minute. The *Herald* office displayed the reports on bulletin boards within 30 seconds of them being received.

Such was the status of The America's Cup that the prolific inventor, Thomas Edison went aboard the *Erin* as guest of Lipton. He admitted he had not before been aboard a yacht of any nature, and knew nothing about sailing.

To the horror of his sailing companions he suggested that it might be possible to rig a sail aloft a yacht that would work on the principle of an aeroplane. To the relief of those on board he assured them he would not take his inventive mind into the realm of sailing.

While waiting for the completion of the first race, the British had time to turn to another element of yachting, this one intensely political — whether Sir Thomas Lipton should be elected a member of that most exclusive of bodies, the Royal Yacht Squadron. Sir Thomas, not of aristocratic stock, was shunned by the club until late in his yachting life. Lipton, on being formally asked, had the pleasure, it was said, of declining.

One classic moment for police during the 1899 challenge was the arrest of gamblers aboard an excursion steamer which had been hired on the pretext that it was taking spectators to the Cup course to view the race.

When the passengers, each charged one dollar, discovered that the steamer was a front for gambling and carried "paid women", they took control of the boat, threw the gambling devices overboard, despite the threats of death from the gamblers, and made it

Columbia and Shamrock battle it out in a 20-knot breeze in the third and final race of the series. It took some time for Columbia to edge ahead. She won eventually by more than six minutes.

back to port. Only one passenger was injured — he was struck on the head with a stool.

As each race proved a fizzer, so the crowds of impatient onlookers dwindled; suggestions were made to conduct the racing off Newport. According to a report from Britain headed LONDON LOSES INTEREST, "War and lack of wind drive Cup Races out of the public mind."

The boredom was broken finally on October 16. Yet it confirmed Britain's worst fears — this challenge would be like the previous. *Columbia*, two feet longer at the waterline than *Shamrock* but with less sail area, won the first race by more than ten minutes.

Shamrock crossed the starting line three seconds ahead of *Columbia*, the only time the British vessel was ahead. *Columbia*, the reports said, was better in

all facets of sailing, long tacks, short stays and to windward. As one report concluded: "The race as a decision of victory was over in the first two tacks.

Shamrock was destined not to win a race, certainly not the second race where she snapped her 60 feet long Oregon pine top mast just moments after the start.

On a port tack, *Shamrock* lost her port topmast shroud, snapping the topmast. Before the series began, it was agreed — at the suggestion of Lipton — that no courtesies be shown either yacht in the event of an accident. *Columbia's* skipper, Charles Barr took *Columbia* over the course and to victory.

When the new mast was fitted, so too was a ton and half of lead which meant that *Shamrock*, after being remeasured, had to allow *Columbia* over 16 seconds. Though in reality little could be done to help *Shamrock*. *Columbia* was clearly the faster boat and after yet another postponement — the eighth of the challenge — *Columbia* won the final race by six minutes.

To the considerable relief of all, the races were conducted in such cordial terms that Sir Thomas Lipton, despite his defeats, was the toast of New York. Several distinguished citizens sent letters to each of the newspapers stating amongst other things that Sir Thomas "has won the admiration of the American people." They then presented him with a loving cup worth more than $5,000.

It wasn't quite the cup he came for, though as history would show, he would return again.... and again.... and again.

Left: Columbia leads Shamrock in the last race of 1899. Above: Columbia's skipper, Charles Barr.

Charles Dixon's impression of Shamrock II and Columbia at the finish of the first race, September 28, 1901.

1901

Back with Another Shamrock

Columbia (NYYC) 3 defeated Shamrock II (Royal Ulster YC) nil

DEEP gloom gripped America in the September of 1901 after the assassination of President William McKinley. McKinley was the third President of the United States to be shot and killed, his second term as President cut short on September 6 during a visit to the Pan-American Exposition in Buffalo. He died eight days later, just two weeks before Sir Thomas Lipton's second challenge for The America's Cup.

Mourners wanted the series cancelled. The America's Cup committee deemed it unwise since Lipton made the long journey across the Atlantic and was already in New York preparing for the event. The committee also saw the need to take American minds off their grief.

Lipton proposed a postponement of the races, a suggestion accepted by the New York Yacht Club committee after a meeting with representatives of the Royal Ulster Yacht Club. The first race would be delayed five days, until September 26.

Lipton's new *Shamrock* cost him close to half a million dollars by the close of the New York summer racing season. He had given an open order to his builders to provide him with the best challenger money could buy. His commercial empire obviously flourished in the wake of his first challenge. To find the key to success, Lipton engaged George L. Watson as designer. Watson had previously designed *Thistle* and Lord Dunraven's *Valkyries*.

While Lipton divided his time between building a new challenger and his immense business interests, a row was brewing in the United States between prospective defence syndicates.

Not unrelated to the old Boston-New York yachting rivalry, the row was now whether Boston yacht club member Thomas Lawson could enter his new boat *Independence* in defence trials though he had no intention of joining the New York Yacht Club.

The Deed of Gift clearly stated that the Cup was to be defended by the club holding it. In previous defences where a Boston boat defended The Cup, representatives of the syndicate belonged to the New York Yacht Club. Lawson, a millionaire, did not see why it was necessary for him to join the Club, nor did he accept that only members of the New York Yacht Club could enter the trials.

Lawson did not inform the club of his intentions when he commissioned the building of the *Independence*. However, when the Cup committee became aware of his intentions they wrote to inform him of the rules of entry and to provide him with an alternative. They would allow him to charter the yacht to a member of the New York Yacht Club. It seemed a reasonable suggestion, for the New York Yacht Club only required that the club's burgee be flown.

Lawson was bitter. He saw such a suggestion as compromising his position in the eyes of his Bostonian colleagues.

The *Independence* was estimated to have cost almost $200,000, and though Lawson could afford it, it was an expensive exercise that threatened to come to nothing.

The rest of Lawson's syndicate withdrew during the haggling with the New York Yacht Club and he was left alone with his yacht. She was designed by a young Bostonian, Bowdoin Crownshield, who had never before attempted a yacht so large, nor had the construction company involved themselves in a yacht of similar lines. *Independence* was on most counts a disaster.

To be competitive in Cup trials, she needed a lot of racing against the other contenders, *Constitution*, a new Herreshoff-design and the old *Columbia*. It was here that Lawson agreed to the New York Yacht Club's terms, though he must have known that unless he could make drastic improvements, he could not hope to win the right to defend the cup.

Above: Clean up and washing time for Shamrock II's crew. Below (from left): the captain, the owner and the designer, Captain Sycamore, Sir Thomas Lipton and G. L. Watson. Right: Shamrock dismasted off Cowes after the bowsprit had carried away. King Edward VII was on board at the time but was not injured.

Independence, because of poor riveting on her hull, leaked like a sieve. She was classed as radical and a scow-type of vessel; her steering gear was defective, she almost sunk in heavy weather off the coast in trials organised by the newly formed Newport Racing Association.

Although 'Hank' Haff was in command, she performed embarrassingly, so much so that she was broken up before the challenge had even started! *Shamrock II* was launched from the yard of William Denny & Brother at Dumbarton, on the River Leven on April 20, she was given three early trials against the first *Shamrock*, and lost them all. Worse was to come. With King Edward VII on board, *Shamrock II*, prepared for her "third formal trial" (fourth overall) around the old Queen's Cup course off Cowes in a moderate sea and a "good sailing breeze."

As the boats manoeuvred at the start with just 60 seconds remaining, they were struck by a moderately strong breeze, normal for that time of year, when according to the *Lawson History*, "suddenly and without warning her whole rig collapsed and went overboard. The yacht in fact was totally dismantled in the space of a minute. Her mast went over the side like an empty paint-tube..."

Thankfully, the fallen mast missed the Prince of Wales. Several sailors carried overboard were rescued and no one was injured.

The accident was not the first for *Shamrock II*. Thirteen days earlier the boat's steel gaff collapsed narrowly missing Lipton. After the second accident, British yachtsmen questioned the new path yacht de-

Columbia leads Shamrock II, a familiar sight, though the margins were relatively close in all three races. Inset: Constitution, an unsuccessful defence contender in 1901.

signing was taking and called for a return to the hardier, older style of yacht.

The accidents, trial defeats and publicised doubts as to the *Shamrock II's* chances against the Americans did little to cheer Sir Thomas.

With new rigging, changes to her spars, *Shamrock II* was put under sail off Cowes early in July .... with far improved results. According to reports, a new pole mast, classed as a novelty in a yacht of Cup class, contributed to her improvement in speed, as did the new sea island cotton sails.

In a series of races over 14 days, she turned the tables on the old *Shamrock*, winning each race, though not by wide margins. But it was an improvement and left the British more buoyant and the Americans, who followed her progress, more wary.

The *Lawson History* points out that before *Shamrock* crossed the Atlantic, Lipton would sack 15 of his crew. The crew members refused to accept a $US40 bonus (above their wages) for the voyage. Concerned about the ocean-sea worthiness of the metal racing machine, they demanded $US75. Lipton, the businessman, sacked them. Under reduced cutter rig, *Shamrock* was towed across by the *Erin*, a trip lasting 16 days. Americans noted the difference in her lines to the two American yachts, *Constitution* and *Columbia*. According to the *Lawson History*: "her ends were longer, her counter and stern finer, and her bow lower, with the fullness carried farther forward, and with more of a 'snub' in the turn of the stem."

A critic writing in *The Scientific American* claimed that "G.L. Watson had designed an entirely original boat" and that, "she has the most refined form ever seen in a cup challenge. Her aft body, from the point of greatest beam, which lies not very aft of the shrouds, to her narrow and shallow stern, has been refined to a degree which makes one ask how it can ever be possible for the boat to carry her great spread of 14,500 square feet of canvas."

Watson aroused considerable interest in New York with news of his tank tested yacht. He had spent nine months with models that weighed as much as "two hundred pounds."

Americans saw *Shamrock's* lightness as a weakness, believing her mast would not stand a big blow. Both *Constitution* and *Columbia* were dismasted during their trials.

After 18 trials, it wasn't the new *Constitution* that was selected for the defence but the old *Columbia*, the first time a defender was retained. Each yacht won nine races, and there seemed little doubt that *Constitution* was the faster boat. But she had inferior sails, and inexplicably she performed brilliantly in one race and abysmally the next.

Columbia was skippered by Charles Barr, a yachtsman without peer among Cup captains of that time. According to historians, he made the races against *Constitution* lessons in tactics, whereas *Constitution* was sailed basically for speed.

Columbia, with the aggressive Barr aboard, was disqualified after a protest by *Constitution's* skipper, Uriah Rhodes, in the last trial race. It did not affect the New York Yacht Club's decision.

The first race, on September 26, was called off through lack of wind with *Columbia* leading *Shamrock II* by more than a mile.

The series had had its affect on Wall Street where *The New York Times* reported that: "The customers' rooms of many brokerage houses were all but deserted." One bet of $5,000 at even money was wagered on *Columbia*, although *Columbia* was popularly rated at 2-1 on for the series.

American confidence was wiped away after the first completed race. In what was classed as the finest light-weather contest in the Cup's history, *Columbia* won by just one minute, 20 seconds after *Shamrock II* led to the windward mark.

In winds of around eight knots, *Shamrock II* confirmed George Watson's decision to building a yacht purely for the light American conditions.

According to one newspaper report: "When they rounded the outer mark, she was 41 seconds ahead of *Columbia*..... and caused several thousand patriotic hearts to sink with dread that the glorious cup was in danger."

The second race was postponed because of lack of wind, but when called off *Shamrock* was in the lead, heightening expectations of the toughest struggle yet.

Luck did not remain with *Shamrock* the next day. *Columbia* won by what was called a "decisive" two minutes 52 seconds in a brisk wind. The reference to the "decisive" victory was a compliment to the challenger for such a victory in past conquests would have been seen as decidedly close. *Columbia* had established a record for the triangular New York Yacht Club course off Sandy Hook, taking three hours 12 minutes 35 seconds.

In the third race, *Shamrock* beat *Columbia* home by two seconds but lost the race by 41 seconds on time allowance. In a classic head to head struggle, *Shamrock* led by 49 seconds at the first mark, but an error in not covering *Columbia*, allowing the defender clear to sail inshore looking for more wind, cost her dearly.

But for such inexcusable tactics, *Shamrock* almost surely would have won. The London Press accorded *Shamrock II* "a splendid failure", and *The New York Times* reported bluntly in a headline, Challenger Loses Her Last Race Through Bad Management.

To the blaring of steam whistles and fog horns Sir Thomas Lipton retired to the cabin of his yacht where he joined his guests, many of them Americans.

At the end of the speeches and after gracious tributes from both sides, Sir Thomas was overcome with emotion and "with hearty handshakes, the little meeting ended in silence."

Lipton, however, would be back. After all, he announced, "a shamrock has three leaves." Just two years later Lipton was back, his popularity with Americans as great as ever.

Reliance running for the finish in the first race against Shamrock III on August 22.

1903

Superboat Retains Cup

Reliance (NYYC) 3 defeated Shamrock III (Royal Ulster YC) nil.

THE 1903 challenge produced the first of the America's Cup "superboats", *Reliance*, another Nat Herreshoff creation. This was not only a radical departure from his earlier designs, but the largest single-masted racing boat ever built.

Herreshoff had developed boat design to such an extent, that at times everything else about The America's Cup, the owners, the players, the characters appeared to be superfluous. All eyes turned to *Reliance*, 144 feet long and with a sail area of more than 16,169 square feet. The sail spread of *Puritan* in 1885, regarded as extreme at the time, was a mere 7,982 square feet.

America's Cup designed yachts had a significant influence on most racing and cruising classes because The Cup was the greatest yachting event of that time, just as it is now.

The closeness of the 1901 challenge renewed the interest of New Yorkers, concerned as much with the struggle as the victory. And there was Sir Thomas Lipton himself, the most popular and recognisable challenger to visit American shores. A week before the first race of the 1903 challenge, Sir Thomas was guest at New York's Majestic Theatre. When he arrived by car, according to one report, the area was "so packed with shouting humanity that three policemen had to be brought into service to pilot the guest of the evening safely through the mob. Inside the theatre, the party went to the boxes on the west side of the house. All during the performance the audience did not lose opportunities to cheer wildly, and the object of their approval smiled back his appreciation."

At the end of the second act, all the men and women on the stage waved British and Shamrock flags. When the comedy was over, Sir Thomas was invited on stage where, after a short speech, he proceeded to kiss every woman member of the cast.

Lipton, buoyed by his previous challenge, had attempted to challenge again with *Shamrock II* in 1902. Such an endeavour was out of the question since the Canadian, Alexander Cuthbert entertained the idea of challenging each 12 months with *Atalanta* in 1882. Because of the severe beatings Cuthbert took and concerned for the prestige of the Cup, the New York Yacht Club had added a clause to the Deed of Gift ensuring that no club could challenge with the same yacht within two years of the previous challenge.

One suspects that the New York Yacht Club might have had differing reasons for denying Lipton his chance. The club no doubt wanted time to regroup after the toughest and tightest struggle in Cup history. This rebuff did not douse Lipton's enthusiasm, though British yachtsmen saw it as another ploy by the always suspected New York Yacht Club.

Lipton went back to William Fife for the design of his new boat. George Watson was by now tired of the strain of producing these racing machines. He declined Lipton's invitation, though he did, in the end, help Fife with the design. The tank tested *Shamrock III* was a fast looking yacht which earned the seal of approval from numerous yachting critics, one of them classing her as "the most beautiful yacht that had ever raced for the Cup."

Shamrock III was white hulled — the other *Shamrocks* were green — and she was the first challenger to have a steering wheel. American defenders had been steered by wheels for some considerable time, and it is remarkable that the British had persisted for so long with the tiller. *Reliance*, for instance, had two wheels.

Built of nickel steel, *Shamrock III*, was not as unwieldy as her predecessor. Launched in March 1903, she had an overall length of 134 feet 4 inches, a water line length of 89 feet 10 inches and was considered more extreme in design than *Shamrock I* and *II*. Like *Shamrock II*, she had her

Reliance in a running sea with Charlie Barr, renowned America's Cup skipper, at the wheel.

rigging problems and lost her mast during trials in Weymouth Bay. One of her crew was carried overboard and drowned.

Shamrock I, and not the second *Shamrock* boat which had performed so remarkably in the 1901 challenge was used as the trial horse, the British optimistic that they may have at last found a challenger to beat the Americans. The new Fife creation was considerably faster in trials, and both yachts were towed across the Atlantic. This was the first time a challenger enjoyed the luxury of taking its own trial yacht into American waters in preparation for The Cup.

Lipton might have given it wings and put it under steam for all the good his decision to bring *Shamrock I* was going to do him. As he later admitted in his memoirs, he did not take long to realise that the Americans had built a bigger and better boat.

Profits from the oil, steel and rail industries made by turn-of-the-century millionaires provided the finance for the new American defender. Cornelius Vanderbilt, from the railroad family, William Rockefeller, of oil fame, Albert Gray, whose family derived its wealth from the steel industry and five other millionaires formed a syndicate and asked Herreshoff to design the yacht, his fifth consecutive American defender.

Again C. Oliver Iselin, who had been in retirement, agreed to act as manager. He influenced Herreshoff into producing a yacht that not only had some of the capabilities of the hapless *Independence* — *Reliance* did not leak, however — but was an improvement on *Columbia*.

Requiring a crew of 64 sailors to handle her, *Reliance* was flat and long with a deep fin keel. She was heavily weighed down and her keel dropped 29 feet below the waterline. Described by yachtsmen as a "skimming dish", she was of such radical design that she was good for little other than America's Cup racing.

These millionaire toys were "thrown away" after the Cup races ended. *Reliance* lasted three months after the final race, when she was broken up for scrap.

The rules governing yacht designs, which led to more stable and safer yachts, particularly after the outcries of the unsafe centreboarders, did not apply to The America's Cup. The Cup committee allowed designers a free hand for they felt they should be allowed to exercise their creative design skills without the restriction of size of yacht and unhindered by other regulations.

Constitution and *Columbia* joined *Reliance* in trials, but *Reliance* won all three and showed herself to be a remarkably fast boat. Charles Barr accepted the role of skipper for the third consecutive defence and the 1903 defending syndicate was as well prepared and as confident as any in The Cup's history.

Despite the immense impression of being far too extreme and unstable, *Reliance* met with no major mishaps. The only cause for concern in preparations

The America's Cup 1851-1987

Shamrock III, the only white hulled Shamrock, was, according to yachtsmen of the time, "one of the most beautiful in America's Cup history." However, she failed to win a race.

was the loss of a sailor off *Columbia*. He was washed overboard and drowned during a lead up race.

Re-measurement of *Shamrock III* on the eve of the first race not only gave her an extra 12 seconds, allowing her one minute 57 seconds overall, but also helped to stimulate betting on the outcome of the series. Wall Street announced that a number of American syndicates laid 2-1 on *Reliance*, one group betting $2000 to $1000 and still prepared to outlay another $20,000. Generally, betting on the outcome, as much a part of the races as the yachts themselves, was reported to be "tame".

The first race was postponed because of lack of wind with the *Reliance* two miles ahead of *Shamrock III*. The next day, in perfect sailing conditions, *Reliance* confirmed her superiority, winning the first race by more than seven minutes after the time allowance was deducted. Three days later, *Reliance* did it again, though this time the difference was one minute 19 seconds. According to *The New York Times*; "So small, however, was *Reliance's* victory, so closely fought the race, so long in doubt as to the final out-

Left: The launch of Reliance at Newport, and (below) the launch of Shamrock III, both with large audiences. Right: Reliance, and some of her 64 crew just visible. She was a radical design and a remarkably fast boat.

come, and so excellent was the showing of the *Shamrock* in those conditions under which *Reliance* is popularly supposed to be at her best, that Sir Thomas will have some justification for his familiar expression, 'I am as confident as ever'."

The race was over a 30 mile triangular course in winds that ranged from five knots to 12 knots and though *Shamrock III's* skipper, Robert Wringe was beaten at the start, he did remarkably well to hold close to *Reliance* on and off the wind.

The yachts had to wait 15 days before the third race could be contested. For the first time — on August 29 — an America's Cup race had to be postponed because of heavy weather. With a strong gale blowing in from the east-northeast, the committee agreed to call off attempts to race.

Heavy seas rolled in off Sandy Hook and the wind was calculated at 28 knots. The decision to postpone the race brought criticism from a number of yachtsmen, particularly those who objected to the new extreme style of racing yacht. They were adamant that the old schooners, such as *Sappho* and *Columbia*, would have raced in such a gale. The committee, however, explained that their reasons for calling off the race was for the safety of the crew, the loss of the crewman overboard from *Columbia* no doubt fresh in their minds.

The irony of the fifteen day wait was that *Shamrock III* did not finish the third race. She became lost in a fog that enveloped the yachts on the second leg. *Reliance* was clearly in command when she emerged from the fog near the finish. *Shamrock* had been a mile behind when they both disappeared and when she re-emerged she was well off course, passing to eastward of the finish line.

It was a disappointing end for Sir Thomas Lipton, his three challengers in four years costing him a reported $2,000,000. He did not hide his disappointment. In his straightforward manner, he explained: "I don't see anything that I really can say except what everybody knows. I got licked by the faster boat." He told newsmen he would return, and that should rumours of a challenge from the Clyde be proved correct, he would do all he could to assist them.

Lipton was true to his word. While the Clyde challenge did not eventuate, Lipton did challenge again, but this time America would have to wait 17 years before the popular Irish knight returned.

The America's Cup 1851-1987

Defender, Resolute, as captured by marine artist R. F. Paterson during the fourth race in 1920.

1920

Closest Challenge Yet

Resolute (NYYC) 3 defeated Shamrock IV (Royal Ulster YC) 2.

SIR Thomas Lipton was on his way across the Atlantic in the *Erin* in August 1914 with *Shamrock IV* in tow when the captain of the *Erin* picked up a wireless message from a German warship that war had been declared. He was left with the decision of turning back or continuing on to New York where the 1914 challenge was to take place. Lipton made for Bermuda, where *Erin* stayed for a short while before continuing on to New York, even though Lipton and his crew were aware that German cruisers were patrolling the Atlantic.

War did intervene and *Shamrock IV* was laid up in Brooklyn on a wooden framework and kept there until hostilities were over. The Cup went ahead six years later, in 1920. Lipton returned *Erin* to England where it was used by the British Government as a hospital ship in the Mediterranean. She was torpedoed and sunk with the loss of six men.

Strenuous efforts were made soon after the 1903 challenge to implement new racing rules, which would produce healthier, more stable yachts. The New York Yacht Club accepted the Universal Rule governing displacement, and excessive sail area which brought a penalty.

The International Rule, a rather more complex formula, was developed by European nations, but was not accepted fully in America until the 1950s when all countries sailed under the one rule. While the New York Yacht Club had accepted the 1903 Universal Rule they did not implement it in The America's Cup.

Lipton wanted to challenge for the Cup in 1907, but only on the condition that the races be held under the new allowance rules which took into consideration displacement of the yacht as well as its length and sail area. Lipton's conditional challenge was refused by the club, which maintained its support of the Deed of Gift allowing defender and challenger to build any type of yacht they wished.

Lipton tried again and again, suggesting that each yacht should be a predetermined size under the new rule, and later after receiving a negative reply, offered to challenge with the maximum waterline length of 75 feet. The New York Yacht Club refused again. Though nine years had passed since Lipton's last challenge he had retained his enthusiasm.

The constant rebuffs by the New York Yacht Club were surprising, particularly in view of Lipton's popularity in America where his sporting attitude to his Cup defeats had endeared him to so many. Strange, too, was the New York Yacht Club committee's admission later that they were not against the Universal Rule. Yet they were wary of any change that might take an advantage away from them. In the meantime Lipton went ahead and built himself a new *Shamrock* in accordance with the International Rule, though it was never intended for The America's Cup. The 75 feet *Shamrock* did well in English racing and won a number of prizes.

In 1913, after sailing in English waters, Lipton made yet another challenge "just for the fun of it."
This time the New York Yacht Club accepted the challenge. Although they finally agreed to abide by the Universal Rule, they still refused to be restricted in the length of their defender. Again the challenge appeared to be back to where it started .... until Lipton stated that his new yacht would be 75 feet long. The New York Yacht Club immediately agreed to make their yacht the same length — which is what Lipton had wanted in the first place.

Lipton took from 1907 to force the New York Yacht Club to accept his challenge. It was a lesson in persistence.

He turned to a new designer, Charles Nicholson for *Shamrock IV*. Nicholson was accepted as one of the brilliant, new designers in England, though he was not as familiar with the Universal

The launch of Shamrock IV on May 26, 1914 with the galleon, Victory as an unusual backdrop.

Rule as its inventor, none other than Nat Herreshoff, a fact that was plainly obvious when the new *Shamrock* reached New York.

Nicholson largely ignored the implications of the penalties one could face under the Universal Rule, for he produced a yacht that was larger than the defender and carried 1,700 square feet more sail area, which meant that *Shamrock IV* would pay heavily in time allowance. There was no doubt *Shamrock IV* was a powerful boat — though not the sleekest, nor the prettiest to sail in The America's Cup. When the yachts were measured *Shamrock IV* had to concede seven minutes one second to the American defender, *Resolute*.

While Nicholson was designing the latest *Shamrock*, the Americans were making their normal resourceful preparations.

Three syndicates joined the defence hunt, including one headed by Cornelius Vanderbilt and Commodore J. P. Morgan, who went back to the master, Nat Herreshoff. The other syndicates engaged designers new to The America's Cup — William Gardner who designed *Vanitie* and Bostonian George Owen who produced *Defiance*.

As one would have expected, the Herreshoff designed yacht, *Resolute*, was faster and more adaptable to all conditions. She won the first three early trials and became lost in the fog in the fourth. Before the

Shamrock IV, with her crew hard at work. She was launched in 1914, but had to wait, because of war, until 1920 to contest The America's Cup.

final trials and even before *Shamrock IV* arrived in New York, war was declared.

Resolute sailed under the guidance of skipper Charles Adams after her launching in 1914. He raced her in the summers of 1915 and 1919, while the *Shamrock* was laid up and untested in Brooklyn. Lipton was undeterred by the disadvantage and the long wait, and moved quickly to renew the challenge.

The war was no sooner over than Lipton was on his way to refit his idle *Shamrock*. The New York Yacht Club warmly accepted his decision to continue with the challenge. The New York Yacht Club wanted the course moved to Newport where the waters would be free of congestion. Lipton rejected the suggestion. Although he was 70, he was still an old limelighter. He enjoyed the social life of New York and the recognition accorded him by the multitudes. He wanted to be in the thick of the action. The challenge went ahead in the familiar Sandy Hook waters.

Unlike her predecessors, *Shamrock IV* was not a "good looking" boat. Even Nicholson, her designer, admitted she was an "ugly duckling". Others were even less complimentary. But as Lipton concluded after his previous challenge, he was not consoled by

The America's Cup 1851-1987

113

Above: Sir Thomas Lipton resting in his favourite cane chair on board his steam boat, Erin. Opposite: There was no rest for Resolute's crew, particularly the crewman high up the mast.

the fact that *Shamrock III* was a beautiful looking boat. He wanted a boat that could wrest The Cup from the Americans, not one that could only win the beauty stakes. If the fourth *Shamrock* was ugly when first built, it was even uglier after six years out of the water waiting for the war to end.

Shamrock IV was placed in charge of William Burton, the first amateur to sail a challenger. His wife, sailed with him, and acted as timekeeper, her presence the cause of some ill-feeling amongst the crew who were against having a woman on board.

Resolute was chosen as the defending yacht after beating *Vanitie* 7-4 in the trial races. The two American yachts and *Shamrock IV* had been built in 1913-14.

For the first time in The Cup's history, the Americans knew what it was like to be close to defeat. *Shamrock IV*, "ugly" and not favoured, won the first two races. She sailed home in the first after *Resolute* broke her main halyard, and the gaff jumped the mast. *Resolute's* skipper Charles Adams was forced to retire her.

In the second race, on July 20, *Shamrock IV*, despite needing a makeshift headsail during the race, sailed past *Resolute* on the first leg of the triangular course and was not headed. She won by two minutes 26 seconds after the seven minutes one second time allowance was deducted.

Despite the years lost by the war, New York's interest did not wane. According to *The New York Times*: "Even Babe Ruth and his home run record had to take second place to yacht races in the public interest." Bulletin boards on either side of Times Square carried the latest sporting results, one telling of The America's Cup race in progress, and the other of the local baseball scores of the day. While such a moment as Babe Ruth's home run record was of some national importance, when Broadway's theatres released their afternoon crowds, the throng around The America's Cup bulletin exceeded by far those keen to learn of Ruth's effort.

While the first two races caused gloom, the next two saw *Resolute* back in favour. She won the third race by her time allowance which meant that *Resolute* and *Shamrock IV* went over the finish line together and the fourth by almost ten minutes.

The fifth and deciding race was to have been sailed on July 25, but with what was described as the "largest gathering of spectators ever," the race was postponed because the weather was too heavy. Local yachtsmen criticised the committee for the decision, claiming that since the water was not rough, yachts of 75 feet should have been able to handle the 25 knot winds.

When the race was concluded two days later, Lipton's *Shamrock IV* would suffer its biggest defeat, 19 mins 45 secs, the widest margin since *Madeleine* beat *Galatea* in 1886. *Shamrock IV* was the first challenger to go the full distance and she did so while having to concede the largest time allowance of any yacht during the years allowances were in operation.

A gracious Sir Thomas Lipton saw his dream washed away. He would never come as close again.

1930

Lipton's Fabulous Era Over

Enterprise (NYYC) 4 defeated Shamrock V (Royal Ulster YC) nil.

NO owner, skipper or designer spanned a greater period of involvement in The America's Cup than Sir Thomas Lipton. He was a weary, yet persistent 80-year-old when he made his final attempt in 1930, 31 years after he sailed his first Shamrock across the Atlantic Ocean, full of hope and believing that yacht racing was meant for enjoyment and recreation. What drove him on? The game itself, ego, publicity for his business interests, the pugnacious urge to be the first to take what he nicknamed, "The Auld Mug" from the Americans ......or was the challenge so deeply in his blood, having first tasted it in 1899, that life without it would lose much of its meaning?

By 1930, there was little doubt that Sir Thomas knew he could have just one last fling. He had seen so many great names of The America's Cup come and go .... Nat Herreshoff, Charles Barr, George L. Watson, C. Oliver Iselin, J. P. Morgan, Hank Haff. For each of his first four challenges, Lipton left British shores confident that he had produced a yacht refined and fast enough to bring the Cup back home. Unfortunately, Lipton and his designers could never match the technological edge enjoyed by the Americans.

The result of the 1930 challenge was no different to his previous attempts. Four times Lipton met defeat and so graciously had he accepted each loss that Americans dubbed him, the "King of Good Losers." Lipton had seen many great yachtsmen come and go and was also witness to, and part of, some drastic changes in yacht designing.

The 1930 challenge introduced the J-class yacht to The America's Cup. The J-class rating varied between 76 feet and 87 feet on the waterline in accordance with the Universal Rule of Measurement. Yachts of the 1920s had taken a new course, with their tall Bermudan or Marconi rigs, and designers discovered through extensive testing that tall narrow sails were far sounder than the short, broader ones used previously in racing boats. America's Cup yachts needed only carry a sail area of around 7,500 square feet to obtain better results than the old boats that carried 16,000 square feet of canvas. What was required was an immensely tall mast carrying a single triangular mainsail. Topsails were needed no more.

The new designs meant that there was no further need for time allowances. Both yachts started with the same basic formula and theoretically should have finished each race together. Of course, such would rarely be the case since there are numerous variables to consider, not the least, for instance, that the yacht selected to defend The Cup, *Enterprise*, was fitted with a duraluminium mast which was held together by 80,000 rivets and which weighed less than two tons. The mast it replaced weighed three tons. The difference in the performance of *Enterprise* in its trials was significant.

Enterprise, designed by W. Starling Burgess, son of Edward, the successful Bostonian designer of the 1880s, featured a number of other remarkable changes. Starling Burgess added a triangular-shaped spar which enabled the foot of the mainsail to be regulated to optimum shape to allow for maximised use of wind flow. The device became known as the Park Avenue boom, since it was wide enough for two men to walk along it abreast.

Starling Burgess had built numerous winches into *Enterprise*, many of them below decks so that eight of the 26-man crew worked below permanently. They were referred to as "the black gang". Such innovation alone did not guarantee *Enterprise* selection as the defending yacht. Historians give as much credit to the professionalism of the yacht's skipper Harold S. T. Vanderbilt for her performances. Vanderbilt left little to chance. He was a hard taskmaster and a man who believed in

Enterprise just after crossing the line at the end of the fourth race, September 18, 1930.

Above: Shamrock V designer, Charles Nicholson checks the sails during a trial. Right: Artist Charles Dixon's impression of a Shamrock V victory. It was not to be. She lost all four races.

the delegation of duties, demanding the same degree of professionalism from his crew as he required of himself.

Vanderbilt organised each of his crew to wear a numbered sweater and when barking orders he would simply call out a number. Should any of the crew be required to change places, they also changed sweaters.

Despite the cold chill of the Wall Street crash of 1929 and the Depression that followed, four American yachts were built for the defence. The cost of *Enterprise* was $630,000 and the total cost of the four estimated at over $2 million. The effect of building four yachts was no doubt of immense value and a decided advantage to the Americans. Each of them differed in length and each allowed the Americans a look at a variety of rigs under differing conditions, a luxury not afforded Lipton. He was stuck with *Shamrock V* no matter what.

The defence trials brought together *Enterprise*, *Weetamoe*, designed by Clinton Crane, a Boston boat called *Yankee*, designed by Frank Paine, the son of General Charles Paine, *Whirlwind*, which had the Herreshoff design on it, this time by Nat Herreshoff's son, Francis and *Vanatie* and *Resolute*, both re-rigged for the trials.

At 80 feet, *Enterprise* had the shortest waterline length — six feet shorter than the longest, belonging to *Whirlwind* — the smallest displacement, yet the largest sail area, 7,583 square feet. *Whirlwind*, the largest of the four, looked the most powerful, though she never proved so in the trials. *Yankee* excelled in heavy weather, yet after extensive trials, *Enterprise* was selected.

Her selection had been far from clear cut, for many hardened yachting men favoured *Weetamoe*, which at

one stage had won more trial races than any of the other yachts. The trials were among the most extensive conducted for American defenders. Victory proved to be harder than winning The Cup itself.

The yachts were raced in pairs to simulate Cup conditions, the pairings changing each day. After the official observation races off Newport, *Weetamoe* had won five races and had been beaten only once, by *Yankee* in a strong breeze. *Enterprise* had won four match races, but she had not beaten *Weetamoe*.

Vanderbilt was far from discouraged and made every effort to improve *Enterprise*. With changes to her rig and sails, *Enterprise* entered the New York Yacht Club cruise where she beat *Weetamoe*, each yacht winning three of the seven races. In the final

Above: Sir Thomas Lipton speaks into the microphone after Shamrock V had been launched by the Countess of Shaftsbury at Gosport. Below: The light alloy mast of Enterprise appears to go on forever. She was called the "mechanical ship."

trials over the Cup course, *Enterprise*, with Vanderbilt pushing his crew, proved to be a better all-round yacht, although it was still felt that had George Nichols handled his crew as well as Vanderbilt, *Weetamoe* might have been the defender.

According to James Robbins, writing in *The New York Times*, *Enterprise* was chosen because of her consistency in all types of weather. "*Enterprise* beat *Weetamoe* twice in soft airs and once in a breeze and a sea. She was there somewhere at all times...."

Two important factors were introduced to The

America's Cup in 1930. The course was moved to Newport — 10 years after Sir Thomas Lipton suggested it — and for the first time, The Cup would be challenged over the best-of-seven races, the first yacht to win four races being declared the winner. The switch to an open sea course off Newport, Rhode Island was not surprising since The America's Cup committee wanted to use an alternative to the old New York course in 1920. Lipton argued strongly against it and the committee relented.

The old Sandy Hook course was impractical since it had been over-run by commerical shipping and it was hardly likely that the busy commercial world would halt proceedings for a few days just for a yacht race, even one as significant as The America's Cup.

Above: Contender Yankee trials for the 1930 defence. Though she excelled in heavy weather she was passed over in favour of Enterprise. Below: From left, Resolute, Vanitie and Enterprise in a defence trial.

Besides, the New York waters had become somewhat fouled, and the winds off Newport were far more dependable. The venue for the race was never to return to New York.

From the time the American yachts began their exhaustive trials, allowing each skipper ample time to readjust and experiment, *Shamrock V* had little chance. Designed by Charles Nicholson, she was built of mahogany planking on steel frame, the last English challenger to be so constructed (the two *Endeavours* that followed her were of steel). She was a

Above: There was little between Enterprise and Shamrock V here. Shamrock was unable to take a race from the defender, the closest margin being 2 minutes 52 seconds in the first race. Right: Shamrock V is already behind Enterprise at the start of the fourth race.

good deal narrower than *Enterprise*, though one foot longer on the waterline, with a hollow spruce mast, heavier than the light alloy mast of *Enterprise*.

It was noted when the two yachts were lying at their moorings in Newport that when a craft passed near the two yachts the swell caused *Shamrock* to roll long after *Enterprise* settled down. The reason given for this phenomenon was in *Shamrock's* hollow spruce mast which was considered to have created a form of aerodynamic oscillation.

While *Enterprise* was referred to as the 'mechanical ship', *Shamrock* had far less winches and relied more on the blood, sweat and tears of its British crew. Another factor was that despite the competence of *Shamrock's* skipper, Ned Heard — the last professional skipper to take the helm in a Cup race — he could not have hoped to match Vanderbilt whose highly rated afterguard included C. Sherman Hoyt, regarded as one of the world's most accomplished helmsmen, Charles 'Bubbles' Havemeyer and navigator Winthrop Aldrich. Combined with *Enterprise's* advanced design, the Americans appeared unbeatable. And so it was.

The largest spectator fleet to gather for The America's Cup congregated off Newport on September 13 ready for the first race. Organisers had more than just the sea to patrol however. For the first time, an air patrol, consisting of four United States Coast Guard seaplanes, were on duty to keep the airways clear of, as one report had it, "any commercial or pleasure planes and blimps that may interfere or 'steal the wind' of the racing yachts."

Though the start was delayed by fog and the airs were sluggishly light, it was obvious that Lipton would need a miracle. Automobiles clogged Newport's normally quiet roadways, its narrow streets were a mass of people and its harbour ventured upon by anyone possessing a pleasure craft.

Sadly for those who had booked a seat on one of the seven chartered seaplanes, the fog prevented them from leaving the ground, though a blimp, carrying newspapermen, ventured out toward the finish of the race when the fog showed signs of lifting.

An estimated 40 Coast Guard boats acted as a cordon of protection, ensuring that the 300 pleasure craft following *Shamrock V* and *Enterprise* did not interfere with the race. The one casualty was Lipton's steam yacht *Erin* which collided with a motor launch.

The mishap further dampened Lipton's spirit for *Shamrock* was beaten by two minutes 52 seconds. Two radio networks, using 150 broadcasting units, carried the full descriptions of the race throughout the United States and to parts of Britain.

There was even less joy for Lipton and the *Shamrock* team after the second race. *Enterprise* won by almost 10 minutes. Fog closed in toward the finish of the race, denying the many motorists who lined Ocean Drive in their fashionable automobiles the chance of seeing the yachts in action.

Shamrock performed best on the final reach where she lost only 24 seconds to the American boat. Although virtually all British hopes had vanished, Lipton restored the ton of lead taken out of *Shamrock* after the first race defeat.

Shamrock lost the next two races, the third of the series after the mainsail halyard parted inside the mast, bringing her sail down. The incident occurred 45 minutes after the start, and under America's Cup rules, *Enterprise* was declared the winner. The fourth race was a mere formality, *Enterprise* winning by more than five minutes. According to *The New York Times*, $2,500,000 was spent by defender and challenger.

In five challenges over 31 years, Lipton had won two of the 18 races he contested, both of them back to back in 1920. It was a measure of his popularity and the significance of The America's Cup in the eyes of the American people that an estimated 20,000 spectators lined the shore at Newport for the last race. Lipton's job had been done, if one considered the tone of the English press, particularly *The Daily Herald*, which explained: "He has helped to weld together two nations in mutual respect and friendship."

When Lipton set out on his challenge in 1899, his good friend the Prince of Wales asked him to encourage sportsmanship, hoping to heel the rift between the two nations after the bitterness of the Dunraven affair.

Sir Thomas succeeded, though reports indicated after *Shamrock V's* final race that he was "tired and worn with the excitement and strain....the twinkle had gone from his eye." He returned home to Scotland after the races to contemplate a sixth challenge. That day did not arrive. At the age of 82, and only shortly after being made a member of the Royal Yacht Squadron, he died.

The America's Cup owes him much, not just for the hand of friendship he brought with him, but for the fact that through his challenges, the contest maintained a continuity that historians doubt would have been possible without him.

He called The America's Cup his "principal recreation for over 30 years." New Yorkers greeted him as they would visiting royalty and Lipton enjoyed the company of the aristocratic classes as much as the adulation from the populace.

With his passing, a new generation of yachtsmen emerged in Britain.....men who preferred to race their yachts themselves. For that reason alone, The America's Cup would not be the same again.

1934

Sopwith Almost Takes Cup

Rainbow (NYYC) 4 defeated Endeavour (Royal Yacht Squadron) 2.

THE quest for The Holy Grail of yachting inspired a new challenger from across the Atlantic — Sir Thomas Octave Murdoch Sopwith, the British millionaire of aircraft fame. His military aircraft, the Sopwith Camel and Triplane became famous in World War I. The Camel, a single-seater fighter plane, was the most successful in the war.

Sopwith taught himself to fly in 1910 and two years later founded the Sopwith Aviation Company. He enjoyed sailing as a pastime and developed into a prominent big-boat skipper in Britain, graduating from 12-metre racing.

He bought *Shamrock V* and raced her for two seasons in English waters before deciding to build a J boat with a view to challenging for The America's Cup in 1933 through the Royal Yacht Squadron. Reaction among the British to Sopwith's challenge was, in most cases, negative.

In 1930, the Wall Street crash and The Depression that followed had not taken sufficient hold to hinder preparations for Sir Thomas Lipton's final challenge. The financial commitment of both challenger and defender had been made before the significance of the crash hit home.

However, by 1934 the economies of Great Britain and the United States had been hit severely. The British felt the time was not opportune for an America's Cup challenge. How could anyone justify a sporting venture involving an outlay of more than a million dollars — perhaps two million — when so many in the U.S., in particular, were poor and destitute.

King George V, Commodore of the Royal Yacht Squadron at the time, despite his deep love for sailing, asked Sopwith to wait until the economic climate improved. He felt certain that the New York Yacht Club would not entertain notions of a new challenge.

Sopwith persisted, explaining that if he did not challenge, he knew of three other syndicates who would. King George relented. The Royal Yacht Squadron issued an official challenge, and what's more, it was accepted. As reports in *The New York Times* and other major daily newspapers clearly indicated sporting endeavours were not cast aside.

For instance, Olympic sprinter Ralph Metcalfe was away in Japan with a United States team when he equalled the world 100 metres record (10.3 seconds); the richest horse race in the world, the Futurity, worth $98,330, was run and won at Belmont by 8-1 shot, Chance Sun. It is a curious fact of horse racing the world over that even during economic depressions and recessions the gambler finds the money and the resilience to continue his passion for the Sport of Kings. Not a dissimilar passion affected yachtsmen.

The constraints of the most savage depression in modern history were noticeable in America's defence efforts. Only one new yacht was built. Not surprisingly it resulted from the combined planning of designer William Starling Burgess, "Mike" Vanderbilt, as the manager-skipper, and Nat Herreshoff.

The name of the boat was *Rainbow*, though for a time, Vanderbilt had trouble finding the money necessary to build her. In the end, 18 names were on the official syndicate list, including three of Vanderbilt's family.

Consideration had been given to using the 1930 defender, *Enterprise*, but changes to rules govening J boats in 1931 eliminated her as a worthwhile defender for the 1934 series. In a bid to build better J boats, an international board ruled that, among other changes, the minimum mast weight should be 5,500lb so as to make the spars more dependable.

Enterprise's aluminium mast weighed 4,000 lb. The International committee also decreed that the

Rainbow during the vital third race after she lost the first two in 1934.

J boats should provide accommodation aboard for the crew. The extra seven or eight tons — some of it above deck — would give *Enterprise* no chance for she was not big enough to carry the extra weight.

Though *Enterprise* never sailed again, a part of her went with the 1934 syndicate. *Rainbow's* sydicate were forced to use much of her gear including some of her expensive sails, a cost cutting venture that allowed Vanderbilt to build and outfit *Rainbow* for a figure somewhere between $380,000 and $420,000, far below the expansive sums spent on the 1930 defenders.

Two of the yachts used in the 1930 American trials, *Weetamoe*, who had gone so close to winning the trials, and *Yankee* were rigged and prepared for the 1934 trials against *Rainbow*. Both of them required extensive alterations to comply with the new rules and while *Yankee*, with *Whirlwind*, was the first to be eliminated in the 1930 trials, she almost won the right to defend against Sopwith's *Endeavour*.

Weetamoe's mast was a duplicate of *Rainbow's*, historians arguing that it was built specifically for the purpose of providing *Rainbow* with a spare in case of accident. *Yankee* had been laid up at Herreshoff's building yard for three years and her alterations were considered dramatic. A Boston boat, her bow was rebuilt to a V rather than the U shape and her sails forward of the mast had to be bigger. Thankfully, *Yankee* was a large yacht and the extra weight provided by the new rules governing J boats was no problem.

Above: Rainbow, her lee rail at the waterline. It was only after increasing her waterline length by adding ballast that she won the defence trials. Right: Endeavour, a George Nicholson design that shocked the Americans.

The changes to *Yankee* gave her a sharper appearance and made her a better all round boat than she had been in 1930. This time she was highly competitive in light airs.

In the preliminary trials and observation races, *Yankee* was clearly the best yacht. *Whirlwind's* alterations did not appear to have helped her and *Yankee* had been beaten only twice by *Rainbow* in two months of sailing.

Burgess and Vanderbilt spent many hours in consultation, looking at every feasible method of overcoming the advantages *Yankee* held over their new boat. They experimented with the ballast, adding extra weight to increase the yacht's waterline length, bigger headsails were made and Burgess and Vanderbilt developed a flexible boom which they considered to be better than the much discussed Park Avenue boom. The new boom could be bent into an aerodynamic curve.

Rainbow was a better boat for the changes even though *Yankee* thrashed her in light airs in their first official trial. However, in the race that ultimately decided the defender, *Rainbow* won by a mere one second. It was enough to prove to the New York Yacht Club committee that, not only was she a faster boat - a fact debated by New Englanders — but that she was

a sounder boat and less likely to suffer gear and structural faults. In many ways, the selection committee stuck with the safer bet. Vanderbilt explained that his problems were far from over for he understood that *Endeavour*, a George Nicholson-designed boat, had proven exceptionally fast in trials in English waters. In most cases during The America's Cup, the defence trials were closer and more exciting than the races themselves. This was one time when the reverse was the case.

Sopwith was the first British yacht owner to command a challenger in an America's Cup series. Until 1934, challengers had been sailed by professional skippers, with the exception of *Shamrock IV's* skipper William Burton who was an amateur representing a non-sailing owner.

Endeavour was already in the water and trialling when the Americans launched *Rainbow*. The British yacht trialled against the older *Velsheda*, another Nicholson design, built in 1933 and seen as a substitute for *Endeavour* if the latter did not come up to scratch. Under a new rule, the challengers could substitute another boat up until a month before September 15, the day of the first race.

Once tuned up, *Endeavour* proved clearly superior to *Velsheda*. The main concern for the British was, the strike by many of *Endeavour's* professional crew just nine days before Sopwith was to leave for America. The crew wanted higher wages. Sopwith refused their demands and hastily recruited a number of strong, young amateur sailors.

Sopwith's afterguard included his wife, who was not out of place behind the wheel; Nicholson, the designer, and Frank Murdoch, an aviation engineer. It became clear during trials in Newport, that there was little difference in looks between *Endeavour*, and the American defender *Rainbow*. *Endeavour* was a slightly larger yacht in every dimension except in sail area, though even then the difference was negligible.

A certain amount of ill feeling — not uncommon in America's Cup racing — developed before the first race when the British discovered, after each yacht's representatives inspected their opponent's boat, that *Rainbow* had been stripped of a considerable amount of its cabin fittings, including the bathtub. The British contended that such an act did not conform to the new rules of racing which stated that each yacht must carry accommodation for its crew. The dispute was finally resolved by removing *Endeavour's* bathtub!

The first race was abandoned because of lack of wind. *Rainbow* led by a mile at the time, leaving the Americans even more unprepared for what was to follow in the next two races. James Robbins of *The New York Times* greeted the first race finish the following day: "Blown like a loosened leaf before a salt wind's flicking goad, the British challenger *Endeavour* today won the first race for The America's Cup, defeating the defender, *Rainbow*, by 2 minutes 9 seconds over 30 miles."

On a rainy and overcast day, *Endeavour* had won only the fourth race by a challenger in America's Cup history. *Rainbow* led by 18 seconds at the end of the

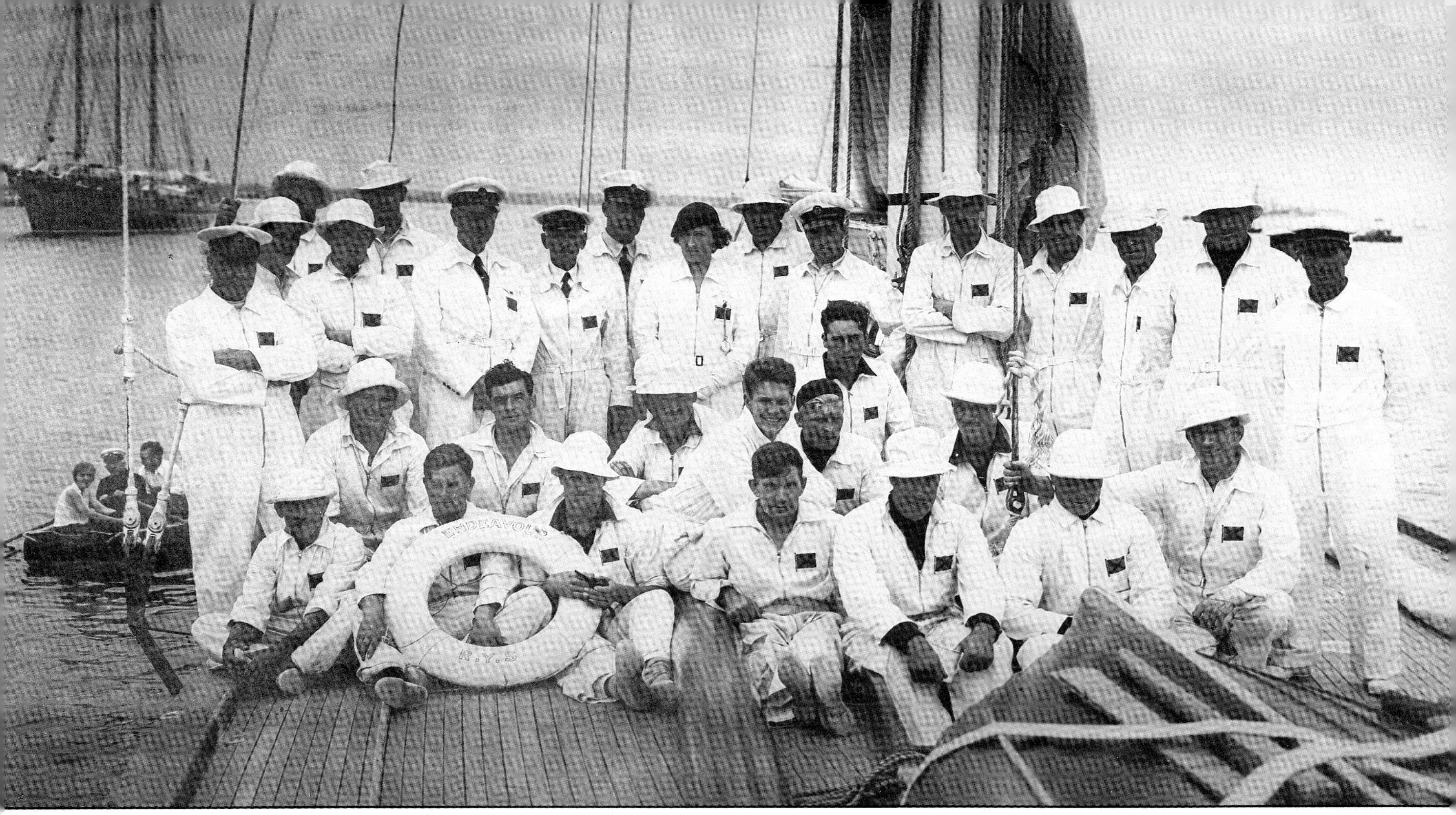

Above: The crew of Endeavour with Thomas Sopwith and his wife.
Below: Endeavour's crew at work, hauling in the mainsail.

windward leg. As President Roosevelt watched the dual, *Endeavour* suddenly closed in. Her great parachute spinnaker was put on her and she caught and passed Rainbow. The following day on the 30-mile triangular course, *Endeavour* won again, this time by 51 seconds. Her time, 3 hours, 9 minutes and one second was the fastest time on record. Sopwith to this point had proved himself an outstanding helmsman and Endeavour became the shortest priced challenger in Cup racing, being quoted at 4-1 on.

This was the point of no return normally faced by the challenger. The news of *Endeavour's* second victory brought immense crowds into the streets of Portsmouth, England and special squads of police to control them.

The only disgruntled Britons were a handful of professional yachtsmen who feared the success of *Endeavour* with its amateur crew would mean the end of professional crews. As the next four races showed, they had no need to despair.

The third race was remarkable. *Rainbow* edged home ahead of *Endeavour* by 3 minutes 26 seconds, although at the end of the leeward leg, *Endeavour* led by almost seven minutes. In one of the great sailing blunders, Sopwith, though still well ahead on the windward leg, tacked to cover *Rainbow* which was under the guidance of Sherman Hoyt. Historians claim that Vanderbilt, in despair, had handed the helm to Hoyt, who had raced against Sopwith in England.

Hoyt stated later that he knew Sopwith to be a helmsman who always tacked to cover his rival's yacht no matter where they were positioned. Hoyt had luffed as a bluff, hoping Sopwith would follow. He did and, unfortunately, hit a calm patch. If Sopwith had stayed on his starboard tack, the race was his.......three races to nil!

In fairness, Sopwith panicked when he saw *Rain-*

Above: Rainbow running before the wind. Below: Sherman Hoyt who took over as helmsmen during the vital third race and pulled off an amazing victory. Below (right): Harold Vanderbilt, one of the great America's Cup skippers.

The America's Cup 1851-1987

bow tack for he was unsure of where the finish line was. Whatever the case, that one race destroyed him.

Both skippers looked at ways to improve their yachts — Sopwith tested a new genoa jib while Vanderbilt added two more tons of ballast and took on board the *Yankee's* new parachute spinnaker to help improve her downwind performance.

The fourth race brought controversy, a protest from Sopwith and more criticism of his handling of the challenger, as *The New York Times* front page article testified: "It was a race which made yachtsmen in the fleet which followed the boats almost cry as they saw the errors into which *Endeavour* was forced. She was the faster boat, she outfooted *Rainbow* ...... but she was beaten because she was mishandled."

The incident that caused Sopwith to protest came at the end of the first mark with *Endeavour* 24 seconds ahead. Sopwith luffed Vanderbilt just after he rounded the mark, passing *Endeavour* to windward. Though several eyewitnesses believed *Rainbow* had no option but to tack, Vanderbilt maintained his course and Sopwith was forced to bear off to avoid a collision. The American boat sailed by and won the race.

Sopwith did not raise his protest flag until near the finish line, alleging that the American representative on board told him it was not necessary to raise the flag until he was within view of the committee boat.

Above: Weetamoe during trials. She had gone close to winning the defence trials in 1930, and her owners decided to try again — again without luck. Below. With spinnakers at work, (from left) Enterprise, Vanitie and Rainbow in one of the many defence trials. Rainbow was successful.

Sopwith explained in his letter to the New York Yacht Club race committee: "I hoisted my protest flag immediately I had decided to make a protest and at the first opportunity that it could be visible to the race committee." Sopwith raised the flag some three hours after the incident and the race committee, relying on technicalities, decreed that the protest could not be heard because the protest flag had not been raised "at the earliest possible moment."

Hardened American yachting experts deplored the New York Yacht Club's decision not to hear the protest. They felt that *Endeavour* should have been awarded the race. Sopwith could have been ahead 3-1, instead of going into the fifth race at 2-all.

Sopwith was forced to accept the decision. He agreed to race the following day and before doing so added a ton and a half of ballast to the boat. Whatever the values of the two yachts, Sopwith and his challenge was doomed. Neither he nor his crew recovered from the second setback.

Rainbow won the fifth and sixth races, the final race by 55 seconds and only after *Endeavour* at one time led by almost three minutes. Better handling of their yacht and the knowledge that Sopwith would attempt to cover *Rainbow* at all costs, gave the Americans victory.

More than 50 years would pass before an America's Cup series would be as close again.

Above: Endeavour on the way to victory. Note her "Park Avenue" boom. Endeavour led the series two races to nil. Below: Rainbow has her revenge. She crosses the line in the fourth race to level the series 2-all. She won the fifth and deciding race the next day.

1937

End of the 'J' Class

Ranger (NYYC) 4 defeated Endeavour II (Royal Yacht Squadron) nil.

NOT since the days of Lord Dunraven had the end of an America's Cup challenge been left with so strong a smell of rancour and ill feeling. Thomas Sopwith made it clear he would never race for The America's Cup again. He was not the first to make such a statement. Nor was he the first to change his mind.

Like many of his predecessors, he looked upon the New York Yacht Club as an overpowering ogre prepared to use all possible means to ensure that the Cup remained in its keeping. The 1934 challenge produced a furore on both sides of the Atlantic, though at first, the Americans were as keen as anyone to quell the fires of controversy that once again threatened the contest.

One simple act of friendliness had more influence in cementing Anglo-American yachting relationships than a thousand words. According to historians, the decision of American yachtsman, George Lambert, owner of *Vanitie*, the beaten yacht in the 1934 defender trials, to take his newly acquired yacht, *Yankee* across the Atlantic for the 1935 British season had much to do with breaking down the barriers.

Lambert developed a friendship with Sopwith during the 1934 Cup challenge. He was not seen as the enemy by the British for he had agreed to trial *Vanitie* against Sopwith's *Endeavour* before the previous challenge.

Lambert's presence in England softened Sopwith's bitterness and the anger of his countrymen, so much so that during the season, Sopwith ordered a new boat from Charles Nicholson with the idea of challenging for The America's Cup in 1936.

Although the New York Yacht Club refused to accept a challenge in 1936 because it coincided with the Presidential elections, Sopwith went ahead with the designing and building of a new yacht anyway. He was happy enough to wait for 1937 for it would give him ample time to prepare and trial the new *Endeavour*.

Nicholson built the biggest boat the rules allowed, and certainly larger than any of his previous J-class yachts. *Endeavour II* was 135 feet overall, 87 feet on the waterline with a beam of $21\frac{1}{2}$ feet, and a draft of 15 feet. Her total sail area was 7,500 feet.

Sopwith saw his next challenge as being even stronger than the previous, basing his judgement on the fact that *Endeavour II* had shown itself to be considerably faster in trials than the first *Endeavour*. He reasoned that since he had gone so close in his first attempt, the Americans would have to find a superboat to beat him.

As previous defences had shown, the British introduced new designs that were, in essence, little advanced on the standards American designers set in the previous Cup races. The Americans simply developed a yacht that was more advanced each time.

In the case of the 1937 challenge, they produced a yacht that was revolutionary. *Ranger* was considered to be the greatest of all America's Cup defenders, the result of a combined designing effort by youthful Olin Stephens and 51-year-old William Starling Burgess, the designer of two previous defenders whose genius was not confined simply to the sea. Burgess designed and built the first plane to fly in New England (in 1910) and opened the first licensed aircraft company in America; he also invented a new type of machine gun, developed by him after serving in the Spanish-American War.

How improbable it might have seemed that two of the world's leading aircraft designers and manufacturers should meet in friendly combat on the sea. Yet the list of defenders and challengers

Ranger, her large spinnaker set, is considered the greatest of all America's Cup yachts.

in The America's Cup is liberally sprinkled with innovators whose inventions and ingenuity brought them instant wealth.

Starling Burgess' *Ranger* co-designer, Stephens was one of the finest young yacht designers in the country, though it was conceded that the major credit for the design of *Ranger* was due more to Burgess than to Stephens.

Owner, Harold Vanderbilt, who had skippered two previous defenders, saw it as imperative that a young designer such as Stephens involve himself in the design of a J-class boat. Burgess would not be around forever and Vanderbilt's decision to incorporate Stephens into the team was a safeguard for the future. Though Burgess gets much of the credit for *Ranger*, Stephens' influence was significant in the production of a yacht of such radical design.

The final design was developed in tank tests carried out at the Stevens Institute of Technology at Hoboken, New Jersey. Burgess and Stephens agreed to combine their talents. They each provided two models for tank testing. No names were given to the models, just the letters, A, B, C and D. After exhaustive testing, model "C" was chosen as the fastest hull.

The identity of the designer of "C" was not divulged at the time and there was little discussion on the subject until many years later when it was erroneously disclosed that Stephens had designed model "C". Stephens publicly acknowledged that Burgess,

The America's Cup 1851-1987

Opposite page (top): Ranger, trialling on the waters off Newport. She was all-steel and displaced 166 tons. (bottom): Owner, Harold Vanderbilt at the wheel watched by his wife. Above: Endeavour II, similar to Ranger in dimensions, but not in performance. Below: Thomas Sopwith and his wife on board Endeavour.

who had died, was the man responsible for the chosen model.

Burgess was fascinated by the results of tank testing and accepted the accuracy of the methods adopted by Professor Kenneth Davidson. Where tank testing was once seen as being too inclined to give false impressions, Professor Davidson developed the system a good deal further, using smaller models and simulating varous wind and sea conditions more accurately than those who had adopted tank testing in the past.

Unwittingly, the British helped in the design of *Ranger*. Charles Nicholson graciously supplied the lines of *Endeavour* some 12 months earlier. When the a model of *Endeavour* was tested in the tank, the results supported the observations of Burgess and other American designers. The tests gave Burgess, in particular, the confidence to accept Professor Davidson's methods. Burgess admitted later that *Ranger* would not have been as revolutionary had he and Stephens not accepted the results of the tests.

The effects of the Great Depression were still sev-

The America's Cup 1851-1987

ere and Vanderbilt struggled to raise the money to build *Ranger*. In the end he was forced to make a $500,000 committment himself. For the first time since 1887, the building of a defender was not placed in the hands of the Herreshoff's.

The Bath Iron Works, in Maine, agreed to build the yacht for little above the cost price. Even millionaires such as Vanderbilt had to watch their pennies in such times. To save further costs, many of *Ranger's* sails were taken from Vanderbilt's previous yachts, *Enterprise* and *Rainbow*, although Arthur Knapp Jnr, who sailed aboard *Ranger*, explained in a later article that Vanderbilt's reason for using the sails was because "he was fond of them", not for any financial reasons.

Ranger, unlike previous defenders, was of all-steel construction. She was huge, displacing 166 tons, and immensely powerful. Yachting experts pointed out that she was not an attractive boat, though as Sir Thomas Lipton once explained after his defeated challenger was classed as a "handsome looking yacht", that he would have much preferred an ugly winner.

Ranger was similar to *Endeavour II* in her dimensions. She was 135ft 2in long; 87 ft at the waterline. Her beam was 21ft and she had a draft of 15ft; her sail area was 7,546 sq ft, three square feet more than the British challenger. *Ranger's* spinnaker measured 18,000 square feet and her displacement was 166 tons, which included 112 tons of lead ballast.

According to Arthur Knapp Jnr, *Ranger* had a much larger forestaysail than any of the other Js, which was accomplished by moving the tack farther forward and the halyard block farther up the mast. Nicholson was proud of *Endeavour II*, the fourth challenger he had designed. But after he had seen *Ranger* for the first time, he realised she was the most revolutionary yacht in 50 years. He knew there and then that Sopwith's hopes of improving on his first challenge were forlorn. Though Nicholson hoped for a miracle, it was not forthcoming. Sopwith was not satisfied with simply taking his new *Endeavour* to Newport. He wanted a trial horse and chartered the old *Endeavour* across the Atlantic. Since Sopwith did not have to declare his challenger until immediately before the start of the first race, he also had the choice of challenging with the first *Endeavour* if *Endeavour II* did not perform well.

Sopwith had no need for such fears. *Endeavour II* proved herself far superior. She was the British challenger to face *Ranger* in the first race on July 31. Sopwith remained highly confident. Time was on his side. He had built *Endeavour II* for a 1936 challenge and had what was a luxury for challengers at the time, the chance to tune up against a trial yacht on the American side of the Atlantic. Sopwith could not complain that he was not well prepared. Both his yachts were hauled out and prepared at Herreshoff's building yards at Bristol, Massachussets, leaving Sopwith with three months in which to ready his challenger.

Ranger swept all before her in the defence trials. She did not lose one trial race, beating *Weetamoe*, *Yankee* and *Rainbow* for the right to defend The Cup. *Rainbow*, the 1930 defender, had been improved, yet was no match for *Ranger*, the superboat.

The first race was devastating for Sopwith. *Ranger* won by 17 minutes 5 seconds, a phenomenal margin in view of the effort and money which had gone into designing and preparing *Endeavour II*.

There was even less joy two days later over the triangular course when *Ranger* defeated *Endeavour II* by 18 minutes 32 seconds, among the worst defeats since *Volunteer* beat *Thistle* in 1887. The light airs of the first two races obviously favoured *Ranger*. It is worth noting that Sopwith won the start in both races, although *Ranger's* crew later claimed that Vanderbilt had been warned by The Cup committee not to risk an incident that would again threaten relationships between the two countries.

The next two races were not as devastating for Sothwith. In stronger winds, the British challenger performed better, though some historians believe Vanderbilt was more keen on keeping the races com-

Opposite: Just after the start of the second race. Endeavour II appears to have a slight lead over Ranger. However, the light airs favoured the defender and she won easily. Above: Ranger forces Endeavour II over the line early at the start of the fourth race. Ranger won again, but the margin was not as devastating as the first two races.

petitive than winning by large margins. Sopwith had two tons of ballast taken from *Endeavour* after the second race and had the boat slipped and re-polished. The four minute margin was at least less humiliating.

In the fourth race, Sopwith was forced across the starting line too early and was recalled. *Endeavour II* appeared faster on the reaches although there was never any question of her overhauling *Ranger*. The margin was the smallest of the four races — 3 minutes 37 seconds.

Vanderbilt handed the job of steering *Ranger* over to the Stephens brothers, Rod and Olin at the finish because of the great job they had done that summer with his yacht.

The Cup series of 1937 was the last for the J-class boats. Many saw them as too specialised — good for nothing else but sailing in limited races — yet that is typical of The America's Cup yacht, as the development of the 12-metre yacht was to emphasise. In time, many yachtsmen regretted their passing.

Sopwith went back to Britain where he continued to race. He and Vanderbilt raced each other again, this time in English waters when Vanderbilt took *Vim*, a 12-metre class yacht, across the Atlantic in 1939. Sopwith had built a 12-metre, *Tomahawk*. *Vim* proved to be the best 12-metre of the year.

By the middle of the Second World War, most of the J-class yachts were thrown on the scrapheap and melted down to be used in the war effort. An exciting era of The America's Cup had passed. The yachting world had to wait almost 20 years for the next defence.

The America's Cup 1851-1987

J-boat

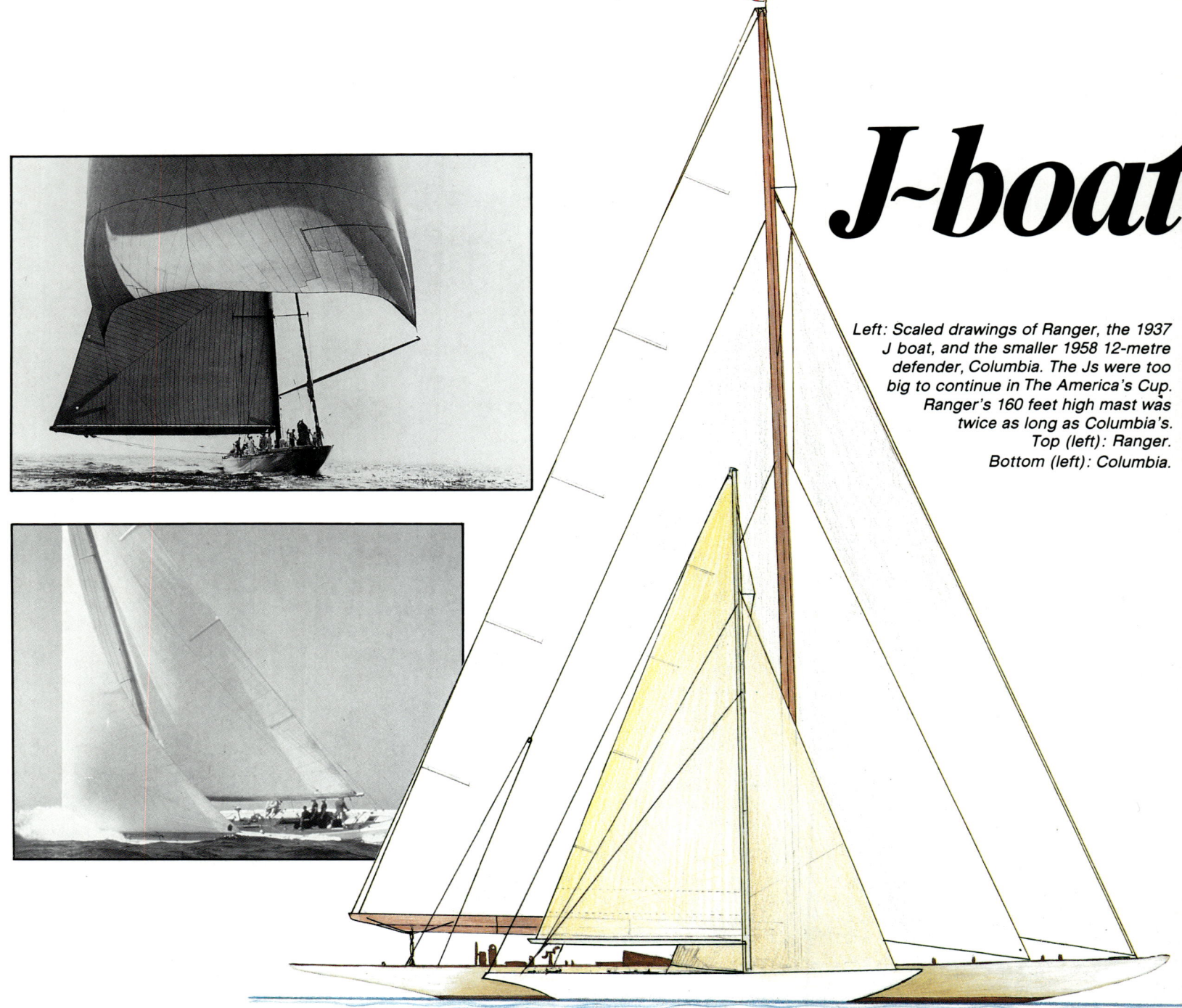

Left: Scaled drawings of Ranger, the 1937 J boat, and the smaller 1958 12-metre defender, Columbia. The Js were too big to continue in The America's Cup. Ranger's 160 feet high mast was twice as long as Columbia's.
Top (left): Ranger.
Bottom (left): Columbia.

IN phasing out the J-boat, quite obviously The America's Cup required a much smaller class of yacht, for financial reasons as much as anything else. Until 1958, The Cup had been contested by yachts of the largest available class.

Not all of them were massive sailing machines. *Mischief*, for instance, the 1881 defender, was 67ft 5in long — 61ft on the waterline. Yet most of the yachts were schooners or cutters and from 1886 to 1958, no defender or challenger measured less than 100 feet.

Reliance, the winner of The Cup in 1903, was the largest America's Cup yacht, measuring 143 feet. In 1937, the last series involving the J-boats, *Ranger* measured 135 ft 2 inches in overall length.

The Js were extravagant racing machines, almost monolithic in comparison to the 12-metre class. They were revered by their owners and the yachtsmen who sailed them for not only were they so uniquely a combination of size and speed, they were popular with the public at large. Owners were among the rich, the J-boat a symbol of that wealth.

The first of the class were raced in America in 1928. *Resolute*, the 1920 defender, and *Vanitie* were built in 1914 and according to Arthur Knapp jnr, sail trimmer on *Ranger* in 1937, they were "gaff-rigged topsail sloops and converted to schooner rigs in the early 'twenties'." In 1928 they were converted to jib-headed marconi rigs.

Only ten Js were ever built, six in America and four in Britain. They raced for eight to ten years, including three America's Cups, 1930, 1934 and 1937. These impressive machines were rated under the American Universal Rule:

$$R = \frac{.18 \, l.w.l. \times \sqrt{s.a.}}{\sqrt[3]{displ.}}$$

Under the Universal Rule, the J-boat needed to have a waterline length of between 76 and 87 feet and the displacement of the yachts grew over the years. *Vanitie* and *Resolute* both displaced 108 tons; *Enterprise* 128 tons, *Reliance* 140 tons, *Endeavour II* 162.5 tons and *Ranger*, the largest displacement of them all, 166 tons.

So many aspects of these giants were impressive. Their mainsails weighed a ton; their masts reached over 160 feet and their spinnakers covered an area as much as 18,000 square feet. *Reliance's* total sail area was 16,159 square feet, by far the largest of any America's Cup yacht. Yet *Ranger*, the last of the J-boats, had a sail span of 7,546 square feet, which was still almost four times the size of the first 12-metre defender, *Columbia* which had a total area of 1,825 square feet.

The strain imposed on the J-boat's mast and rig-

to 12 metre

ging was enormous. According to one account: "The compression on the masts could amount to nearly 200 tons. Once sailing they could carry their way for miles — one J won a race in extremely light airs by simply ignoring the direction of the wind when it had almost dropped to nothing and heading straight for the line — and they could take up to five minutes to rack and regain their speed." Yet they were sensitive to the touch of a hand on the wheel.

It became evident after the war that the J-boats would not race again. Technology advances were beginning to take Cup racing into another dimension. Such materials as aluminium, plutonium and titanium were being used in yacht building and, like new sail cloth, they were expensive. While British Js were made of steel, the Americans used the expensive metal, tobin bronze. The Americans, with their highly developed engineering and design skills, tended to disregard cost when building Cup yachts.

To build, race and outfit a yacht the size of *Ranger* would have been overbearingly expensive, even for the wealthiest. Estimates were put at around $1.5 million, the cost of building alone being $500,000.

The cost of building and racing the 1930 defender, *Enterprise* was almost one million dollars and in that year Americans built four Js for the challenge, *Enterprise, Yankee, Weetamoe* and *Whirlwind*. There were six other Js — *Shamrock V, Velsheda, Rainbow, Endeavour, Endeavour II* and *Ranger*. Even though other yachts raced in the J-class, according to one writer: "To call any yacht other than these (the ten above) a J is a misnomer."

It was quite some time after the war when the yachting fraternity began to think seriously again of The America's Cup. The J-boats were gone — that much was certain. Though no one seemed to notice the demise at the time, they virtually finished in Britain at the death of King George V. After the king's death, his cutter *Britannia*, was towed out into the middle of the Channel and scuttled. J boats raced no more in British waters.

The 12s were a contrast. Even before the Second World War, the 12-metre yacht had begun to establish itself as the premier class. They were no modern child of yacht racing. They were reported to have been seen on the Clyde in 1908. After the Second World War, Harold Vanderbilt invested in the smaller 12-metre class, obviously looking for the action. The boat was designed to the International Rule which had been Europe's system for classifying yachts for more than 30 years.

However, the entry of the 12-metre class meant a new Deed of Gift. The Deed as it stood allowed for yachts of a minimum 65 feet on the waterline. The largest yachts racing in the mid-50s were little more than 70 feet long overall and with a maximum waterline length of no more than 52 feet.

No American or British owner had a yacht to meet the specifications of the Deed. Nor were they inclined to build one, again the cost of building large yachts too exorbitant. The most acceptable class of yacht was, therefore, the 12-metre. It's overall length was 70 feet, with a waterline length of 45 feet, and the comparison below between *Ranger* and *Columbia* underlines the major differences.

	Ranger	Columbia
Overall length:	135' 2"	69' 5"
Waterline length:	87'	45' 6"
Beam:	20' 10"	11' 10"
Draft:	15'	8' 11"
Sail Area:	7546 sq ft	1825 sq ft
Displacement (tons):	166	28.4
Mast height:	160'	82'

The modified Deed of Gift paved the way for the entry of 12-metre yachts. The term 12-metre is often confusing, since many believe it to be the length of the yacht. Indeed, there is nothing about the 12-metre that measures 12 metres. The basic formula for determining the rating of the class equals 39.37 feet, or 12 metres. That formula is based on the following quotation:

$$R = \frac{L + 2d + SA - F}{2.37}$$

R = Rating (12 metres)
L = Length of hull measured at a point approximately 7 inches above the waterline length, with certain corrections
d = Girth measurement, determined by the difference between measurements on the hull from sheer to keel
SA = Sail area
F = Freeboard
2.37 = Mathematical constant.

The formula of the International Rule is precise. Factors within the formula balance each other and it is necessary to remain within the strict limits. Extremes were discouraged. For instance, if the length of the hull is increased, the sail area would be decreased in order to remain within the 39.37 rating. Otherwise, the yacht would no longer be in the 12-metre class.

In 1974, rules were modified to allow for a number of openings on deck. Though it was a simple method of reducing weight, the 12s were considered to be unsafe in heavy weather and limits were placed on the number and dimensions of the openings.

Bendy masts became trendy in 1980, firstly because of their use by the British and then by the Australians. However, they had a short life. The mast allowed for a larger mainsail which under existing rules did not require a penalty. When a rule was introduced limiting the mainsail at varying heights, the bendy masts disappeared.

In these modern times, it is hard to imagine The America's Cup without 12-metres. They are the greyhounds of sailing, the classic thoroughbreds in an event that is universally regarded as the greatest sailing event of them all.

1958

New Columbia, Same Result

Columbia (NYYC) 4 defeated Sceptre (Royal Yacht Squadron) nil.

PROSPERITY returned to the world in the 1950s after the ravages of the most devastating war in history. It was a time also for the yachting world to think again of The America's Cup.

There were three long periods of inactivity in The Cup's history — 1851 to 1870, 1903 to 1920 and the longest, 1937 to 1958. Not even the passing of a landmark, such as the 100th anniversary of The Cup, in 1951, proved sufficient a motive to move either America or Britain from their understandable reluctance to race again. It wasn't that The Cup had been forgotten — far from it.

The first post-war discussions were held in 1946 between Captain John Illingworth, Commodore of England's Royal Ocean Racing Club and members of the New York Yacht Club. Illingworth was keen for the series to be resumed in ocean-racing yachts which, although not as large as the J boats, would have a minimum waterline length of 65 feet and would still be fit for pleasure sailing.

The trend since the war was to smaller ocean racers and a number of classes, from the 6 metres (overall length about 36 feet) to the largest class (about 72 feet), enjoyed a renewal of international competition. Illingworth obtained an unofficial agreement from the then Commodore of the New York Yacht Club, DeCoursey Fales, to conduct The America's Cup in yachts with a waterline length of 65 feet as designated by the Deed of Gift.

Neither the British nor the Americans was anxious to build large yachts anymore. Nor was the New York Yacht Club interested, initially, in changing the Deed of Gift, the holy scroll of yachting which had caused so much dissension between defenders and challengers in the past.

By the mid-1950s, Henry Sears, Commodore of the New York Yacht Club, again raised the question of applying to have the Deed of Gift amended to allow a smaller class of yacht to enter Cup races. This time, Sears gained approval from his committee. He produced what was the fourth Deed of Gift. This was approved by the Supreme Court of New York in December 1956. What's more, the Royal Yacht Squadron indicated that it was prepared to challenge in 12-metre class yachts.

Two important amendments were made to the deed — the boats would have a minimum waterline length of 44 feet and no longer did the challenging yacht have to be sailed to the defending country.

The transformation from the J boats, sailing monoliths if you like, to the sleeker, smaller 12-metre yachts was inevitable and, in retrospect, the only choice. Yacht building had undergone immense changes since the war, as much because of the new technologies which allowed boat builders a greater choice of materials with which to work as any other reason.

The 12-metre class yacht was not new. The first one had been built as far back as the turn of the century — the first 12-metre built in Britain was in 1907. The 12s were the thoroughbreds of the classes, a true racing machine and it is worth noting that the early 12-metre yachts lasted for decades. Many built in the early years were still around when the 1958 challenge was sailed. Most of them had been converted by their owners to cruising vessels.

The twelve's were designed to comply with the International Rule rather than the Universal Rule, which the Americans had used as their guideline for America's Cup racing. The International Rule, accepted as Europe's rating system since the early 1920s, encouraged a narrower, sleeker yacht with smaller sail areas than the Universal Rule.

However, neither the British nor the Americans appeared anxious to rely on 12-metre yachts, for racing in the class in both countries was hardly at its peak. Few, if any, new 12s had been built

Columbia, skippered by Briggs Cunningham, was the first 12-metre defender.

since the war, the last well known 12-metre to be built was *Vim*, designed by Olin Stephens and built in the summer of 1939. *Vim* was taken to Britain by her owner Rod Stephens where she won 19 races before returning to the United States.

She was laid up at City Island for 11 years and finally bought by a shipping magnate, John Matthews. When Matthews realised in 1957 that he had a possible America's Cup defender, he re-fitted her, adding new winches, a lightweight boom and virtually restoring her to her original trim. Her new sails were of Dacron, a synthetic material stronger than the Egyptian cotton used until then. More importantly, the sails were water resistant and lighter.

Vim was considered a great 12-metre yacht, and although built some 19 years before the defence, she went within a whisk of being the defender. Americans were not exactly eager when invitations to defence syndicates went out. Because of this, Commodore Sears, fearful of being embarrassed by having no defender at all, built one himself. He went to the best, Olin Stephens for his new yacht. The result was *Columbia*, skippered by Briggs Cunningham, who had sailed *Vim* for Harold Vanderbilt in 1939 and 1940.

Two other syndicates came forward with potential defenders, ironically, because each had heard that Sears was struggling to raise funds. One yacht was *Easterner*, owned by Hovey Chandler, the one-time owner of *Rainbow* and *Weetamoe*, and an elder statesman of American yachting. He was a Bostonian, who felt it was time that the old New York-Boston rivalry was renewed.

The other yacht was *Weatherly*, skippered by Arthur Knapp Jr., and funded by Henry Mercer, who admitted knowing nothing about racing ocean yachts. Once again the Americans had four possible defenders, and the advantage of another intense series of trials to tune their eventual representative yacht.

One can understand the reluctance of the British to find a challenger. Most of the 12-metre yachts had either left Britain or were being used for cruising. The Royal Yacht Squadron did not take up the challenge

The mighty Vim, built 19 years before the defence series, is seen here re-fitted for the trials. She didn't qualify for defender, but she is considered the prototype for 12-metre yachts.

until nearly a year after the changes to the Deed of Gift.

Recent English yachting had been poor. They had not won an Olympic yachting gold medal at either the 1952 Helsinki Games, or the Melbourne Games of 1956. The best performance was a silver medal to Colonel S. Perry in the 5.5 metre class in Melbourne. Perry was technical advisor to the Hugh Goodson syndicate which had agreed to challenge through the Royal Yacht Squadron. Perry later resigned when his advice was ignored.

The British syndicate looked to the country's best designers for a revolutionary yacht that would lift British yachting out of its doldrums. The British were neither lacking in sailing expertise nor designers, but critics lamented the quality of the tank testing carried out in the search for a worthy challenger. Poor simulations and insufficient time in the tanks at East Cowes meant that the British embarked on a mission impossible even before the new yacht, *Sceptre*, designed by David Boyd, reached the water.

When the Americans saw the British yacht they knew that only the most dramatic of mishaps would allow the British to take The Cup. The American defenders had been through some of the best match races ever sailed, with *Vim* and *Columbia* proving themselves superior to both *Easterner* and *Weatherly*.

As time and experience have shown, it is not the boat with the fastest hull that emerges triumphant — crew performance and sails have an integral bearing on the outcome of races. So it was with the 1958 defender trials. According to experts, *Easterner* appeared to have the fastest hull, but she turned out to be the slowest yacht. *Vim* was rated as having the slowest hull, yet she went close to earning the right to defend.

Vim's performance was a tribute to the aggressive sailing of their skipper, Emil "Bus" Mosbacher, supplemented by a young, diligent crew. *Vim* performed

best in light weather, and for a time, appeared likely to win selection.

The final trial races between *Columbia* and *Vim* were locked at two-all when *Columbia* won the fifth race, and then the deciding sixth race by a mere 12 seconds after the lead changed twice. *Columbia* sailed 40 trial races. Only the last of them gave her the right to defend The Cup.

Few believed that the Defence series would be as exciting, or as close. The British had brought with them a yacht incapable of matching the technically advanced Americans. Nor did *Sceptre* have the advantage of an intense summer of trials; her crew was selected from men in the armed forces for the reason that they could afford a summer away from home. They were young (the British syndicate decreed that the crew had to be under 30); they were big and strong, all the wrong reasons according to historians.

Watched by President Eisenhower and his wife, *Columbia* thrashed *Sceptre* by almost eight minutes in the first race and 11 minutes 42 seconds in the second, which had been re-sailed after lack of wind caused a postponement.

Though the wind freshened for the third race, *Sceptre* lost again, this time by 8 minutes and 20 seconds. The British saved the best until last — they lost by 7 minutes and 5 seconds, the smallest margin in the series!

The 17th challenge was over and the America's Cup was back in vogue again after 21 years. *Sceptre*, if nothing else, was a symbol of the renewal.

Opposite: British challenger Sceptre, as she was in later years. She was crewed by men from the armed forces and was insufficiently prepared. Below: A view of Sceptre's deck while in Newport before the hard racing began.

U.S. defender, Weatherly, modified for the 1967 series, was expertly sailed by Bus Mosbacher in 1962.

1962

The First Aussie Challenge

Weatherly (NYYC) 4 defeated Gretel (Royal Sydney Yacht Squadron) 1

THE summer of '62 brought with it winds of change and the first challenge by the men from Down Under. Australia, a mysterious, far away land to most Americans, took up the chance to enter international sailing.

Not since Canada's *Atalanta* was thrashed so comprehensively by *Mischief* in 1881 had another country outside of Britain challenged for The Cup.

Though there was hint of Australia's interest in Newport during *Sceptre's* challenge, the official request from the Royal Sydney Yacht Squadron, when it came, caused indignation and resentment in Britain where the British were already preparing for their own challenge. They sometimes treated a new challenge as their inalienable right since they had kept the races going for almost 80 years without another challenging country to interrupt them.

Australia, on the other hand, had no tradition in world yachting. The nation's only previous contest in a major international event was in 1898 when Mark Foy's 24-foot long *Irex*, built in 1886, was beaten by British yacht, *Maid of Kent* in four consecutive races for what was known as the Anglo-Australian Shield.

A later challenge by Foy in *Southerly Buster*, a boat he had specially built for the race, was refused by the defending club, the Medway Yacht Club, on the basis that Foy's crew raced for cash and were, therefore, professionals. The Shield was forfeited to the Australians.

Yachting in Australia was lively, if nothing else. Racing was limited mainly to Sydney Harbour where thousands often lined the harbour shores at weekends to watch the day's events. Yet Australian yachtsmen had earned a reputation as skilful tacticians and helmsmen and their ocean sailing qualities were not in doubt since the Sydney to Hobart race, which was in its 18th year, had established itself as a world ocean classic.

Besides, Australia won its first Olympic sailing medals two years earlier in Melbourne, Roly Tasker winning a silver in the 12-metre class and Alex "Jock" Sturrock a bronze medal in the 5.5 metre. The background was promising. Nothing, however, had occurred in Australian yachting to prepare her for the immensely sophisticated approach required for The America's Cup.

There appeared little anxiety among American yachtsmen that their beloved trophy would leave its resting place in the New York Yacht Club. They accepted the Australian challenge for little other reason than that The Cup needed a breath of fresh air. The Sceptre challenge had been so disastrous that the Americans felt a similar defeat against the British might wipe away all interest in The Cup.

When it became clear to the British that the Australian challenge would be accepted, they sought a Commonwealth substitution. The Duke of Edinburgh later wrote to the Australian Yachting Federation seeking a combined effort. Ironically, His Royal Highness was the patron of the Royal Sydney Yacht Squadron!

Sir Frank Packer, the head of the Australian syndicate, refused the British request, as those who knew him, expected he would. Packer was a blunt, stubborn, high powered newspaper magnate. He had a reputation for tough dealings. He was born rich and learned quickly to be domineering and, in the eyes of many of those who worked with him and against him, often ruthless. In many ways he treated his involvement in The America's Cup as he did his business. Success in one, however, did not guarantee success in the other.

Packer cabled the Commodore of the Royal Thames Yacht Club, Captain John Illingworth, explaining:"I see no reason for Australia to withdraw from its right and just position as the valid and the first challenger for the 1962 series....Maybe we won't do any better, but every now and again you have to give the young fellow in the family his head...."

An Australian syndicate member, Sir William Northam, who won an Olympic sailing gold medal at Tokyo in 1964 at the age of 60, faced the British, including the Duke of Edinburgh, at a meeting in London in May 1960. Northam was asked to discuss the possibility of a co-ordinated challenge. After the meeting, however, the British finally accepted that the Australians had a right to sole challenge. In many ways, Northam had calmed the rough waters.

Appeasing the British was the least of the Australians' problems, however. Their lack of experience in designing, building and sailing 12-metre yachts was always going to be a decided drawback.

Packer chartered the veteran 12 metre, *Vim* as a training yacht for Australian crewmen many of whom would have moved the Sydney Harbour Bridge for the chance to sail in Australia's first challenge. The search for a designer stopped at Alan Payne, an unassuming and modest man and the only professional yacht designer in Australia at the time. He was soundly trained in hydrodynamics and in naval architecture, having served at Australia's most important naval shipbuilding yard at Cockatoo Island in Sydney Harbour.

Payne, as the challenge was to prove, was one of the finest designers in America's Cup history, his attention to detail and the practicalities of each yacht he designed, the foundation for his success. Bob Bavier, who defended The Cup in *Constellation* two years after *Gretel's* challenge, said of Payne in his book, *America's Cup Fever*: "He loves boats, has an instinctive feel about them to supplement his technical savvy....he is unassuming and so modest about his own ability that one has to find out for oneself that he is one of the world's finest yacht designers."

Payne produced a yacht that was faster than America's defender, *Weatherly*. Having studied the designs of a number of American 12-metre yachts, Payne reasoned that to be competitive, the Australian boat would need American rigging, particularly the sails. Although a test tank existed in Sydney, he persuaded the New York Yacht Club to change its rules and allow him to use the more sophisticated tank at the Stevens Institute in New York, as well as allowing the Australians to use American sail cloth, which was far superior to Australian and British cloth. They were significant concessions and perhaps indicative of the complacency that had developed in the Americans.

The New York Yacht Club changed the rules after the *Gretel* challenge. In all future series, the challenging yacht had to be built, designed, tested and equipped in the originating country.

Gretel, the Australian challenger, surprised the Americans. She was considered a faster boat than Weatherly, although she lost the series.

Secrecy surrounded *Gretel*, just as it had with defenders and challengers before and after 1962. Even the name of the yacht was kept a secret until the official launching on February 19, 1962. *Gretel* was named in memory of Sir Frank Packer's wife, who died in August 1960.

Built by the Halvorsens, a Sydney family enterprise established on the shores of Sydney Harbour in the 1920s, *Gretel* did not show her true sailing capabilities in early trials with *Vim*. In fact, their were howls of disappointment from sections of Australian yachting concerned that the challenge would prove an acute embarrassment.

After a time, *Gretel* began to beat *Vim*, though not at every outing. While Payne had built a fast boat, there was more to America's Cup racing than boat speed. It had to be manned with the right crew and the Australians had to know just how fast it could go in certain conditions. According to historians, they did not find out in time. More than one reference was made during the series that had the Australians known just what *Gretel* could do, they might not have lost the series.

Gretel, together with *Vim*, did not arrive in Newport until two months before the challenge, insufficient time to allow a challenger to prepare thoroughly. The Australians suffered, too, from not knowing the name of their helmsman and crew until

Spinnakers are set as the old faces the new in 1962 defence trials. Columbia, the 1958 defender, leads Nefertiti, the only American yacht built specifically for the 1962 series. Neither of them qualified.

the eve of the first race.

It was one of the failings of Packer that he concealed such information, thereby depriving the crew of valuable preparation time as a team. Jock Sturrock and Archie Robertson alternated as skippers in trials. When the day of the first race arrived, Sturrock was the man chosen.

A straight shooter and hard worker with a fine sense of humour, Sturrock lamented that he and his crew did not have more time together. Yet he had little reason to criticise Packer's handling of the challenge. While many felt Packer interfered far too much, Sturrock explained that Packer contributed in a positive manner. "If there was anything needed that he thought might improve the boat he got it in double quick time," Sturrock explained.

According to Sturrock, Packer did not make decisions on his own, as had been believed the case. "Packer had an afterguard, an advisory committee, comprising Alan Payne, Fryge Halvorsen and Archie Robertson. The picture people have of Packer is quite wrong. He always went to his committee for advice. And I must say I got on very well with him."

By the time of the first race, the Australians had

The mansions of Newport, Rhode Island, a millionaire's hideaway, except during America's Cup defence series.

done remarkably well. Unknown as 12-metre yachtsmen and under-prepared compared to the immensely thorough Americans, they were ready to show the yachting world that the "young fellow" of the family was prepared for the big time.

Only one new yacht, *Nefertiti*, was built for the defence, further indication that the Americans did not fear the new boys. A Boston boat, she was designed by Ted Hood, a talented man who also acted as co-skipper. She was claimed to be Hood's first 12-metre design, a radical, broad yacht with a short keel. *Nefertiti* was at her best in fresh winds. Her helmsman Don McNamara was an aggressive skipper who had many "stormy moments" with the New York Yacht Club and later left the syndicate.

Nefertiti faced three tried 12s in trials, *Easterner*, *Columbia* and *Weatherly*. *Columbia* had changed hands since the previous defence and had done little sailing. *Weatherly* was modified at Luders yards, though there had been the temptation for shipping magnate Henry Mercer, who had commissioned *Weatherly* for the 1958 defence, to build a new boat. He preferred to modify her.

Bus Mosbacher, one of the greatest of America's Cup skippers, was the helmsman on *Easterner* until in 1962 he accepted the role as *Weatherly's* skipper. *Easterner*, with George O'Day as helmsman, and *Columbia* were eliminated from the final trials, leaving the new boat *Nefertiti* and the old, *Weatherly* to fight for the role of defender.

Though *Nefertiti* was faster on the reaches, she could never get the better of *Weatherly* to windward. Mosbacher was a master at controlling his crew and he was fortunate that his crew was settled. The *Weatherly* syndicate committee spent considerable time through summer refining and altering their yacht, to the point where it stood out as the obvious defender. It had taken Mercer four years to tune his yacht to the stage of qualifying for the defence, a significant fact considering the short period of the Australians' challenge.

The Australians did not stop looking for improvements in *Gretel*. Even up to two weeks before the race Payne moved *Gretel's* mast 19 inches forward to help improve her balance. One other innovation of Payne's was to install coffee-grinder winches in *Gretel* which were linked together by a clutch to allow four men instead of two on the handles. Sturrock's crew were heavyweights compared to Mosbacher's "midgets" and they were able to trim *Gretel's* sails faster than *Weatherly's* crew could trim her's.

Packer was chided by American reporters for replacing Terry Hammond with inexperienced navigator Magnus Halvorsen on the morning of the first race. They later criticised Halvorsen for holding "a losing tack for two minutes" on the first leg.

The start of the first race was delayed an hour while an exasperated Coast Guard tried to clear one of the largest spectator fleets to watch a race. Figures ranged from 2,500 to 4,000 boats (around 35,000 spectators). Sturrock claimed *Gretel* had been affected by unthinking spectators who at one point sailed their craft between the two yachts. On the first leg, Sturrock was forced to tack back to Mosbacher to avoid the fleet.

Once behind, *Gretel* had little chance against the wily Mosbacher, and defeat by three minutes, 43 seconds was a credit to them and to Payne, who by this time was accepted by the Americans as having designed a faster boat than *Weatherly*. Sturrock had actually won the start, but according to Norris Hoyt in his book, *The Twelve Metre Challenges for the America's Cup*: "Sturrock didn't know his boat, and didn't realise the extent to which the spectator fleet would box him in."

On the final run to the finish, *Gretel's* slim hopes of catching *Weatherly* were dashed altogether when her backstay parted. Sadly for the Australians they were still learning about their boat. Noyt wrote: "The pattern of defeat emerges. The first Cup race is very late to be learning your boat — but how can you learn if there's no competition with reality? Also, the spectator fleet made good competition impossible. Packer decreed that *Gretel* would ask for a layday after every race, mainly to wear out the spectators, but also to practise the lessons learned in the actual race."

What followed in the second race belongs to history. *Gretel* won. The course was triangular and *Gretel* had a new navigator — not the original, Hammond, but Robertson, who at one stage, seemed likely to be helmsman. In a westerly, gusting up to 25 knots and with a much thinner spectator fleet (this was Monday as opposed to Saturday's first race day), the Australians saw their chances skyrocket. This was the weather they had been hoping for.

Though the Australians tacked too short for the first mark, *Gretel* trailed by only 12 seconds; by the second mark, she was only 14 seconds behind. On the final leg, as *Weatherly* ran into trouble with her spinnaker which dragged water, *Gretel* caught hold of a monster wave that roared out of nowhere. Riding waves was something Australians could handle and forward hands Peter O'Donnell and Mick York stood near the mast and let out an almighty shriek as *Gretel* zoomed past a helpless *Weatherly*. Sturrock felt a moment of panic believing at first, when he heard the loud yells of his forward hands, that the mast of *Gretel* was about to fall. "I went crook on them later. I thought something terrible had happened, like losing the bloody mast."

Gretel sailed to a 47 second victory. That night Newport's "little Australia" celebrated. *Gretel's* win was the first by a challenger since *Endeavour* beat *Rainbow* in 1934 in the second of its two victories on September 18, 28 years ago to the day. Sturrock joined in the roaring celebrations, though he cautioned his crew that further victories would be even more difficult.

The fear the Americans now held of the Australians was no better illustrated than this story told by

Norris Hoyt some years after *Gretel's* victory.

"Bus Mosbacher invited me over for a drink, met me at the door, took me into a private room and told me in firm terms that I was a reporter, not a tactical adviser, and that my comments on the radio were to be limited to what was happening and what had happened, not what he or Sturrock might do.

"'This is the biggest poker game in the world,'" he (Mosbacher) said, "'and if he ever gets the notion that he can beat us on a point of sailing, he might just sail off by himself and do it.' Then I got the drink."

The Australians called a rest day the next day and unfortunately for them, the wind blew at 30 knots. Sturrock waited more than 10 years after the series to ask Mosbacher would he have called for a layday had the Australians wanted to race. Mosbacher told him: "It's something you will never know."

The following day, the winds calmed and *Gretel's* chances went with them. The light breezes not only left the Australians perplexed as to the type of rigging they should use, but were far more suitable to *Weatherly*. The result was a resounding 8 minutes, 40 seconds victory to the defender. There were no roaring celebrations from the Australians that night. *Gretel's* margin of defeat was reasonable only when one considers that at the end of the second leg she trailed *Weatherly* by 24 minutes.

Sturrock and his crew gleaned a good deal from the defeat, however. They were excited at the manner

Weatherly, her lee rail under water as gusty 25 knot winds whipped up the seas during the second race. Not suited by the conditions, she lost the race. It was her only defeat.

in which *Gretel* had made up so much time in light airs. The fourth race began in winds of 8 to 10 knots. Sturrock tacked 23 times on the first leg, yet trailed at the end of it by one minute, 26 seconds.

Gretel reduced the lead to 48 seconds by the second mark and, such was the speed of *Gretel* that Australian supporters saw an inevitable second victory. Making runs on small waves and making full use of a breeze that had freshened to 16 knots, *Gretel* closed in on *Weatherly*.

Mosbacher's reputation as one of the world's finest helmsman was not won overnight. He saw only one measure that would save *Weatherly*. According to historians, Mosbacher set a genoa and reached away, hoping to entice Sturrock to do the same. Hoyt recorded that: "At first, Sturrock hoisted his genoa inside his spinnaker and accelerated, eating away at Mosbacher's lead at almost a third better speed. For two minutes he was actually closer to the finish line than *Weatherly*, but he sharpened still more on to Mosbacher's course, took down his spinnaker, and dropped speed. Mosbacher gauged his move exactly, set spinnaker, dropped genoa and ran for the mark."

Mosbacher had played for time and won. Though *Gretel* was closing again at the finish, *Weatherly* had won by just 26 seconds, still the smallest winning margin in The Cup's history.

Gretel had her chances again in the fifth race. American observers, though understanding the lack of experience of the Australians, wondered at the manner in which they were forced to allow Mosbacher to call the tune. Mosbacher knew the wind shifts of Newport. No visiting yachtsmen could have expected to match him.

There were times during the final race when *Gretel* rocketed along at a rate that seemed certain to put Weatherly behind her. Yet Mosbacher's understanding of the conditions and his tactical brilliance were always enough to maintain an ascendency. *Gretel* lost the fifth race by 3 minutes, 40 seconds.

Though the 1962 series was called the most closely fought of all the America's Cup series, it certainly wasn't closer than the 1934 challenge in which the American defender *Rainbow* trailed Sopwith's *Endeavour* two races to none and only won the third after an error of judgement by the British. Yet the 4-1 defeat of Gretel did not reflect truthfully just how close the 1962 series had been. It was a lesson for the future. Australia had arrived in a flurry as a worthy America's Cup nation. There was every indication from the first attempt that one day the Americans may be playing the role of challenger.

The America's Cup 1851-1987

1964

No Sovereign Rule for British

Constellation (NYYC) 4 defeated Sovereign (Royal Thames YC) nil.

AUSTRALIAN yachting was paid the highest compliment of all after the 1962 series between Weatherly and Gretel — the New York Yacht Club altered the Deed of Gift. The strength of a challenge could almost always be gauged by the alterations, if any, deemed necessary by the New York Yacht club. The closeness of the series is usually directly proportional to the magnitude of those changes.

Less than three months after the challenge finished, the New York Yacht Club moved to slam shut what they conceived as loopholes in the Deed. The Cup would become even more unattainable. The club's board of trustees, entrusted with the right to interpret the Deed of Gift as they saw fit, decreed that, in future, the equipment on board the challenging yacht must originate from the challenger's own nation. No longer could a challenger use American sails or spars. No longer could the yacht be designed other than in the originating country, nor could they tank test the boat at the Stevens Institute.

Justification of the changes was simple. The New York Yacht Club felt they were upholding an interpretation of the Original Deed Of Gift which had been neglected until 1962.

The British were the first to "pay" the price of *Gretel's* excellent showing, though they beat the system in that their new challenger *Sovereign* had been tank tested at the Stevens Institute before the New York Yacht Club altered the Deed of Gift. Designed by David Boyd, who had been responsible for *Sceptre*, *Sovereign's* lines were too well advanced to withdraw. The Americans accepted the British challenge as long as all other aspects of *Sovereign* originated in England.

Despite the disaster of their 1958 challenge, the British were by no means reluctant to return to the waters off Newport. They were somewhat indignant at the Australian challenge and the readiness with which the New York Yacht Club accepted it. Having missed out on the 1962 defence, the British syndicate, headed by a young self-made millionaire, Anthony Boyden, had planned their new challenge from 1960, basing their attempt on the assumption that the new boys from Down Under would go the way of all previous challengers.

Without access to American technologies, the British underlined the enormous gap in the standards of designing and outfitting 12-metre yachts. Few challenging syndicates prepare themselves as far in advance as did Boyden, described by Norris Hoyt in his book, *The Twelve Metre Challengers* for the America's Cup, as " a self-made thirty-five-year-old roaring boy, entirely innocent of sailing experience at any level of competition."

He prepared for a 1963 attempt, believing initially that the New York Yacht Club were keen to accept a defence that year. But all notions of such a challenge were swept away in the closeness of the struggle with *Gretel*.

The New York Yacht Club needed time to recuperate. Emotionally exhausted, the Americans agreed to host the Cup the following year. Boyden, therefore, had 16 months in which to tune *Sovereign* to racing pitch. Launched in July 1963, *Sovereign* lacked, among other things, a new 12-metre trial horse. A revamped *Sceptre* was the only alternative and her performances against *Sovereign* served to show the British that their new challenger stood little chance against the Americans.

While Boyden considered a new boat, the Livingstone brothers, Australian cattle men living in England, agreed to build a sister-boat to *Sovereign* called *Kurrewa V*. Though not the ideal trial-boat, she was better than nothing. British observers were critical of the inadequacies of their

Constellation, a failure in early defence trials, improved with time. She thrashed the British challenger, Sovereign 4-0.

challenge, specifically saying that Boyd should not have been the designer after the disaster of *Sceptre*, nor was there complete confidence in skipper Peter Scott, son of famous Antarctic explorer Robert Falcon Scott, who reached the South Pole in 1912, and died on the return journey.

A British Olympian and acknowledged as a brilliant yachtsman, young Scott lacked experience in 12-metre sailing.

Sovereign, for all her similarities to *Kurrewa V*, proved to be the faster once they reached Newport, even allowing that her sails were inadequate. The British also took the unjustifiable course of hiring big, brawny, Rugby players as crewmen, believing brute strength to be the prerequisite.

The tight 1962 defence revived and stimulated American interest. They had, in general, become blasé about the Cup. While the British searched for a way out of their difficulties, the Americans found four syndicates willing to take up the challenge against *Sovereign*. Two of the boats, *American Eagle* and *Constellation* were built specifically for the challenge, while two old warriors, *Nefertiti* and *Columbia* also returned to the scene.

Nefertiti, redesigned by Ted Hood, had only just failed to defend the Cup in 1962. *Columbia* was the first yacht from the west coast of America to enter defence trials. Sold to a Californian, Pat Dougan, the 1958 defender was skippered by Briggs Cunningham. Both *Nefertiti* and *Columbia* started off the season promisingly, while the ultimate defender, *Constellation* performed dismally.

In the end, it boiled down to the two new boats, *American Eagle* and *Constellation*, with *American Eagle* at one stage holding a 16 races to six advantage in early and mid-season racing. A curious change came over *Constellation* toward the end of the New York Yacht Club cruise and it took a self-effacing decision by partowner and helmsman Eric Ridder to correct the problem.

Ridder, a six-metre yachtsman who had won a gold medal in the class at the 1960 Rome Olympics, surmised that he might have been the reason for *Constellation's* lack of early success and handed the helm gradually to his relief skipper Bob Bavier. Historians class Bavier as the official skipper of *Constellation*, but Bavier in his book, *America's Cup Fever*, writes: "Most books and articles on the America's Cup record that I was skipper of *Constellation* in 1964. Not so. Eric Ridder was. It's true that in the final trials and in the match itself I not only was helmsman but also called the shots.....Still Eric retained the title of skipper." Bavier was given more of each trial race until *Constellations's* remarkable improvement forced Ridder and his syndicate to allow Bavier full authority. Ridder was the titular head. Bavier explained: "I demurred at first because I felt it might be difficult to assume the role of skipper without being acknowledged as same. But once assured by Eric that I was to have a free hand, I agreed."

Constellation was a different boat under his control. Where *American Eagle* had won 14 straight races

The America's Cup 1851-1987

Opposite: A forward hand helps with the bright red spinnaker of British challenger, Sovereign. Above: Sovereign trails Constellation during the Defence series.

against *Constellation* before Bavier took the helm, her record under Bavier's command was 13 wins and three losses. Bavier had raced small boats since he was 11. He enjoyed ocean racing and was a skilled 12-metre skipper, another example of the importance of having a 12-metre controlled by helmsmen who understand the special tactics needed in match-racing.

American Eagle's skipper Bill Cox was another highly rated skipper, although by the end of the official trials Bavier's aggression was seen as the difference between the two yachts. Once Bavier applied pressure, he was able to sap all the confidence built up in Cox and his crew during the early victories. In only his second race as skipper, Bavier engaged in a tacking duel (he tacked 42 times on the final leg) described as one of the fiercest in defence trials. *Constellation* won by one minute 8 seconds. *American Eagle* won only one more race.

Among the changes to The America's Cup in 1964 was the decision of the New York Yacht Club to abandon the traditional triangular and windward to leeward courses in favour of the six-leg Olympic course. While the length of the course remained at 24 miles, tactics and sailhandling became even more important. More legs meant more buoys to round. It was also decided that after 1964, challenges could be made once every three years.

For Britain and *Sovereign*, the 1964 series was even more calamitous than 1958. Bavier, by race time, well in charge of *Constellation*, decided to be aggressive from the start of the first race. While indications were that *Sovereign* would be no match for the American defender, Bavier wanted to take no chances.

Constellation won the start by several lengths. One of the most lopsided defences in America's Cup history was underway. *Constellation* won the first race by five minutes 34 seconds. The second race was won by 20 minutes 24 seconds, the largest winning margin since *Mayflower* beat the English challenger *Galatea* in 1886.

The third race provided no relief — a six and a half minute defeat. It proved to be a telling insight into the fever generated by The America's Cup. Bavier recalled the feeling of achievement after *Constellation* had rounded the last mark with a lead of 12 minutes 26 seconds: "We were staying between *Sovereign* and the finish, making a loose cover and we were opening

The America's Cup 1851-1987

up distance with every passing minute......the strange part was that I could feel the growing excitement among our crew....I was steering with all the intensity as if *Sovereign* was one length astern and gaining. We had decided long ago, as soon as we determined that *Constellation* was faster, that no matter how far ahead we got we would never hold back in order to make the race look more respectable. Many times in the series we rooted for *Sovereign* to make it closer after we had a commanding lead. We agonized when we saw her make a desperation tack or jibe which we knew full well would put her even further behind.....No other sailing event could engender such excitement when the outcome was so obvious. But this was not just some other sailing event. This was the America's Cup, and we were about to win it and we suddenly wanted to win it in style."

Above: Constellation was a "dawdler" in early trials. But when the aggressive Bob Bavier took the helm, she grew another sail. She won the second race of the defence series by more than 20 minutes. Opposite: An unusual shot of work aboard Constellation, looking aft. A good view of Constellation's bendy boom.

And so they did. Bavier was true to his word. He showed *Sovereign* no mercy, *Constellation* increasing her lead by more than three minutes, winning eventually by 15 minutes 40 seconds.

The devastating loss took the sting out of the British. Scott faced an unenviable task in a decidedly slower boat. He rarely raced a boat after the series had ended and certainly was not about to try The America's Cup again with an inferior instrument. It would be 16 years before the British entered the fray again, although up to 1983 no British yacht had reached the defence series.

Intrepid on the windward leg during the third race. She won by 4 minutes 41 seconds.

1967

Intrepid Destroys the Dame

Intrepid (NYYC) 4 defeated Dame Pattie (Royal Sydney Yacht Squadron) nil.

SIR Frank Packer wasted no time posting Australia's second challenge. He had been at Newport in 1964 with Alan Payne watching *Sovereign's* demise and could see little prospect in the British returning in the immediate future for another challenge. The prediction by one American yachting writer before the challenge that it would be an "horrendous mismatch" was exact.

Australia had the 1967 challenge on its own. Packer, however, did not. Instead of the British opposing him, as they did so testily in 1962, Packer found opposition from within Australia.

Emil Christensen, a director of one of Australia's largest food processing and packing firms and a member of the Royal Melbourne Yacht Club, gathered together a Victorian syndicate which included many prominent Australian businessmen and yachtsmen. They commissioned Warwick Hood, a Sydney yachtsman and Payne's assistant in the construction of *Gretel*, as designer and signed Jock Sturrock, *Gretel's* skipper, as helmsman.

To qualify, the Victorian syndicate's boat had to race *Gretel* in trials off Sydney Heads for the right to represent the Royal Sydney Yacht Squadron. Built at Bill Barnett's shipyards on the foreshores of Sydney Harbour, the new yacht had to be of all Australian construction and rigging.

Packer, however, was fortunate that a clause in the Deed of Gift allowed him to use existing equipment in the advent of challenging with a yacht from a previous challenge. *Gretel* had been placed in cold storage for three years. In the secrecy of Halvorsen's boatyard, her designer, Alan Payne and Trygve Halvorsen modified her, aware that she almost certainly would be needed for another challenge.

A metre had been sliced off her stern, her mast was moved forward 10 inches and her underbody redesigned. She had a new boom and a revised sail plan. Packer had lost Sturrock, his 1962 helmsman, to the opposition syndicate and when trials began in the Australian spring and summer of 1966, disharmony and apparent mismanagement combined to sink *Gretel's* chances.

The new Australian boat, *Dame Pattie*, named after the wife of the former Prime Minister of Australia, Sir Robert Menzies, beat *Gretel* 6-1 in the first trial series and 3-0 in the final series. *Gretel's* only victory came after *Dame Pattie* lost her mast overboard. *Dame Pattie* was 200 metres from the finish of the third race and was leading by four minutes when the mast broke. Although the alterations improved *Gretel's* windward performance, *Dame Pattie's* superior management easily accounted for her.

In Newport, the prospect of a new Australian challenge gave the Americans a feeling of urgency and anticipation. *Gretel's* performance had awakened them to the new 12-metre nation from the Antipodes. When *Dame Pattie* comprehensively beat *Gretel* in the first series of challenge trials, they wondered at this new and well-funded syndicate from Down Under.

Not all Australian yachtsmen, however, were convinced that *Dame Pattie* was a better boat than *Gretel*. They reasoned that *Gretel's* relatively novice skippers, Trygve Halvorsen and Gordon Ingate were no match for an experienced match race tactician such as Sturrock. Both Halvorsen and Ingate were fine yachtsmen but without experience in 12-metre match racing.

The rule barring challengers using American made equipment, particularly the acron sailcloth was disconcerting to the Australians. Christensen and his syndicate hired technicians from a number of companies to tackle the problem. They found what they thought was the answer in 1966 when Bradford Cotton Mills Ltd unveiled their new cloth KAdron.

Though the cloth was lighter and stronger than anything used previously, it did not appear to perform to expectations, one American claiming: "Her sails did not hold up in a breeze." Besides, the Americans had made advances and, as had been the case so many times before, the challenging nation only appeared to be able to reach the standards set by the Americans at the previous series.

When it became certain that *Gretel* could not match *Dame Pattie*, Packer decided against taking her to Newport for further trials. Instead, he offered Christensen and Sturrock use of any equipment that might help them. Sturrock went aboard *Gretel* for the first time since the 1962 series. He selected a mainsail and two headsails to take to Newport.

The Americans produced one of their "superboats". It is accepted that three superboats raced in The America's Cup, *Reliance* in 1903, *Ranger* in 1937 and *Intrepid* in 1967.

Like the other two, *Intrepid*, was an ugly duckling. Her designer, Olin Stephens, took 12-metre yachts to a new dimension and he was fortunate in having a man in charge of the syndicate, William Strawbridge, who allowed him time to develop his concepts. Strawbridge understood from some mismanagement in the *American Eagle* campaign during the previous series, that a firm, strong management policy was vital to the success of a defender.

Stephens, therefore, experienced little of the pressures placed on many designers to complete their work within unacceptable time limits and spent considerable time tank testing at the Stevens Institute. Over a period of 18 months, seven models were tested before Stephens was satisfied with his new concept. The result was worth waiting for.

Above (left): Olin Stephens, one of the greatest designers in America's Cup history. Above (right): Intrepid's skipper Bus Mosbacher at the wheel. Opposite: Dame Pattie running before a breeze. She didn't run fast enough for the Aussies. Inset: Jock Sturrock, skipper in his second challenge.

Stephens introduced a number of innovations. The new yacht had a separate rudder and keel, a main rudder and a smaller trim rudder; she was two metres shorter than previous 12s and she had less keel than earlier boats; almost all winches were below deck (only the helmsman, tactician and two others would have their heads in sunlight); her boom was lowered almost to the level of Bus Mosbacher's shoulder; she had a snubbed nose and her deck appeared absurdly clear of equipment. Another innovation was the double steering wheel, one for each of the rudders.

When news of the radical design reached Sydney, *The Sun*, an afternoon newspaper, carried on its front page a cartoon type diagram showing two yachtsmen sitting together on a foot pedal said to generate hydraulic power! A number of Australian yachting writers questioned Stephens' principles, the theory being that since all great designers have their flops along with their successes, *Intrepid* might be one of the former.

How unlikely that should seem, particularly now. Here were the world's greatest designer, sailmaker and 12-metre helmsman armed with a blank cheque from a syndicate that understood the meaning of good management, sailing on their home waters against a challenger with limited preparation in Newport. Yet confidence and expectations in Australia were high. Yachting writers, in the main, believed the new Australian boat to be better prepared and in with a better chance of victory than *Gretel* in 1962.

Dame Pattie's arrival in New York for the 1967 series — a traditional entrance for Cup challengers.

Intrepid innovations of Olin Stephens. Above, the twin rudders, a main rudder and a small trim rudder, and right, the double steering wheel, one for each of the rudders.

Once *Dame Pattie* reached Newport, Australian editors filled their sports pages with The America's Cup, not the least mentioned belief being that *Dame Pattie* would give the Americans their toughest challenge. Even some American newspapers began to believe the publicity.

The Washington Daily News reported: "...the tough sailors from Down Under at last will have a boat worthy of their skills — but U.S. yachtsmen are becoming dimly aware that the challenge this year may be the most formidable in the 116-year history of America's Cup races."

Mosbacher spent many days agonising over whether he should accept the invitation to join the Intrepid syndicate. One condition he wanted was to have a hand in designing the boat's lay out. He also had to be certain that he was being offered the fastest 12-metre afloat. Mosbacher remarked after guiding *Weatherly* to victory over a faster *Gretel* in 1962 that he would not return to 12-metre racing unless he had the fastest yacht.

For all the confidence he had in *Intrepid*, he still treated the Australians with respect. If some of his colleagues saw *Intrepid* first and daylight second, Mosbacher saw the pitfalls of one who had most to lose. Not only had he helped in *Intrepid's* design, thereby sharing in any criticisms for a boat that might turn out to be a flop, he was defending the most sought after trophy in yachting. He did not want to be the first American skipper beaten for The Cup.

There appeared little doubt from the moment of the first series of trials that *Intrepid* would be the defender. She opened her campaign by winning all three of the Philip Roosevelt races and in June won four out of five races in the observation series. In all she won 19 of her 20 trial races against *Constellation*, *American Eagle*, *Columbia* and *Weatherly*, although *Weatherly* did not enter the final trials.

While the Americans eliminated their unwanted, the Australians looked for ways to improve *Dame Pattie* and to familiarise themselves with the vagaries of Newport's weather. Sturrock and his team sailed the course whenever the Americans were not using it, evaluating weather patterns and endeavouring to come to grips with Newport's notably fickle and unpredictable wind shifts. The handicap the Australians faced was explained by Norris Hoyt: "Even though Sturrock had slipped from under Packer's thumb, he still had the insuperable handicap of any challenger; there was no genuine competition to tune against......Christensen and his syndicate gave Sturrock excellent financial support and gave splendid parties for the twelve meter crowd and their guests and friends in Newport, but they were not sailors and could not offer advice or tactical assurance to their helmsman."

The distant cordiality and mutual respect between the challenging and defending parties was broken abruptly by an Australian protest before the series began. Warwick Hood issued a formal protest on behalf of the Australians claiming that *Intrepid* had been improperly measured.

On official measurement day, the Americans took a

Right: Historic meeting of Bus Mosbacher (left) and Australian skipper Jock Sturrock aboard the America after a misunderstanding strained relationships. *Below:* Dame Pattie well to leeward of Intrepid.

number of winches off *Intrepid*. The Australians saw this as illegal and asked that the American yacht be re-measured — with all the winches on board. The protest angered Mosbacher who felt the Australians, particularly Sturrock, had gone behind his back. "If the Australians wanted to make a complaint they should have conferred with us," Mosbacher claimed.

He was particularly upset with Sturrock. They had been friends for many years and Mosbacher felt that Sturrock had gone behind his back. Moreover, Mosbacher was angry that he had lost a day's tuning while re-measurement took place, not to mention the Australian crew eating his crew's lunches while waiting for the re-measurement. Sturrock merely explained that the protest had nothing to do with him, and left it at that. A public reconciliation on board the 104-foot replica of the *America* smoothed relations between the two syndicates, though the incident in no way matched the rancour and ill feeling of some of the early series.

It took the Australians one race to understand that Stephens' design, far from being a flop, was indeed the superboat its revolutionary design suggested. *Intrepid* won the race by 5 minutes, 58 seconds in a wind consistently over 15 knots. Sturrock led at the start, but for the rest of the race had to be content to watch *Intrepid's* stern.

American observers criticised the need for three destroyers, one carrying President Kennedy, to be among the spectator fleet. They shielded some of the winds, thereby confusing the two skippers. Thankfully, the President decided he had had enough after the first leg and the destroyers returned to Newport.

Dame Pattie was considered a good light weather boat and even faster than *Intrepid* downwind, but Sturrock's problem was staying in striking distance. The only race in which Sturrock felt he had a chance was the second. "We started well, the wind was lighter. We cut across *Intrepid* and kept on top of him. Then the breeze came in again and freshened. She just sailed away."

Intrepid led by 53 seconds at the first mark. *Dame Pattie* could not get close enough to make any impact on the reaching legs. The spectator craft again hampered the trailing boat and *Dame Pattie* was far from disgraced in finishing less than four minutes behind.

Criticisms poured in from American experts, one claiming the Australians were "Sunday sailors." Larry Merchant, of *The New York Post* wrote: "The Australian challenger did everything wrong but go under." Another described *Dame Pattie's* performance as a game of "follow-the-leader."

So telling was *Intrepid's* superiority that in the third race, Mosbacher wasted 40 seconds, as much in avoiding the downdraught of a helicopter which flew in to rescue two men from a capsized sailing boat as the craft itself, yet still won by 4 minutes, 41 seconds.

Though the Australians got the light breezes they wanted in the fourth race, which had been postponed the previous day because of heavy seas, *Intrepid* won comfortably by 3 minutes, 35 seconds. Sturrock won

the start and led by four boat lengths. The lead lasted ten minutes.

Sturrock confided that he knew after the first race that the Americans had a superior boat. He admitted that it was deflating to face each race aware that there was little the Australians could do about *Intrepid's* superiority. "We always hoped for the best after each race....that you might get light winds....you might get lucky. But you knew deep down in your heart that unless an accident happened you weren't going to win the race." Numerous reasons were given for de-

When the day is done. Dame Pattie silhouetted against the twilight. Inset (left): The Australians found the pond of their living quarters, Vernon Court, the perfect place to clean their sails. Inset (right): Dame Pattie's crew outside Vernon Court.

feat — the mainsail was inadequate, the headsails stretched disastrously, poor tactical sailing. Sturrock was more to the point: "We were beaten by a better boat, a better man (Mosbacher) and a better crew."

Mosbacher retired from America's Cup racing after the series, having won at first on a slower boat and then on a faster one. The needs of a challenger, however, were becoming clearer to more and more people. For the following defence, Sir Frank Packer would return with a faster and better all-round boat and French millionaire Baron Bich, an observer in Newport in 1967, had decided he meet him in a series of challenge races. Such challenge races meant a more thorough preparation, and carefully honed design and yachting skills. The gap between defender and challenger could be, and was, narrowed.

The America's Cup 1851-1987

Intrepid returns again as defender, this time with Bill Ficker as skipper.

1970

Faster Aussies Beaten Again

Intrepid (NYYC) 4 defeated Gretel II (Royal Sydney Yacht Squadron) one.

THE 1970 America's Cup series was perhaps the last in a particular era of races for the New York Yacht Club's slightly dented but ornate silver ewer.

Although it did not lack controversy, the series was marked by displays of sportsmanship that transcended the international rivalries and there was still something Corinthian about the manner in which the competitors prepared for the battle to decide which yacht club, or in that year's series, which millionaire, would challenge the New York Yacht Club's selection in the final races.

The 21st Match for The America's Cup had brought new blood into the arena in the comic opera figure of Baron Marcel Bich, the French plastics tycoon perhaps best-known for the ballpoint pen he marketed under his family name (he had purchased the patent from a Hungarian named Biro in 1953). Baron Bich's interest in 12-metre sailing had begun just five years earlier when he had purchased an aged 12-metre, *Kurrewa V*, for his family of nine children to sail on the Mediterranean.

He had been intrigued by the prospect of racing a modern 12-metre and spared no effort to obtain the services of the best available brains and talent though his approach was less than diplomatic.

In Australia, Sir Frank Packer, was preparing to sponsor his third 12-metre. In 1962, *Gretel* had won a race against the defender, *Weatherly*, becoming the first post-war challenger to take any of the best-of-four races from the Americans. Sir Frank had not had much success since then however. He had asked the British syndicate for permission to sail against their yacht *Sovereign* in 1964 but had been brushed aside. In 1967 he had Sydney designer Alan Payne re-work his original design for *Gretel* and come up with an entirely new underbody, and entered her in trials against the new Australian 12-metre *Dame Pattie*, skippered by Jock Sturrock, who had achieved the small victory with *Gretel* five years earlier.

Sir Frank changed his skippers during the course of the trials and *Dame Pattie* went on to Newport and ignominious defeat by *Intrepid*, skippered by Bus Mosbacher.

In 1970, Sir Frank was ready to try again with a new boat, *Gretel II*, and a new skipper, Jim (now Sir James) Hardy.

Payne, who was responsible for the cross-linked winches in the original *Gretel*, had incorporated several innovations in the new boat, including dual wheels for the helmsman to enable him to obtain a clearer view of the sails to facilitate sail trimming, and collapsible spreaders, which enabled the genoa sail to be sheeted in further to give it a flatter and faster shape.

The French entrant, *France*, was the second Baron Bich had built. The first, Chancegger, was designed by a young American, Britton Chance Jnr, and constructed by the Swiss boatbuilder Herman Egger. She was the pattern for the blue-hulled *France*, which was designed by the French designer Andre Mauric, to satisfy the rule which demands that challengers be designed and built in the country of origin of the challenge.

Baron Bich also bought *Sovereign* and the 1964 winner *Constellation* to maximise his crew's minimal 12-metre experience.

The selection series began with Hardy at the helm of *Gretel II* and the veteran French skipper Louis Noverraz at the helm of *France*. Noverraz, at 67, was just two years older than the Baron.

In a sign of things to come in the French camp, the Baron replaced Noverraz after *France* was defeated in the first race with another top-liner, Poppy Delfour, the French 505 champion — but to no apparent advantage. The Australians won the second race, though the boats did change lead several times.

Had the Baron's third skipper, Jean-Marie Le Guillou, a 5.5 metre champion, stayed in Newport, he might have steered in the third race, but he and two crewmen had quit the French camp earlier, tired of the continual changes being made to the crew by the Baron.

Noverraz was at the helm for the third race, a race which the Australians won though one of *Gretel II*'s foredeck hands, David Forbes, was swept off the deck into the sea after he helped set the first spinnaker of the race.

Gretel II was running at 10 knots when Forbes went over but he had the presence of mind to grab the mainsheet as the yacht swept past and wrap four turns around his wrist as he was towed through the sea.

"I said to myself, 'I'll drown before I let go.'

"I knew I'd get back on board sooner or later and it was just a question of how long I could hold out.

"Martin Visser and someone else leant over the topsides and almost tore the shirt off my back trying to drag me back aboard," Forbes said.

Three races down in the best-of-seven series, the Baron made a Napoleonic decision, possibly the only choice he had under the circumstances. His crew was near mutiny and feelings were running hot along the waterfront.

Sir Frank Packer had upset the French syndicate at their initial meeting in Newport with a show of gamesmanship in the manner of the mutual enemy, the New York Yacht Club. Sir Frank had challenged the legality of the French yacht's measurements, questioning the inclusion of extended hull fairings, much to the obvious distress of the Baron who felt his personal integrity was being put to the test by the Antipodean. As it happened the series was to end before the question would be decided by the International Yacht Racing Union — in the Baron's favour.

Though Baron Bich had stated he was prepared to return to Newport again and again if it were necessary to win the Cup, he realised early that his defeat would be at the hands of the more experienced Australians rather than the American defenders. Thus it was that he decided to take the helm himself for the fourth race.

Fog was already swirling over the course as the boats arrived for the start, the Baron, dressed in his cream uniform with the emblem of the Yacht Club D'Hyeres on its pocket, and wearing white kid gloves saluted Hardy across the water. He had already sent him a message: "Don't be too kind. Treat me as a skipper."

It was hard to believe "Gentleman Jim" would have treated Baron Bich any differently but the weather had the upper hand and treated the French millionaire with contempt.

It was *Gretel II*'s race from the start. Before the

cannon sounded, the Baron had allowed himself to be placed across the starting line, necessitating a long run back and a re-start after the gun ... by which time Hardy and *Gretel II* had disappeared into the blanketing fog.

Gretel II reached the first buoy 4 minutes 17 seconds ahead of the French yacht. At the second mark, the Australians had stretched the time to 5 minutes 28 seconds. On the third leg, the French managed to clip some time, rounding 4 minutes and 44 seconds astern.

Left: Baron Bich enters The America's Cup arena with Andre Mauric's design, France. Above: The Baron on board his challenge contender off Newport.

The real drama began on the second windward leg, when in the thick fog, the French navigation went sadly awry. The French were lost. Their yacht was in the middle of the spectator fleet. They moved toward the buoy but seemed unable to see it. The Baron ordered several sweeping reaches across the course before the crew located the bright orange buoy — 24 minutes and 15 seconds astern of *Gretel II*.

The French were able to trim this ridiculous margin back to 23 minutes and 5 seconds at the leeward mark but the outcome of the race was in no doubt.

Gretel II was almost two-thirds of the way to the finish when *France* rounded the final mark, largely due to the expertise of navigator Bill Fesq.

Gretel II took the winner's cannon and dropped her sails. The crew picked up a tow and pulled on their sweaters to await the French and give them three cheers. After 42 minutes, it was learned that the Baron had signalled "abandon race," and shortly after the dejected French crew emerged, beaten, from the fog.

The Australian victory was popular in Newport where the Aussie crew had won the admiration of the local townspeople, but worse was in store for the Baron. He was pilloried by the Press, the French Press in particular, because the French verb for abandon is not a polite word to use in connection with a sportsman. Baron Bich was piqued. He accused the International Race Committee of dishonouring him; he maintained the race should never have been started — and he may have had a point in that. But the Committee said that the U.S. Coastguard had not requested a postponement, conveniently shifting the responsibility, but not convincing spectators.

Baron Bich did turn his boats over to the Australians for use in their practice before the final series however, and it was reckoned by all in Newport that the champagne ball he held that season was the best in the years the Cup was sailed off Newport.

The U.S. defender candidates had not followed the foreign trials closely, though *Gretel II* had tuned against *American Eagle*, sailed by Ted Turner, before the foreign series began. It was Turner's initiation in 12-metre match racing and it whetted his appetite as later series proved.

The America's Cup 1851-1987

Intrepid (left) about to be passed by Gretel II during the fourth race. Inset above: Gretel II's owner, Sir Frank Packer and skipper, Sir James Hardy interviewed dockside in Newport. Insets right: (Top), Gretel II hard on Intrepid during race one. (Middle), Intrepid across the line a clear winner in race one and (bottom), The start in race three. Intrepid won by just over a minute.

Opposite: Gretel II showing the form that withstood elimination races against France and won a race against Intrepid. Above: A quick overhaul for Gretel II before racing.

There had been two new U.S. boats built — *Valiant* and *Heritage* — but the elderly *Intrepid*, with modifications designed by Britton Chance, was to prove the faster boat. *Weatherly* was also included in the trials to make the racing schedule more manageable, but the new yachts were the focus of the attention.

That illustrates one of the best lessons about America's Cup racing. In this series experience counts at least one third, with the boat and crew making up the other two-thirds of the sum. *Intrepid's* syndicate manager, Bill Strawbridge, selected the successful skipper of *Constellation*, Bill Ficker, and almost immediately, "Ficker is Quicker" buttons surfaced in Newport.

Heritage was eliminated along with *Weatherly* early in the defender series. *Valiant*, with an experienced afterguard led by George Hinman and skippered by a leading figure in the New York Yacht Club, Bob McCullough, was beaten six races to one by *Intrepid*, which became the first previous defender to be selected again for the honour since 1901, and the Herreshoff yacht, *Columbia*.

The 1970 America's Cup races have gone down in history as classic examples of matches which could have gone either way and probably should have gone Australia's way but for continual errors and extremely poor luck.

The statistics, which show that *Intrepid* beat *Gretel II* four races to one, do not reflect the closeness of the series. Since that summer in Newport, a number of leading U.S. sailors, including Bob Bavier, the skipper of *Constellation* in 1964, conceded that there was little to choose between the yachts in winds of 12 to 15 knots, except for the fact that *Gretel II* accelerated better coming out of a tack, and should have fared better in tacking duels. In winds of more than 12 knots, *Gretel II* performed far better than *Intrepid*, not only accelerating faster but in terms of pure boatspeed, especially upwind.

However, it seemed that from the start of the series, the Australians were going to find it heavy going, and only in the first and third races did the weather favour them.

The America's Cup 1851-1987

Intrepid led to the first mark in the first race from a better start, but it would not have mattered. The Australians failed to hoist their spinnaker properly at the weather mark and broke the spinnaker pole. The twisted spinnaker took six minutes to unravel and *Intrepid* was well and truly in front. On the second reach, foredeck boss, Paul Salmon was swept overboard and *Gretel II* had to return and pick him up losing more valuable time. The crowding of the course by the spectator fleet didn't help either and Bill Strawbridge said later that the management of the course was "the worst ever."

Both yachts finished the race with protest flags flying, an indication of friction between the camps and the tension behind the series, but they were dismissed, giving *Intrepid* one win. In the second race, *Gretel II* led at the first two marks and was close behind at the third, at which point the race was abandoned because of fog which made the conditions unsafe, particularly in view of the large spectator fleet. It was considered a good thing that the race was called off when *Intrepid* was in front, as everyone believed Sir Frank Packer would have protested most vociferously if the race had been stopped when the Australians were leading.

The incident that most Australian yachtsmen recall and which still provokes arguments in yacht clubs around the world took place at the start of the new, second race.

Hardy had been taken off the helm for the start and replaced by Martin Visser, who many of his fellow crewmen felt lacked the calm temperament necessary in a helmsman. Indeed, John Bertrand, who was later to be at the helm of *Australia II*, remembers the day clearly from his position as port sail trimmer.

"I remember *Intrepid* being to weather as we were coming in at the weather end of the starting line. We were coming up to the committee boat, and *Intrepid* had nowhere to go — except around our stern (which meant we would have won the start easily) or between us and the committee boat which was a fast closing gap).

"They elected to dive for the gap, but it was an incredible gamble. If you have no room there, you have no room there — and you are out! They missed the committee boat by a couple of feet.

"Martin was so involved emotionally that he literally had blood in his eyes," Bertrand, who was to value this experience in his own championship season 13 years later, recalls.

"He struggled desperately to block *Intrepid's* way, but he went too far and luffed the sails to beyond closehauled which meant he was no longer in control or even sailing on a proper course ... which is against all the rules.

"We hit *Intrepid* with an almighty thump and smashed our bow. The artificial coating covering the front of the bow crashed away but amazingly we went on to win the race."

The protest committee of the New York Yacht Club was assembled by the time the boats returned to

Bill Ficker, skipper of Intrepid. Opposite: Bill Ficker and Jim Hardy duel for honours at the start. The Australians made the series one to remember, crossing the finish line first twice, but having one race taken from them after a protest.

their docks. Their decision might just as well have been pre-printed, but the committee seemed to want to make the Australians suffer, so the protest was not heard till the following morning.

All evening the waterfront bars buzzed with opinions from partisans. Some believed the Australians should be given the race for their "sportsmanship". Others felt that they had only won because *Intrepid's* tactician Steve van Dyck had been lifted off the U.S. yacht after being stung by a bee on the lip shortly before the start of the race. There was plenty to argue about, then, but there was more after the Australian protest was dismissed and the Australians disqualified.

Sir Frank Packer claimed that protesting to the New York Yacht Club was like complaining to your mother-in-law about your wife. He had a point and all protests in future America's Cup matches were heard by an international jury.

With the score two to zero in *Intrepid's* favour, the Australians may have looked beaten but they were still fighting.

Ficker forced Visser over early at the start of the third race, and though he was also over, managed to duck back across the line and so get a commanding start. *Gretel II* was outsailed in what should have

been her weather, 10 knots building to 18 at the finish.

The fourth race was again *Gretel II's* weather but again *Intrepid* took the lead and stayed ahead for five legs.

Hardy, at the helm again, took *Gretel II* out on a lift and *Intrepid* failed to cover. The wind shifted through 90 degrees as both yachts tacked parallel with the finish but the shift favoured the Australian boat and enabled them to lay the line, giving them a clear win by 1 minute 2 seconds.

The fifth race in the series is reckoned by those who watched as one of the classic 12-metre races, only bettered by the final race in the 1983 series which saw the Cup change hands.

Norris Hoyt, the mathematician and Newport historian, described it as "one of the most brilliant ever sailed." Bob Bavier rated it as "the best sailed race in 12-metre history, a race where the slower boat won despite great odds."

The race was again sailed in 10 knots, dropping to five at the finish. But the wind was swinging and the local knowledge Ficker and van Dyck had accumulated through the summer paid off. Hardy took the start, to windward with a one second lead, but almost immediately the Americans tacked close under *Gretel II's* stern. If Hardy had tacked then on top of *Intrepid* he might have been able to guard the favoured side of the course. Once Ficker gained the upper hand, though it was by the smallest of margins, he covered the Australian yacht incessantly.

Better knowledge of the weather conditions on Rhode Island Sound and better boat handling meant victory again for the Americans, who went on to win the final race of the 1970 series by 1 minute and 44 seconds.

The America's Cup 1851-1987

American defender, Courageous to leeward of Southern Cross at the start of the second race. She went on to win by just 51 seconds.

1974

Courageous Right to the End

Courageous (NYYC) 4 defeated Southern Cross (Royal Perth YC) nil.

IF 1970 saw the end of the era of wooden yachts competing for The America's Cup, 1974 ushered in the era of space-age exotic materials, aluminium 12-metre yachts, Kevlar fibres incorporated in the sail cloth and rudimentary onboard computers to aid the tacticians and navigators.

The 1974 America's Cup also introduced a new challenger from Australia who was later to play a profound role in the history of The Auld Mug.

In June, 1974, Alan Bond, a stocky, pugnacious self-made millionaire from Perth, in Western Australia, arrived in Newport with his crew and a new 12-metre yacht named *Southern Cross*, designed by Bob Miller, who was later to change his name to Ben Lexcen. Bond had been a sign painter and he was active in real estate speculation. In fact, the transom of his yellow-hulled yacht bore as its hailing port Yanchep Sun City, the name of a Bond development in the arid sand hills to the north of Perth facing the Indian Ocean.

Bond was a highly-charged, highly-motivated individual and he ran his campaign as if it were an extension of his business, forgetting that his experience lay more in wheeling and dealing ashore than in the rarified atmosphere of 12-metre yacht racing.

He had worked up his new crew and new boat with two trial horses, *Gretel* and *Gretel II*, which he had purchased from Sir Frank Packer, before the media tycoon died, his vision of seeing The America's Cup won by Australians still unfulfilled.

In hindsight, the Bond challenge suffered a major flaw from the beginning. Everyone involved was too close to the project to see that all the energy was being devoted to *Southern Cross* and not enough to ensuring that her trial horses were fast and up-to-date. The consequence was that *Southern Cross* skipper John Cuneo had the pick of the sails and crewmen, while Jim Hardy, sailing *Gretel II*, made do with the leftovers.

Cuneo, an Olympic gold medallist in the Dragon Class, was a superb sailor but he lacked the leadership qualities essential for communicating with a team of 10 crewmen aboard a racing yacht in the often tense moments of match competition. He was replaced at the helm of *Southern Cross* by Jim Hardy soon after the team arrived in Newport.

But that was just one of the battles in the Bond camp. There was also the question of which yacht club the West Australian boat represented — the official nominees, the Royal Perth Yacht Club, or Bond's development. The Royal Perth Yacht Club won the day — not without some rancour.

The other foreign challenger was again Baron Bich, determined to redeem the honour he felt he had lost in the 1970 series, and ready to demonstrate Gallic superiority in the matter of 12-metre yacht racing.

He had appointed the Danish Olympic helmsman Pal Elvstrom, the only man to have won four Olympic gold medals in yachting, to head his effort. Andre Mauric was again to build the yacht, but strident nationalism from sections of the French media, encouraged by leading French sailors, threatened the Baron's efforts.

One of the early rumours to surface in Europe was that Elvstrom planned to have a Scandinavian crew on board, not a French one, a reversion to the days of the J-boats with their paid Scandinavian hands, often fishermen, who were referred to as "Swedish steam." Naturally all potential French helmsmen felt embittered toward the enterprise.

Elvstrom also enraged the French with a series of other tactical blunders — training in *Columbia* in Danish waters, and later, as he was having *Chancegger* and *France* towed back to Le Havre via the

Opposite: Southern Cross revelling in the breeze, though she was never fast enough to stop Courageous winning all four defence races. Inset: A happy Jim Hardy and Alan Bond. Above: The Ben Lexcen designed Southern Cross being offloaded. Right: Southern Cross and Gretel II in trials off Sydney Heads.

Kiel Canal and the North Sea, *France* sank in a further flurry of pointed articles.

To add to the problem, Elvstrom's own racing record began to suffer under the pressure. He was beaten in the 1972 Olympics and the 1973 Half-ton World Championships by Frenchmen.

The final and most savage blow was a cruel campaign of speculation about Elvstrom's mental health — it was well-known in racing circles that he was afflicted with a nervous illness — but the campaign persuaded Baron Bich to all but halt his challenge. He cancelled the new boat he had ordered from Herman Egger and sent Jean-Marie Le Guillou, who had quit his crew angrily in 1970, with the refloated *France* to Newport to gain experience for a future challenge.

Southern Cross demolished the French effort in four straight races to earn the right to challenge the American defender. The ease with which the French were beaten did not help the Australians however who needed stiff competition.

Miller had designed the yacht with an articulated rudder, which in theory would enable the boat to turn more swiftly, by bending much as a fish's tail does. Neither he nor the crew had any idea how fast their yacht could turn in comparison with the U.S. boats.

The defenders were having almost as much trouble assessing their effort. The New York Yacht Club's selectors were conducting elimination series between two new yachts, *Mariner* and *Courageous*, and the revamped warhorse, *Intrepid*.

Mariner, a Britton Chance design, was perhaps the most unusual, with a radical, steeply stepped stern.

Mariner was steered by Ted Turner, the Atlanta television magnate who had assisted the Australians with his yacht *American Eagle* in 1970.

The attention was focussed on *Mariner's* crew initially, because they were having so much trouble in the elimination series. It was apparent that something was radically wrong with the boat early in the summer. Chance refused to acknowledge there was a problem, preferring instead to point to the charts developed during tank testing, and then, to criticise Turner's helmsmanship.

When the yacht should have been reaching a competitive level and sailing fairly evenly against the other two U.S. yachts, she was not. So at the height of the U.S. trials she was returned to her builders for major surgery — the replacement of her radical aft underbody with something more conventional. While she was out of action, Turner, ever flamboyant,

The America's Cup 1851-1987

hired a light aircraft to fly over the course where the yacht club was conducting its elimination races, with the banner: "*Mariner* will return". It didn't matter. Turner was replaced as helmsman by Dennis Conner, but the change was immaterial and the yacht was excused.

Though not an America's Cup defender, *Mariner* did give rise to a piece of dialogue which will last forever in America's Cup lore, a comment from Turner to the hapless designer: "My God, Brit, fishes are pointed at both ends, don't you know that even turds are tapered?"

Aboard *Courageous*, the veteran US sailmaker and designer Ted Hood, was placed at the helm. He took over from Bob Bavier who had been skipper and who also had been driving the boat on the downwind legs.

With the collapse of the *Mariner* syndicate, Dennis Conner was invited to join *Courageous* as starting helmsman, a move that angered Alan Bond.

Bond claimed that Conner, a successful Congressional Cup skipper, would introduce "rodeo tactics afloat," he painted scenes of "masts crashing and crewmen injured" in an extravagant press release he personally delivered to the Rhode Island State Armoury in Newport where the Press was traditionally housed.

Bond said Conner's "pressure tactics" approach, apart from being "unsportsmanlike," would bring a "definite element of danger to the safety of the crews and boats."

His statement read: "We are extremely apprehensive and concerned to learn of Conner's appointment specifically in the role of starting helmsman.

"Conner has a reputation as an aggressive helmsman in Congressional Cup match racing and we are fearful that fouling and striking tactics will be introduced to America's Cup starts.

"These tactics are an accepted part of Congressional Cup racing but would prove extremely dangerous if used in actual America's Cup events.

"We deplore this approach, which is degrading to the dignity and prestige of the America's Cup as one of the world's most important sporting events.

"We are most concerned that this style of racing could be condoned by the New York Yacht Club, to seriously disadvantage our efforts.

"Apart from the unsportsmanlike nature of this approach, there is a definite element of danger to the safety of the crews and boats by adoption of rodeo tactics afloat."

Bond was showing the brash one-upmanship he was to become noted for — at a time when *Courageous* was still to be selected as the U.S. defender.

Within the week, however, on almost the last possible day the Americans conduct their trials, *Courageous* defeated *Intrepid* in strong winds to seal her selection. The last wooden US 12-metre to compete in defender trials retired.

On September 10, *Southern Cross* met *Courageous* in light airs, not to the liking of the Australians perhaps but the U.S. victory was decisive. The new yellow-hulled Australian contender was not pointing

as high (sailing as close to the direction of the wind) or sailing as fast as *Courageous*. The Australians returned to their base, Chastellux Mansion, cowed.

The day had begun inauspiciously with two postponements, the first because of fog and the second because of lack of wind. At one point, the international jury was considering cancelling the race but the Australians were not so lucky. There were no errors and no brilliant tactics, just prayers for stronger winds for the rest of the races to prove that the boat was at least competitive.

Bond joined his crew aboard for the second race, the first syndicate chief to do so since Harold

Left: Britton Chance, designer of defence contender, Mariner. Above: Southern Cross, to windward of the blue-hulled France after the start of the elimination races.

Vanderbilt had sailed aboard the J-boat *Ranger* in 1937, but the second match was as total a rout as the first had been.

When someone asked Jim Hardy how he had slept after losing the first race, he had replied: "Like a baby. I woke up every two hours and cried." But for Bond, losing face was perhaps more important. He reacted with characteristic action. He sacked both the tactician Hugh Treharne and the navigator Ron Packer, replacing him with Jack Baxter.

In the most incredible move, however he replaced Treharne with Cuneo, the man he had passed over earlier as skipper in favour of Hardy.

While Baxter's appointment was viewed as a good decision, Cuneo's placement on board was the subject of hot debate in Newport's waterfront bars.

Cuneo had created a sensation in the small port city a week earlier when he had been caught aboard *Courageous*, taking notes and measurements, by a security guard late at night. He had not worked before with Hardy as tactician and he and Hardy had barely been on speaking terms since the crew arrived in the U.S.

Treharne was obviously the scapegoat for the boat's early failures, particularly tactical mistakes which it was claimed lost *Southern Cross* the lead in the first two races.

The crew changes were not the only factors Bond wanted to talk about on the eve of the third race, however. He also levelled the ridiculous charge that *Courageous* had the advantage of local knowledge. He said that Southern Cross had been denied access to the course before the series and, therefore, his crew was not as experienced in picking the wind shifts on that course as the Americans. It was nonsense of course, but it was typical of Bond to attempt to present a blustery excuse for the failure of his yacht.

The Australian crew had more than three months and unlimited opportunity to study the conditions on the course. Indeed, some Australians had even used The America's Cup buoy as a diving platform, to the annoyance of the New York Yacht Club.

The re-hiring of John Cuneo also created another problem, the tactician's stations in *Southern Cross* had been built for tall men — originally for John Bertrand (who resigned to take the mainsheet because of difficulties experienced with Cuneo) and then Treharne. When Cuneo came aboard again he found himself in a deep well beside the helmsman, out of which he could barely see the water.

The third race was lost by a 5 minute 27 second margin and the fourth race saw *Southern Cross* defeated *Courageous* by a margin of 7 minutes 21 seconds.

The best racing of the summer had been between the U.S. yachts fighting for the right to be defender. U.S. boatbuilder, Bob Derecktor, was one of those amazed at the poor showing of *Southern Cross*. He had sailed with several of the more experienced Australian crewmen, and later said: "Five of those guys on their crew are the best sailors you could find anywhere. I would be happy to have them on my crew. I don't know what happened. It was so bad I couldn't bring myself to ask them."

Perhaps Alan Bond knew what to say better than anyone else. Certainly, he had more right to say it as it had been his money after all.

After seeing his yellow-hulled yacht ignominiously defeated despite massive hype from the Australian media and several well-known yachting writers, Bond modestly conceded: "It's very hard to come to a foreign country and take away something that has been here for 123 years. We were outsailed."

When *Southern Cross* had lost the first race, Bond brashly predicted: "We shall rise from the ashes!" After the second defeat, he said, *Southern Cross*, his "boomerang" would "bounce back".

With a four to nil record at the end of the series, Bond promised: "We'll learn by our mistakes. We'll be back."

Southern Cross was the first mark on a long learning curve for Bond and his designer Miller (Lexcen). The boat was longer than the conventional 12-metre yachts being built by the Americans, and sufficiently different (without being as radical as *Mariner*) to provoke discussion. Perhaps in the stronger winds off the West Australian coast her hull shape would have counted for something?

Olin Stephens, the doyen of U.S. America's Cup designers, with a list of defenders from his drawing board beginning with the giant J-boat *Ranger*, in the 1930s, and the 12-metres *Columbia, Constellation, In-*

Intrepid, revamped and skippered by Gerry Driscoll, leads Courageous in defender elimination trials. Intrepid defended the Cup in 1967 and 1970. This time it was Courageous' turn.

trepid and now *Courageous*, showed clearly what the Australians were up against in the design area. Ted Hood, the late change on the helm of the U.S. yacht, showed the challengers what they had to match in sailing skills.

Alan Bond, who still had to consider the fate of the Yanchep land development, talked boldly of hosting a $25,000 World Cup for 12-metre yachts off Sun City in 1976. He put in a last plug for the place by saying that if anyone watching his challenge had learned anything about Western Australia, then he felt *Southern Cross* had won anyway.

Some felt that The America's Cup matches had been so costly that future series would be sailed in less-expensive designs which could easily be converted to ocean-racing after the competition. Some even speculated that unless the appeal of The America's Cup could be broadened to make it more competitive, even millionaires like Baron Bich and Alan Bond would weary of throwing money at it.

But 1974 was valuable for the participants from each sydnicate. As the future would show, Bond, Miller (Lexcen), Turner and even in a small way, Baron Bich, gained from the expensive experience.

The New York Yacht Club had marked Dennis Conner as a future helmsman, and an international jury had heard protests for the first time.

But probably the greatest benefits of that summer were reaped by the people of Newport itself. The community, which had turned against President Richard Nixon in the 1972 elections, and had felt his vindictive nature immediately afterward when he personally ordered the transfer of the Atlantic Fleet's base from Newport to Norfolk, Virginia, in a move that withdrew the economic underpinnings from Newport, had found a new source of income.

Newport's mansions were nationally recognised tourist attractions but the waterfront area had been neglected. The America's Cup and, in particular, the Australians' participation had been key to the reconstruction program that attracted tourists and development capital back to the wharves; long the haunt of the shore patrol and fishermen.

The 1974 season saw Newport turn back towards its harbour as a source of income. Old buildings were moved in their entirety to the water's edge to become restaurants, bars and discos. Students flocked in to take the summer service jobs, as bartenders, waiters and waitresses. Boutiques flourished, new arcades were developed, a long-term plan for the redevelopment of the city was formulated.

Southern Cross (yellow hull) and Courageous look for wind after the start. The Australians were disappointed that the closest they could get at the finish of any of the four defence races was 51 seconds.

Newport lost its charm as a provincial backwater favoured by the very rich and the amateur yachtsmen, corner stores were replaced with supermarkets, older wooden clapboard houses were replaced by blocks of flats. The Portugese and black fishermen who had lounged along Thames Street disappeared and with them went the smoky little strip joints and bars which the crews of *Gretel, Dame Pattie* and *Gretel II* had known.

President Nixon, who resigned his office in disgrace just weeks before The America's Cup, was probably unaware of the upset he created within the community. His departure was cheered by Newporters around the town. His legacy — the enforced re-evaluation of the city's prospects was to be a benefit to Newport long after The America's Cup was gone.

Courageous, another Olin Stephens design. She defended the Cup successfully twice.

1977

Cup Stays in New York

Courageous (NYYC) 4 defeated Australia (Royal Perth YC) nil

THE 23rd match for The America's Cup in 1977 saw the emergence of a new challenge from Sweden, but the summer in Newport was undoubtedly dominated by Ted Turner, the "Mouth of the South."

Turner, who is never but never at a loss for words except when asleep — and even then some of his ocean-racing friends claim they can still hear him — was the darling of the media because of the outrageous quotes he gave so freely, and the bane of the New York Yacht Club for the same reason.

But if it had not been for Turner, the New York Yacht Club's match race for the battered silver ewer would hardly have been known to the American public at large.

As the owner of the Atlanta Braves baseball team and the Atlanta Hawks basketball team, Turner enjoyed a high profile in the world beyond the waterfront. But when he put on his engine driver's cap and stood behind the helm of *Courageous* or his personal ocean racer *Tenacious*, the fans identified with him totally.

For the public, 1977 represented a battle between Turner and the stiff-necked geriatrics who ran the New York Yacht Club and dominated the Eastern U.S. sailing establishment.

Beating the foreigners was another thing, but they were sure Turner was capable of that — just as soon as he had humbled those New Yorkers!

The foreigners weren't lying down however. A syndicate headed by Gordon Ingate challenged through the Royal Sydney Yacht Squadron with *Gretel II* joining the Royal Goteborg Yacht Club in bringing new competition to the challenge.

The Swedish yacht, *Sverige*, was designed and sailed by the Olympic yachtsman, Pelle Petterson, who had the backing of a formidable number of Swedish business interests.

Gretel II, sailed by a crew of veterans, quickly earned the syndicate the nickname "Dad's Navy."

On the West Coast of Australia, Alan Bond was putting together his second challenge with a new boat designed by Bob Miller (Lexcen) and a young Dutchman, Johan Valentijn, who had previously worked with Sparkman and Stephens in New York. The new boat, to be called *Australia*, was conventional compared with *Southern Cross*.

She was designed to excel in light to medium conditions and as a result was smaller and lighter with a large sail plan. Her skipper was Noel Robbins, a national and world champion small boat sailor.

Baron Bich had also returned, and his large barquentine *Shenandoah* dominated the waterfront. He had asked Andre Mauric to design a new 12-metre yacht, *France II*, but the new hull had not been tank-tested and from the start was unable to beat her ageing sister *France I*.

Alan Payne, who had designed *Gretel* and *Gretel II*, designed a spar for the French boat which was very similar to the mast he had designed for *Gretel II* but it did not improve the new French yacht's capabilities. When it became apparent that the new boat was not competitive, the French asked for and received permission from the New York Yacht Club to rebuild *France I* in the U.S. — a costly operation in terms of valuable sail training time lost.

The Swedes' presence in Newport was made apparent by the masses of blue and gold bunting that appeared everywhere but their yacht was kept at an abandoned installation on the opposite side of Narragansett Bay to the town and their training went largely unobserved. They had initially attempted to purchase *Intrepid*, which would have given them a good trial horse, but the New York Yacht Club made it clear to *Intrepid's* owners that such a sale was not considered in the best

interests of the competition. *Intrepid's* owners reconsidered their imprudent decision and the Swedes were forced to rely on the 1958 defender *Columbia* as a trial horse.

Petterson had built a light weather boat in which the winches were to be powered by pedals but *Sverige's* most unusual feature was that it had a tiller instead of a wheel for the helmsman. Petterson, a small boat sailor felt he would be able to steer the yacht more precisely with tiller steering — particularly in the pre-race manouevring which takes place in the 10 minutes before the starting cannon is fired.

With so many foreign yachts competing, the New York Yacht Club might justifiably have been concerned about keeping the Cup, but the Commodores had enough on their plate sorting out the defender contenders. Apart from Turner, who was sailing a slightly altered *Courageous*, there were two new yachts, *Independence* and *Enterprise* from the East and West Coasts of the U.S.

Courageous was to be sailed as a trial horse to *Independence* — but under Turner, the white-hulled yacht with the cool green deck took on a new life. In 1976, Ted Hood, who had obtained *Courageous'* lines from Sparkman and Stephens to develop *Independence*, discovered that *Courageous* had been as much as 1800lb underweight during the 1974 series — more than twice as much as her designer's certificate allowed for with miscalculations.

The figure declared on the designer's certificate is the minimum allowed without penalty, so *Courageous* had a waterline six inches too long and carried some 84 square feet too much sail area throughout the 1974 series. The alterations made to *Courageous* to enable her to conform to the 12-metre rule certainly didn't hinder her ability.

After the 1974 series, the New York Yacht Club had decided to encourage a type of yacht which would be more seaworthy and theoretically, could, after its 12-metre days, be converted for ocean-racing. To this end, self-draining cockpits were made obligatory, deck openings restricted and winches re-appeared on deck.

While Turner had been tuning against *Independence* — though the New York Yacht Club hoped it would be the other way — *Enterprise*, skippered by sailmaker Lowell North, was tuning against another veteran, *Intrepid*.

Turner had initially been asked to sail *Courageous* solely as a trial horse skipper, and if *Courageous* were to turn out to be faster than the new 12-metre, he would turn the yacht over to Hood for the final selection series.

It was not the sort of deal a man with Turner's pride could wear, so he made a counter-offer to the *Independence* syndicate — he would pay for the up-grading and legitimisation of *Courageous* but the boat must be his to sail.

Turner, who had been refused membership of the New York Yacht Club twice, did not seem likely to win. So the agreement was accepted. But as one of those who had voted against Turner's admission to the Club said: "If he is selected, he will be the first skipper in the history of the Cup to appear on the starting line wearing a muzzle."

Courageous then proceeded to dominate the preliminary selection trials, causing those who had

Opposite (far left): France II. She was so disappointing that Baron Bich preferred France I for the 1977 series. Left: Enterprise, a new boat from America's West Coast, in a defender trial. Above: Gretel II leads Sweden's innovative Sverige (to her stern) in light airs. Right: The sometimes outrageous, yet talented Ted Turner, in a quieter moment aboard Courageous.

spoken so disparagingly of its skipper to reconsider their position. The final trials were closer — *Independence* was eliminated after first being beaten by *Courageous* and then losing twice to *Enterprise*. *Courageous* then turned and beat *Enterprise* once before being selected.

Under the guidance of the Yacht Club d'Hyeres, the foreign elimination series proceeded with some confusion. It was the first time two clubs from the same nation (Australia) had contested the right to challenge for The America's Cup and there were no set rules on how to decide which yacht should be selected.

After a series of round robin events held to determine the relative capabilities of the yachts, it was decided that *Australia*, which was clearly the superior boat, should meet *France I*, and *Gretel* should face *Sverige* in semi-finals, the winners of which would meet in a best-of-seven cup type series.

Australia dispatched *France I* with no problem whatsoever but *Gretel II* and *Sverige* were far more evenly matched. The Swedes won the first race, lost the second, and the third when their mast buckled and went overboard. They won the fourth to tie the series two-all, lost the fifth and won the sixth and then the seventh, though it had seemed that there might have been a chance that the two Australian yachts would meet each other in the challengers' finals. In fact, the two Australian yachts stayed well apart in Newport, meeting only once when *Gretel II*

The America's Cup 1851-1987

Opposite: Gretel II, shows her class seven years after challenging for the Cup in 1970. She was only narrowly beaten by Sverige in the eliminations in 1977. Above: Sweden's Sverige. She made the elimination challenge final but was no match for Australia.

beat *Australia*, creating headlines at home and raising the hopes of loyal *Gretel* supporters.

In the finals, *Australia* beat *Sverige* four-nil. The victory was seen as proof that the Australian crew's experience was paying off and that possibly *Australia's* design team had put together a competitive yacht.

The final races were not as anti-climactic as the 1970 series had been. Turner was feuding with almost everyone, including his tactician Gary Jobson, but more particularly the *Independence* syndicate chief Lee Loomis, and the New York Yacht Club. His caustic comments often found their mark with telling effect, but his crew — most of whom sailed with him on *Tenacious* — adored him.

Noel Robbins on the other hand had little to give him a distinctive personality. He was pleasant and soft-spoken but at no time did he exhibit the same sort of fierce determination to win as Turner did.

John Bertrand, who declined an invitation to sail aboard *Australia*, later said he felt the crew lacked the killer instinct — as previous Australian crews had done.

Robbins started the boat proficiently but they were not aggressive. Bob Bavier, the former U.S. Cup skipper, said they lacked the aggression needed from a challenger who expected his boat to be slower.

"The Australians lost a great chance to win in the third race when Turner went too far away from the line with just minutes to go. When he started back, Robbins, who was nearer the line, instead of tacking on *Courageous'* wind fell in on her weather beam. *Courageous* from that time on went full out for the line but was still twenty-two seconds late, and with a safe leeward on *Australia*. Had Robbins tacked on her wind he could have slowed *Courageous* down enough to win the start by thirty seconds. Had he covered well thereafter he should have been able to stay on top because *Australia* was going well in that race, and after getting behind early lost only two seconds on the last five legs of the course. It was a golden opportunity to capitalise on the one big error made by Turner in the whole series."

Bavier summed up: "Most observers thought the match was a rout. I will admit the outcome seemed inevitable after the first leg of the first race, but I feel that if the crews had switched boats and jibs, the Americans still would have won."

Bertrand, who was setting up his sail-making business in Melbourne, described the series as a "massacre."

But perhaps the competition itself was the winner, though the score was four to nil, because Turner breathed new life into the defence. He restored interest in The America's Cup within America by bringing to it the same sort of fans as those who watched his baseball and basketball teams. In doing so he scandalised a portion of the sailing community which

The America's Cup 1851-1987

Ted Turner, at the helm of U.S. defender Courageous, *and his crew keep an eye on Australia in this close up view of life aboard the American boat during the defence series.*

many thought deserved to be scandalised, or at least taken down a peg or two.

Turner's greatest performance, however, was to take place after the final race of the series. For the first time in the history of the Cup there was a crowd of fans waiting to see the winning skipper — and Turner did not let them down.

After a traditional ducking, along with the rest of the crew at *Courageous'* Bannister's Wharf berth, and liberal swigs of champagne, rum and whatever else well-wishers pressed upon him, Turner led his crew and supporters to the final Press conference of the summer in Newport's Armoury.

He was exhilarated, and drunk. He had humiliated the people who had banned him from the New York Yacht Club for so long and he had successfully defended their Cup for them. He could do no wrong in the eyes of the Press or the public and when he slipped from his seat at the press conference, clutching a bottle of akvavit, pressed upon by a Swedish supporter, the crowd cheered.

He did not join the New York Yacht Club race committee that night for the traditional dinner. He and his crew celebrated in style, however, at the mansion where they were quartered for the summer.

Turner represented the last of the gentleman sailors to be involved in The America's Cup defence. Professional sailors would take the helm in the future, and he enjoyed the role to the utmost.

The Australians and Swedes knew they had seen the best America had to offer. Surprisingly, it did not seem to hurt that much being beaten by Turner because in his own rebellious way he was a friend to the Australians throughout the campaign.

And the Australians remembered the assistance he had given *Gretel II* in 1970 with the use of *American Eagle* as a trial horse. Turner for his part was impressed with the *Australia* crew and several of the crewmen stayed in the U.S. to sail with him after the series, including Steve Ward, who was to build a new breed of 12-metre yachts in Australia. The 1977 America's Cup would be remembered for its professional defence, its lack of gimmicky "secret weapons", and for the humour that Turner brought to the proceedings.

Immediately after the series was wrapped up, Alan Bond announced he would challenge again.

America's Cup fever had struck not only Baron Bich, who also felt it necessary to emulate Sir Thomas Lipton and his five challenges, but the bluff Australian millionaire as well.

Turner also wanted more of the same magic and applied to the Trustees of the Kings Point Fund (the tax deductable foundation through which *Courageous* had been bankrolled) to purchase *Courageous*.

He wished to become the only man in the modern history of the Cup to skipper the same yacht to successive victories.

Harold Vanderbilt, the millionaire yachtsman, had taken three giant J-boats to victory in the thirties and the professional skipper, Charles Barr, had driven the 1899, 1901 and 1903 winners to successful defences — and Turner wished to join the ranks of the greatest sailors America had ever produced.

Australia, co-designed by Bob Miller (later Ben Lexcen) and Johan Valentijn, lost all four races and was not helped by the light winds. Below: Victory parade for Ted Turner and his Courageous crew. No one celebrated quite like Turner, his first — and only — role as defence skipper.

Freedom, one of the most thoroughly tuned defenders in Cup history. She won the series 4-1.

1980

Freedom Wins, Loses a Race

Freedom (NYYC) 4 defeated Australia (Royal Perth YC) 1

THE 1980 America's Cup challenge brought fresh impetus to the competition, the autumn winds seemed to cool Newport earlier, bringing a keener edge to the competition between foreign challenge contenders and the American defence contenders alike.

The British, for the first time since 1964 were entering a yacht, *Lionheart*, the Swedes were back with a revised version of *Sverige*, Baron Bich had returned with a new yacht, *France III*, and Alan Bond had come back again with *Australia* — also slightly altered by Ben Lexcen.

Dennis Conner, whose starting tactics had caused Bond to issue a written caution three years earlier, had spent the summer jousting with three other U.S. yachts, the ageing *Courageous*, sailed by Ted Turner and the same crew he had assembled for his 1977 victory, *Clipper*, a new 12-metre sailed by Russell Long, son of the owner of the famous ocean-racer, *Ondine*, and *Enterprise*, which acted largely as a trial horse but was sailed competitively by sailmaker Lowell North.

The French and Swedish challengers were of little account. The Swedes had set up a store-front trade bureau along Thames Street near the wharf where *Australia* was berthed and seemed more interested in marketing sweaters and carved wooden objects, than racing. Several members of the Swedish Royal Family were due to visit Newport and the concentration of the Royal Goteborg Yacht Club seemed to have wandered from the task in hand.

Similarly, Baron Bich was relying almost solely on his eldest son, Bruno, to run his campaign, but Bruno was also running Bich's North American operation in Connecticut and couldn't devote himself fully to the effort. It may not have mattered, for as French skipper Bruno Trouble was wont to remark that summer: "Put 11 Americans on a boat and you have a crew, put eleven Frenchmen on a boat and you have 11 Frenchmen on a boat."

The British were different, in a British sort of way. The challenge came from the Royal Thames Yacht Club, but the principal figure behind it was an oil futures speculator named Peter de Savary, a short, tough talking figure not dissimilar from Alan Bond in many ways, who affected Churchillian-sized cigars and fast motor launches.

He had plenty of front, and he was in Newport as much for the social scene as the yacht racing. His picture appeared more frequently in the social pages of the newspapers than his yacht did in the sports pages, but he seemed happy with the trade-off.

Jim Hardy had been selected to skipper the revamped *Australia*, which had been given a fast, conventional hull. His tactician was Ben Lexcen, who as Bob Miller had designed *Southern Cross* and with Johan Valentijn, had designed the original *Australia*.

Valentijn, who was born a Dutchman, had taken Australian citizenship to work on *Australia* and had subsequently adopted French citizenship in order to design *France III*, to accommodate the section of the Deed of Gift which specifies that designers must be citizens in the country of origin of the challenge or defence. Valentijn would change his citizenship again.

John Bertrand, who had been anticipating sailing in the 1980 Olympics, came aboard as port trimmer when *Australia* joined the boycott of the Moscow Olympics following the Soviet Union's invasion of Afghanistan.

In all, it appeared that the Australians had a winning combination — or at least the potential. The boat was fast, the crew was experienced and the shore management, Bond and his lieutenant, Warren Jones, ran things as professionally as possible.

The foreign competition was dispatched without a blink, except for the British yacht, *Lionheart*.

Right: The crew of defence contender, Clipper, at work on a windward leg of an elimination trial. Above: Lionheart, the British challenge contender, showed promise in light airs with her bendy mast. Left: Freedom, with Clipper close on her in defender trials.

Freedom during one of the elimination races. She was a Sparkman and Stephens design and was skippered by Dennis Conner.

And for one reason alone. The British had taken an idea developed by Ben Lexcen and gone one further with it. *Lionheart* had a fibre-glass tipped mast, a spar which had extraordinary bend in its upper section.

Australia's mast had a pronounced but fixed curvature. The theory was that the top of the mainsail could be made larger to provide more power to the boat, particularly across the lighter ranges of winds expected during September when the races were sailed. The curvature also permitted the building of mainsails that were wider across the middle — a dimension that is unrestricted in the 12-metre formula.

Lionheart's performance with a conventional mast was woeful. She trailed *Australia* by up to 15 minutes and more, but when her bendy mast went in, she matched *Australia's* speed in light conditions.

After watching the British boat's new performance,

Above: Freedom to windward of Australia. Opposite: Australia and her spinnaker. She raced in nine defence races, winning one — the second race of 1980. Inset: Dutchman, Johan Valentijn, who took out Australian citizenship to co-design Australia.

mast as follows: "I don't know anyone who would take the rig out of a winning boat as we have and run the risk of the yachting world calling them foolish like we have.

"But they haven't been in two America's Cups as we have and they don't realise to win The America's Cup you must be innovative. Ultimately innovation will win it.

"And we may have the weapon in our hands. You would never forgive yourself if you walked away and left it."

With that sentiment, the Australians went into the first race against the Americans.

Conner and *Freedom* had been selected after first *Courageous*, the popular boat, was excused from trials and then *Clipper* and *Enterprise*. Conner was very much the New York Yacht Club's choice.

The first race was most telling. A section of *Freedom's* steering quadrant buckled at the start and Conner was forced to steer with the assistance of the trim tab, the small flap which assists the larger rudder alter the angle of the yacht.

Australia crossed the starting line five seconds ahead of *Freedom* but at the leeward end of the line. With a favourable wind shift, *Freedom* was 52 seconds ahead at the first mark.

On the second leg, a Press helicopter flew low over *Australia*, interfering with her spinnaker, according to Alan Bond, and *Freedom* had a lead of 1 minute 33 seconds at the second mark.

Another wind shift caught *Australia* off-guard, a sail change was ordered but the halyards were crossed and bowman Scott McAllister was hoisted up the mast to clear the scrambled lines, giving *Freedom* a further 15 seconds to round the mark 1 minute 48 seconds ahead.

On the fourth leg, *Australia* sailed too close to the huge spectator fleet, and wash from the power boats interfered with her run through the water. *Freedom* gained more time, to round the buoy 2 minutes 14 seconds before *Australia*.

Australia did hold her own, to a point, on the square run, losing just three more seconds and on the final leg she picked up 25 seconds, to finish 1 minute and 52 seconds behind the crippled U.S. defender.

It was a humiliating loss in any terms. The bendy mast was taken out of *Australia* as soon as she docked — but only for repairs.

"We were very satisfied with the mast", Bond said. "We had a small problem with the lower spreaders but nothing very major."

The Australians were well used to pulling and stepping their new mast. In the previous week, they had removed it to repair the mainsail track on the mast and they had replaced it. They then had to pull it out again a day later when the jumpers, the upper struts on the mast, broke, and back in again it went. No mast in the history of The America's Cup had been removed and replaced so frequently.

Bond also accused Conner of receiving a secret radio transmission from *Freedom's* tender *Chaperone*, when the yacht was in the hands of the starting com-

mittee. Conner brushed the complaint aside and went out and celebrated his first victory in the series.

There was a lay day, called by the Australians and then the yachts met again in a race which was extremely encouraging for the crew and backers.

Australia and *Freedom* met in a race that began in five knots of wind, the minimum required to begin a race, but from that moment on, the conditions flattened. *Australia* trailed *Freedom* over the starting line but suffered several problems at that point. First, the jib, a lightweight laminated sail made of a fabric chemically bonded to a heavier acron material, began to separate as the boat made its way up the first windward leg. A sail change was made but then further equipment failure prevented *Australia* from jibing smoothly. She trailed *Freedom* around the buoys to the bottom mark where she was 1 minute 9 seconds behind, but in the light, fading airs, her huge mainsail showed enormous potential and the gap closed quickly.

In the drifting conditions, she passed *Freedom* and started to move to the finish, but she was beaten by the clock. There is a 5 hour 15 minute time limit for America's Cup races and *Australia* ran out of time. Aboard *Freedom*, navigator Halsey Herreshoff programmed the yacht's onboard computer with the boat's speed, the distance remaining to be sailed and the time allowable and told the crew *Freedom* would have to average 220 mph to finish within the time limit.

There was no question *Australia* had promise but the conditions obviously had to be optimum.

On Friday, September 19, they were. *Australia* became the first challenger in a decade to take a race from the defender.

Again it was a race against the clock in dying breezes but *Australia* did finish 28 seconds ahead of *Freedom*, as the sun was setting. Conner had intended lodging a protest (his protest flag was flying as *Freedom* came over the line) against *Australia*'s apparent lack of a stern light, but was dissuaded by his crew from doing so.

Nevertheless, it was not an easy race as the Australians battled the clock and *Freedom*. Lexcen admitted that there had almost been a "punch-up" aboard over strategy on the second leg.

"We were undecided which way to go and we were in a high state of depression," he said.

Hardy had led around the first four marks of the course, but then the wrong spinnaker was set, and worst of all failed to stay on top of *Freedom* as they raced downwind. A tacking duel on the final leg permitted *Australia* to slide ahead by about six boat lengths.

The winds were freshening though and despite incredible problems in the third race, *Freedom* and her crew proved vastly superior.

A spinnaker on the U.S. yacht ripped in half, but the crew had the tatters down and a new spinnaker in place in seconds, then *Freedom*'s genoa ripped, and later the replacement spinnaker and pole were dragged in the water for over two minutes.

With all this, the Americans still managed to win by 53 seconds in weather that should have suited *Australia*.

The race had been very even, as Conner later admitted. *Freedom* had the start by three seconds and the first leg by 45 seconds when *Australia* started to whittle away at the margin, reducing it 26 seconds on the second leg and 20 seconds on the third. *Freedom* clawed her way to a commanding 51 second lead on the fourth leg, but the gear failure allowed *Australia* to round the mark just eight seconds behind.

Then the Americans slapped a tight cover on Hardy and his crew and outsailed them.

Conner later admitted that he and his crew were taking new measure of the Australian yacht.

"There is no doubt that *Australia*'s mast is a real breakthrough," he said "I don't have a crystal ball, but I'd say bendy masts are here to stay.

It was polite, perhaps, to show concern, but *Freedom* tore away in the final two races, winning by 3 minutes 48 seconds and 3 minutes 38 seconds — huge margins in 12-metre yacht racing, to end the series four races to one.

Conner proved to be wrong about bendy masts. The U.S. Yacht Racing Union pressed the International Yacht Racing Union not to accept the innovation at a meeting later in 1980.

However, the summer hadn't been a total waste of time to the Australian team in Newport. Alan Bond and Warren Jones had studied the U.S. effort — not without some awe perhaps — and decided that if they were to win they needed the same sort of preparation as the defenders.

The primary difference between the Australians and Americans they felt was that Conner had had two yachts to work with throughout the year preceding the races and had been free to select the faster boat.

Thus, after the last race, Alan Bond commissioned Ben Lexcen to design two new 12-metres for the 1983 series and he publicly named John Bertrand as the skipper of the boat which would challenge.

It was a new approach for the Australians, but it was not a new plan for Bond. Ten years earlier he had said he would build two 12-metre yachts to challenge for The America's Cup, and have them designed by Lexcen (then known as Bob Miller).

His plan, as outlined in an interview published in *The Australian* newspaper on December 2, 1970, was simple: "Bob Miller has got a far greater vision than most people imagine," he said. "He'll supervise the building of two 12-metre boats.

"One will be quite conventional in design, the other will be unconventional so, to start with, we hope to have a better boat.

"What we need is more match racing experience. Our trial boats will be built early and we'll train our crews for a full two years."

So, ten years on, Bond was ready to implement the plan he had formulated a decade earlier.

Opposite: A classic shot of Freedom and Australia at close quarters during one of the defence races. Inset: The second race of the series, won by Australia. The Australian boat has rounded the buoy and is taking down her spinnaker.

1983

They Said it Couldn't be Done

Australia II 4 (Royal Perth YC) defeated Liberty (NYYC) 3

NO event in the history of sport captured the imagination of the world as thoroughly as the final race in the 1983 America's Cup series: not a baseball series, not a Superbowl, not a battle for cricket's Ashes.

It is almost impossible to reach the point of exaggeration when describing the intense interest that was generated in what is — or was — a sporting trophy which had been held by one yacht club for 125 years.

But the story of those final four hours, 15 minutes and 45 seconds, really began 13 years earlier when Alan Bond and his designer Ben Lexcen (known at that time as Bob Miller) were peremptorily asked to leave a dock at City Island, New York, because an America's Cup defence contender was being worked on there.

Bond, who at that point had never seen a 12-metre yacht but could not help admiring the graceful lines of the boat, was naturally outraged at the inhospitable treatment he received. The incident did pique his interest. What, he wanted to know, were these boats and where did they race?

Till then he had committed his sporting interests to support of the South Fremantle Australian Football Club, which he took from the bottom of the league ladder to the top, via a simple incentive scheme — he offered cash to the players when they won and not a penny when they lost.

Personally, he was interested in challenges. He had swum the Badger Creek Rapids of the Grand Canyon (which President John Kennedy also swam) and also a turbulent stretch known as the Granite Narrows, to prove to himself he could do it.

But the America's Cup interest was sparked that day in New York more by the disagreeable manner he was shown off the dock than anything else. In essence, Bond decided he would show the Americans where they could get off.

After three disheartening challenges, ranging from the absurd to the hopeful, the team, led by Bond, his executive chief Warren Jones, the designer Ben Lexcen and the skipper John Bertrand, was ready.

First, the men had to put into place the essential pieces of what was to have been Bond's ultimate challenge.

They wanted two new boats, one experimental and one conventional, with which to practise for the series. They wanted time to gain match-racing experience in 12-metre yachts. They wanted a sparring partner that would be sailed as fiercely as they were prepared to sail, and they wanted a crew that was as good as, if not better than the American crews they had met in the years they had so futilely trekked to Newport.

They wanted computer systems as advanced as those available to the Americans. They wanted sails as good as the Americans and they wanted weather information that would match that of the Americans.

They wanted a lot, but their experience through the 1974, 1977 and 1980 campaigns had shown them the way to approach the problem. Professionally and analytically Bond, Jones, Lexcen and Bertrand set out to put into practice what they knew to be the correct method of wresting the Cup from the New York Yacht Club.

Australia II, a wing-keeled wonder, was duly designed as the "radical" component in the two boat equation. *Challenge 12*, another Lexcen design, was the conventional counter-balance.

Historic and unthinkable, Australia II wins The America's Cup. Inset: They couldn't stop laughing, skipper, John Bertrand (left) and owner Alan Bond.

Australia II was controlled by the Bond syndicate but *Challenge 12* was managed by a syndicate headed by Richard Pratt, a businessman from Melbourne, Victoria.

A third Australian 12-metre was built by a syndicate headed by Sydney businessman and yachtsman Syd Fischer. *Advance*, as that boat was called, was never really in contention.

The Bond syndicate had also secured another outstanding asset in Tom Schnackenberg, one of the foremost sailmakers in the world, an individual who combined an innate eye for a good sail with a thorough understanding of computer technology and an unstinting devotion to work that saw him in the sail loft from dusk till dawn.

Other foreign challengers were *Victory 83*, from the Royal Burnham Yacht Club; *France III*, from Yacht Club de France; *Azzurra*, the first Italian challenge from the Yacht Club Costa Smeralda; *Canada*, from the Secret Cove Yacht Club of Vancouver.

The Americans had two defence syndicates, each with two boats. Dennis Conner, who had rejected *Magic* and *Spirit of America*, before whittling his choice down to two boats — *Freedom* and *Liberty*.

The other US syndicate, the *Defender/Courageous* syndicate had two top U.S. helmsmen working for it as well — Tom Blackaller at the helm of *Defender* and John Kolius, aboard *Courageous*.

The foreign eliminations were more closely watched than ever before, as the rumours of *Australia II's* mystery keel had spread before it as oil spreads on water.

But the Americans were no less closely studied, particularly because of the undisguised rivalry between Conner, the veteran defender and Kolius, the newcomer from Texas.

The pressure being applied to Conner by Kolius was nothing to the pressure being exerted on the helmsman by the New York Yacht Club because of *Australia II's* mystery keel. Few people outside the crew had seen it, but the myth surrounding its power, its supposed ability to lift the yacht higher and faster through the water, sent chills through the crew of *Liberty* long before they had to meet it.

The psychology of the *Australia II* challenge weighed heavily on the commodores of the New York Yacht Club as well. A campaign to have *Australia II* declared illegal began to gain momentum from the moment the foreign challenge trials began.

Australia II was skippered by John Bertrand except for a brief period when he was recuperating from a neck injury incurred during a volleyball game at Founders Hall, the *Australia II* crew house.

John Savage, the Melbourne sailor, skippered *Challenge 12* and Sydney 18-footer champion Iain Murray drove *Advance*.

The majority of the other foreign competitors were more colourful than competitive. *France III* was backed by a soft-core porn film producer named Yves Rousset-Rouard. His skipper was Bruno Troublé, who had helmed *France II* for Baron Bich.

Harold Cudmore, the skipper of *Victory 83*, the British challenge's yacht, which was again backed by Peter de Savary, was of great assistance to the *Australia II* challenge, because of his match-racing skills. He was able to maintain the pressure on the crew that had been keeping them sharp since they began sailing against *Challenge 12* on the waters of Melbourne's Port Phillip Bay.

Cino Ricci, the skipper of *Azzurra*, a beautifully-built azure-hulled yacht and Terry McLaughlin, who sailed *Canada*, which was designed by Bruce Kirby, the designer of the Laser, one of the most popular classes in the world, were the other two skippers competing in the foreign elimination series.

The foreign yachts were to sail in a complicated series of three round robins, after which three boats were eliminated. The remaining four yachts then went into another round robin series, after which two further boats were dropped and the two survivors sailed a best-of-seven series along the lines of the actual races.

The races provided *Australia II* with the match-racing experience the Australians had complained of lacking to their disadvantage in previous years. *Australia II* scored a 48 to 6 record, having lost to all the other yachts once, including forfeiting a race to *Canada*, when the mast-head mainsail crane buckled, chopping down onto the left arm of Scotty McAllister, who had been hoisted aloft to clear what was thought to be a jammed halyard.

In an heroic feat, mainsheet hand Colin Beashel was hauled up to bring the injured and unconscious bowman down. In winds gusting to 22 knots, Beashel manoeuvred the limp body down onto the pitching deck from where he was taken ashore for treatment by the head of the *Victory 83* syndicate in a fast and powerful launch.

It was the end of racing for McAllister, who was replaced as bowman by a young crewman from *Challenge 12*, Damien Fewster.

In the final foreign elimination series, *Australia II* defeated *Victory 83* by four races to one. The battle with the New York Yacht Club over the legality of *Australia II's* keel was, however, just beginning.

Halsey Herreshoff, the navigator on *Liberty* had said in an interview during the foreign eliminations when it was apparent that *Australia II* was having little difficulty dealing with the opposition, that the Australian yacht would probably win The America's Cup if she were permitted to race "as rated."

This extraordinary statement spurred the New York Yacht Club's efforts to have the yacht disallowed at any cost.

The principal protagonist, from the technical side, was thought to be Johan Valentijn, who had designed *Magic* and who was, with Dennis Conner and Halsey Herreshoff, the co-designer of *Liberty*, Valentijn had changed his nationality yet again.

Since July, Warren Jones, *Australia II's* syndicate manager, had been receiving correspondence on an almost daily basis from the New York Yacht Club America's Cup Committee's chairman, Bob McCullough, the committee's legal adviser, James Michael and the club secretary, Voctyor Romagna.

The New York Yacht Club had earlier in the summer passed up the opportunity to view *Australia II's* keel at the official measuring, but as it became

Canada I, the first Canadian yacht in more than a century to attempt an America's Cup challenge.

obvious that *Australia II* would be the boat to meet *Liberty*, the campaign to have the yacht disqualified intensified.

The New York Yacht Club questioned the legitimacy of the keel to the United States Yacht Racing Union and then the International Yacht Racing Union. McCullough claimed that *Australia II* was unfairly rated as a 12-metre as she would have a greater draught when heeled than when measured upright.

He was supported in his claim by the U.S. representative on the international measurement committee, Mark Vinbury. The other two members, Tony Watts, Canada, and Jack Savage, Australia, had other views. But in a letter to Watts, Vinbury suggested that while the measurers had rated *Australia II*'s keel according to the 12-metre rule, the rule itself was not able to assess the unusual shape of the keel and thereby fairly rate the yacht. He wanted the I.Y.R.U.'s keelboat technical committee to decide the matter as soon as possible.

The New York Yacht Club seized upon his letter and immediately submitted its own request to the I.Y.R.U.'s technical committee chairman, George Andreadis, for a ruling. In the 34-page document, Halsey Herreshoff stated: "If the closely guarded keel design of *Australia II* is allowed to remain in competition, or is allowed to continue to be rated without penalty, the yacht will likely win the foreign trials and will be likely to win The America's Cup in September."

James Michael, the New York Yacht Club's legal authority, said the following four points were inescapable:

The appendages to the keel of *Australia II* constitute a peculiarity within the meaning and intent of the terms "any peculiarity" as used in Rule 27 and Measurement Instruction 7 of the Rating Rule;

The appendages give the yacht decided benefits and advantages, as witness her performance record;

The appendages are either illegal under the Rating Rule, or, at the very least, are not fairly rated thereunder;

And, therefore, it is required that the keelboat technical committee award it such certificate of rating as is "equitable."

Michael also enclosed a copy of the letter Vinbury had sent to Watts and copies of other correspondence from other interested parties who supported the New York Yacht Club's view, including a letter from the U.S. designer Britton Chance, who said *Australia II* was improperly measured.

A week later, on August 10, the United States Yacht Racing Union formally requested a ruling from the International Yacht Racing Union, at the request of the New York Yacht Club's America's Cup committee. On the same day, the three-man international measurement committee reaffirmed its measurement of *Australia II*.

Still the New York Yacht Club did not stop prosecuting the case. On August 12, the United States Yacht Racing Union again requested that the inter-

national body make an urgent ruling on the matter of *Australia II*'s keel.

The New York Yacht Club stressed that it was hoped the *Australia II* syndicate would assist the International Yacht Racing Union, if it were to proceed with a full examination.

Returning the fire, Warren Jones revealed that one of the U.S. syndicates had approached the Netherlands Ship Model Basin, where Ben Lexcen had tank tested his new yacht, in an attempt to purchase a similar keel.

Lexcen had worked with Dr. Peter van Oossanen and Joop Sloof during various stages of the design

After the race is over. Australia II and her crew. The ecstacy of victory came later. Inset: Australia II's winged keel, the centre of much controversy at Newport. It wasn't unveiled to the public until after the series.

but there was no doubt that he was the originator of the winged keel, an idea he had been toying with for almost 20 years.

Jones also tendered an opinion from the foremost authority on 12-metre yachts in the world, Olin Stephens, who said that *Australia II* was rated correctly and that furthermore, her designer should be congratulated for the innovative concepts he had employed.

"Stephens added that he would hate to see *Australia II* removed from competition merely because she was too fast," Jones said.

The *Australia II* syndicate was well prepared for the legal sparring and fired off a protest of its own to Dr. Beppe Croce, the president of the International Yacht Racing Union, drawing his attention to the attempts of the New York Yacht Club to change retrospectively the rules relating to the measurement of 12-metre yachts.

On August 17, the I.Y.R.U. said it would call a meeting when evidence from the Australian Yachting Federation was available. The following day it an-

The America's Cup 1851-1987

nounced that the meeting would be held in London on August 30.

On August 22, the head of the *Victory 83* syndicate, Peter de Savary, came out with an ace on behalf of the Australians. De Savary had several years earlier paid a design fee to Johan Valentijn, the multi-national 12-metre designer, and had then received a letter from the New York Yacht Club telling him he could use none of it because Valentijn had become a U.S. citizen and was designing an American defender.

The incident had galled him and now he exacted his revenge. He called a Press conference and announced that his syndicate had been experimenting with winged keels since January, 1982.

Furthermore, the British designer, Ian Howlett, said he had written to the I.Y.R.U. on July 28, 1982, asking them whether wings were permitted on keels and what restrictions would apply, particularly relating to their fixed or adjustable nature.

A quorum of the Keel Boat Technical Committee, Tony Watts, James McGruer and Sir Gordon Smith, had met and decided the following:

TIP wings were permitted, so long as the static draft was not exceeded.

ADJUSTMENT of the angle of incidence was not allowed.

WINGLETS may not be retracted.

The interpretation was given to Howlett in confidence and would not normally have been made public until November, 1983. The 12-metre class is a developmental class and interpretations of the rating rule are kept confidential until after The America's Cup matches.

Keel fins had in fact been fitted to *Victory 83* for the final race of the semi-finals against *Australia II* during the foreign elimination race on August 22. They had been inspected by the U.S. measurer Mark Vinbury, in confidence, and he had decided that no re-measurement of the British yacht was necessary.

On August 25, Dr. van Oossanen told the Australians he had received another request from the New York Yacht Club, this time from a delegation including Richard Latham, a member of the New York Yacht Club's America's Cup committee, and Will Valentijn, a relative of the designer. The delegation presented Dr. van Oossanen with an affidavit which contained untrue charges — primarily the allegation that Lexcen was not the sole designer of *Australia II*.

The Dutch engineer said the Americans persisted in presenting him with a draft affidavit despite his repeated claim that Lexcen was the sole designer of the yacht.

"There would be absolutely no truth to a claim that *Australia II* was designed by anyone other than Mr. Lexcen," he said.

On August 26, the New York Yacht Club capitulated. They advised the United States Yacht Racing that they didn't need answers to their submissions on *Australia II's* keel until November, after the races.

"We have concluded that the evidence available to us to date is insufficient to press the matter further at this time. With these matters resolved we now can all focus on the match itself to be settled on the water and may the better yacht win," the New York Yacht Club statement said.

The real action was finally about to begin.

On September 14, *Australia II* met *Liberty* for the first time in the historic 1983 America's Cup series.

As was the practice, the yachts were towed out to the course by their tenders, along with their trial horses for final tuning in the weather of the day.

Opposite: Dennis Conner at the helm of the red-hulled Liberty. Above (Top): Conner in a happy mood before the series began. Above (left): Tom Blackaller, skipper of defence contender, Defender, and arch rival to Conner. Above (right): John Kolius, skipper of Courageous.

The *Australia II* crew, were given an extra boost when their tender skipper Phil Judge slipped a cassette of music by the Australian rock group Men at Work onto his boat's cassette player, linked to powerful speakers on deck.

"Do you come from a land Down Under, Where women glow and men plunder? Can't you hear, can't you hear the thunder? You'd better run, you'd better take cover."

The song was to become the powerful theme of the *Australia II* crew, boosting them as they left for the course each race day.

The New York Yacht Club's race committee, aboard the 75-foot motor yacht *Black Knight*, set the course signals at 11.50, hoping for a midday start to the final 10 minute pre-race manoeuvres. At noon both yachts entered the starting area between the newly-painted red America's Cup buoy, 7.9 miles east of Brenton Reef light, a major navigational aid in the area, and *Black Knight*.

The America's Cup 1851-1987

The America's Cup match had been scheduled to begin the previous day, but shifting winds had made it difficult, if not impossible, for the New York Yacht Club race committee to set a course. During pre-race manoeuvres, however, *Australia II* did show her potential for fast tacking, an asset that did not go unnoticed by Dennis Conner.

"We should have taken our sails down immediately the race was abandoned so no-one could have noticed how far ahead *Australia II* was," he said, when that race was postponed.

On the 14th, the wind was a steady 18 knots, when the cannon sounded. There were no pre-race confrontations as Conner elected to stay clear of the Australian yacht.

Australia II crossed the line with a three second margin ahead of *Liberty* and took an early lead up the first windward leg. Nine minutes into the leg, Conner initiated a tacking duel and successfully broke through the Australians' cover to gain a half a length lead.

Close to the top mark, Bertrand swung *Australia II* back from the right hand side of the course where it had been riding a favourable wind shift, and crossed *Liberty* on a starboard tack, to take a three-metre lead at the top mark, rounding eight seconds ahead of the red-hulled U.S. yacht.

Speculation that *Australia II*'s winged keel would not assist the boat on the reaching legs was upset as she managed to not only retain her lead but increase it by two seconds on the second leg.

Bertrand made a critical miscalculation on the third leg, when Conner brought *Liberty* up on *Australia II* on the second reach, using a staysail under the spinnaker to advantage.

The big red yacht climbed through *Australia II*'s air and rounded the mark sixteen seconds ahead. The Australians attempted to lure Conner into a tacking duel but he wouldn't be drawn. By the top mark, through skilful reading of the wind shifts, the Americans were 28 seconds ahead.

With a spinnaker set, *Australia II* bore down on *Liberty* on the square run. Conner, on a port tack, came over onto starboard, crossing *Australia II*'s bow by about one and a quarter boat lengths.

About a quarter of a mile from the fifth mark, Bertrand appeared to panic. He swung the helm violently, hoping to tack *Liberty*'s stern.

The strain on the steering gear broke the bracket for one of the pulleys through which the steering cables pass from the wheel to the rudder, nearly ending the race for the challenger. *Australia II*'s spinnaker pole rocketed up and Bertrand was forced to jibe away. He cleared the mark using the trim tab while mainsheet hand Colin Beashel effected emergency repairs, but *Liberty* had stretched her lead to 35 seconds.

The American yacht ploughed on, winning the first race by 1 minute 10 seconds.

Dennis Conner said the big factor in the race appeared to be luck. "The breaks went our way," he

Opposite: Spinnakers set as Liberty leads Australia II narrowly in a freshening breeze. Above and opposite (inset): Racing was close in conditions that suited the Australian challenger. Liberty drops her spinnaker as the two yachts prepare for the windward leg.

acknowledged. He said he had found *Australia II* "pretty damned fast."

"We can't control their ability to turn rapidly," he said. "We shall have to concentrate on things we can control."

But the mystery of the keel was obviously still needling the taciturn U.S. skipper who said racing a boat with a masked keel was like "racing a thoroughbred with blankets around its legs."

That night, *Australia II*'s shore crew headed by Ken Beashel, a veteran of the 1967 *Dame Pattie* campaign, rewelded the broken pulley bracket and rechecked every other fitting on the yacht.

On September 15, there was a 17 knot breeze blowing as the yachts met in pre-start manoeuvres, but minutes before the yachts were sent across the starting line a 25 knot gust struck *Australia II* before her mainsail was correctly pulled taut.

Colin Beashel was hoisted aloft immediately where he found that a high tensile bolt that should have locked the mainsail into position at the top of the mast had sheared and the mainsail had dropped about half a metre.

With Beashel at the top of the mast, which was raked as far forward as possible to give the mainsail optimum shape, the race began.

Australia II was five seconds behind *Liberty* as she crossed the line, her boom almost on the deck. In one of the most remarkable 12-metre races ever, *Australia II* held the U.S. defender to the first mark with a 45 second lead, despite the mainsail problem.

Like a crippled bird, the white-hulled yacht pulled through the water, her huge mainsail never completely under control, as Liberty ate into her margin. At the second mark, the Australians were only 31 sec-

onds ahead, and at the third, *Liberty* had taken another ten seconds from her lead.

On the fourth leg, Conner acted. The wind had started to lighten and in the fluky conditions he had brought *Liberty* up into a position where he could "slam dunk" *Australia II*, tacking on top of her. The Australians hoisted a protest flag immediately.

Conner rounded the top mark 48 seconds ahead of the challenger, and slammed a cover on her. The Australians managed to win back 17 seconds by the fifth mark but *Liberty* found fresher breezes all the way home, to finish 1 minute and 33 seconds ahead.

The following morning the international jury met to consider two protests lodged by the Australians. Bertrand claimed that Conner had tacked too close to *Australia II* forcing her to change course, and that the *Liberty* crew had hoisted code flat "N" signalling a desire for a lay day, before the Australians — though the lay day had been officially set down as an Australian request.

The jury threw the protests out. After hearing from crewmembers of both yachts and a member of the New York Yacht Club selection committee, Bob Bavier, and after viewing television film of the incident — the committee said *Liberty* was clear of *Australia II* when she tacked. Telephoto lenses, they believed, on evidence from Bavier, made the boats look closer than they were.

Liberty, they also decided, had raised her flag for a lay day one second after the Australians hoisted their own.

With a score of two to nil, the Australians attacked the defenders on September 17, as though they would be sent home on the next plane if they lost.

It was a Saturday, and an armada of yachts followed the 12-metres out to sea, *Liberty* leading *Australia II*, which had the huge boxing kangaroo flag flying from her forestay.

On the course, the wind was light, averaging 10 knots, *Australia II's* weather. At noon, the 10-minute gun sounded and Bertrand took charge of the pre-start area, driving *Liberty* away from the favoured starboard end of the starting line.

The challenger was 11 seconds ahead of *Liberty* by the time the U.S. yacht crossed, and she easily moved away opening up a huge 1 minute and 15 second margin at the top mark.

The lead gave the clue to what was happening. Just as in 1980, *Australia II* was going to have her biggest battle against the clock. The dying wind carried *Australia* around the course with unreasonable margins, two minutes at the wing mark, 1 minute 58 at the bottom, 1 minute 46 at the top and 5 minutes 57 at the fifth mark.

The boom was lowered on *Australia II*, but the crew were not disappointed with their performance. They enjoyed the psychological drubbing they had given to the Americans and were sitting on the boom cheekily when the time limit expired.

On September 18, the forecast was for winds as light as those which had seen the previous day's race finish without result.

Australia II heads for victory over Liberty in the fifth race.

Wind shifts delayed the start to the last minute permissable and the race committee sent the yachts away at 2 p.m. Conner crossed the line with a margin of eight seconds, but *Liberty* was not in clear water and the challenger glided by her, taking the left hand side of the course and finding a breeze.

It was a spectacular race for the Australians. The crew work, tactics and sails all combined to bring *Australia II* to her full potential. Despite a tacking duel, *Australia II* was 1 minute and 14 seconds ahead at the first mark.

Liberty took 22 seconds from that lead on the second leg, and a further 10 seconds on the next leg but the Australians covered well to keep the defender under control. At the fourth mark she had opened the lead again to 1 minute and 15 seconds after 29 tacks.

The Australians glided further in front on the square run, rounding 2 minutes and 47 seconds ahead of *Liberty* before going on to win by 3 minutes and 14 seconds, the biggest margin in an America's Cup race since 1958, when the Cup races resumed after the war in 12-metre yachts.

After a lay day, racing resumed on September 20. The heavier weather Conner had been hoping for failed to materialise and the New York Yacht Club's race committee started the boats in 10 knots.

The win two days previously had apparently unsettled Bertrand who blew the start, badly mistiming the distance from the starting line and following *Liberty* over six seconds behind. Conner said later he

fully realised the potential of *Australia II* and was determined not to allow her to have clear air through the race. He tailed a tight cover on the challenger and kept it there for the next three and a half hours.

The race was *Liberty's*, beautifully sailed, by 36 seconds at the first mark, 48 seconds at the wing mark, 48 at the next mark and 46 at the bottom.

Conner handed the Australians a sailing lesson and finished a smart 43 seconds ahead.

The Australians were down, three races to one. The New York Yacht Club race committee ordered champagne to be chilled for what they believed would be the final race.

Dennis Conner, a little more wary, said: "I guess God works on Tuesday."

Said Bertrand: "Nothing's changed. We still have to win three races to win the Cup."

On September 21, *Liberty* and *Australia II* met in fresh 18 knot winds. The Australians had but one option, victory, or they would be out of the series as hopelessly as the 24 challengers had been before them.

Fate dealt them a good hand, just before the start, a hydraulic ram which controlled mast bend in the upper portion of *Liberty's* mast, buckled.

It was replaced minutes before the start but then the luff tape on the defender's headsail, and the bag it was stored in, went overboard.

Conner took the start by 37 seconds, after Bertrand went over early and had to bring *Australia II* back and start again. Fifteen minutes later, *Australia II* went for the left hand side of the course, generally unfavoured and Conner let them go there alone.

It was his mistake and though *Liberty* rounded the top mark 23 seconds ahead, *Australia II* took back a full minute to lead *Liberty* by 23 seconds at the second mark.

The upper mast trouble continued to dog *Liberty* but the Australians went on relentlessly. *Australia II* led by 18 seconds at the third mark, and 1 minute 11 seconds at the fourth mark. At the fifth she was still a safe 52 seconds ahead, despite a course change.

Bertrand made up for his earlier mistake by keeping a close cover on *Liberty*, rounding 52 seconds ahead at the fifth mark and going on to a 1 minute and 47 seconds victory.

The former U.S. America's Cup skipper Bill Ficker paid Bertrand a great compliment. "The situation was a real test of how much confidence the crew had in its skipper," he said. "If the crew doesn't have confidence, they will lay back and blame him for losing the race. I think it is to Bertrand's credit that they fought back after losing the start and came back to win."

The yachts raced again the following day, starting in 12 knot winds. Again Bertrand lost the start, but was saved from disgrace by a fortuitous wind-shift that lifted them to a lead of 2 minutes and 29 seconds ahead of *Liberty* at the first mark.

Liberty took but one second at the second mark from *Australia II* and the crew from Down Under stretched their lead to 3 minutes and 46 seconds at the third mark. A course change was signalled at the fourth mark and as the challenger set her spinnaker on the new course, it became obvious that Conner would attempt to foul the Australian yacht.

The tactic failed, but the Australia crew's sailing adviser, Sir James Hardy, who had helmed three previous challengers was outraged at the dismal sportsmanship. He let fly a spate of salty abuse at the New York Yacht Club's race committee that astonished those around him.

The fouling tactic failed and *Australia II* rounded the mark 3 minutes and 22 seconds ahead of *Liberty*. At the fifth mark she was 4 minutes and 8 seconds ahead and racing for the line.

Just before 4 pm, *Australia II* tied the series three all, with a 3 minute 25 second lead. The fleet of spectator craft erupted in a storm of sirens and whistles, history was being made.

After a lay day during which Bertrand practised starts against Harold Cudmore, the skipper of *Victory 83*, and the crew of *Liberty* took their yacht to have it reballasted and remeasured under one of the three rating certificates with which it had been issued — one for light, heavy and moderate conditions. The final race day dawned, but the moment of truth was postponed by fickle weather conditions.

The tension was palpable but the shifting weather made it impossible to start the race with certainty. As soon as the postponement flag was hoisted, however, Conner applied for a lay day. He wanted to change his yacht's rating again.

The Australians again practised starts with Cudmore, and late that day, Conner had changed his mind. He would not alter his yacht's rating.

September 26. A still morning, the first attempt to start the race was halted seven minutes into the starting sequence and a postponement ordered because of the wind shifts. At 12.45 p.m., the sequence began again.

Australia II's manoeuvrability showed as the two yachts spun on each other's sterns, *Australia II* dominating the start though she crossed the starting line eight seconds behind *Liberty*.

The white-hulled yacht had the speed and crossed the defender about half a boat length ahead on her first tack.

But the Australians then made a mistake, they failed to cover Conner, and the American found a wind-shift which he rode to take the lead from the Australians.

Liberty rounded the top mark 29 seconds ahead of *Australia II*, and out in the spectator fleet, the people behind the challenger — Alan Bond, Ben Lexcen, Tom Schnackenberg, closed their eyes. At the wing mark, *Liberty* was 45 seconds ahead.

On the third leg, *Australia II* began to make a dent in *Liberty's* lead, she took 23 seconds from the American, but *Liberty* relished the next windward leg and rounded the top mark 57 seconds ahead.

On the fifth leg, the most amazing in the history of the Cup, *Australia II* sailed outside *Liberty* and took the lead. Bertrand had picked up two wind shifts and he reached in for the mark, rounding it 21 seconds ahead of *Liberty*.

In desperation, Conner initiated a tacking duel, he threw his yacht from port to starboard and back 47 times, hoping to break the *Australia II* crew, but to no avail.

At 45 seconds after 5.20 p.m., *Australia II* broke the longest winning streak in the history of sport when she beat *Liberty* by 41 seconds, taking The America's Cup by four races to three.

There was chaos on the water and there was pandemonium on the dock as the victorious challenger returned to Newport. Sirens and cannon, every conceivable noise-making device was employed to salute the visitors, and in Australia, a nation that had stayed awake all night to watch the historic race, the Prime Minister, Bob Hawke, warned employers in his now famous quote: "Any employer who sacks an employee for not turning up to work today, is a bum."

It was a glorious end to a most nerve-wracking but exhilarating summer.

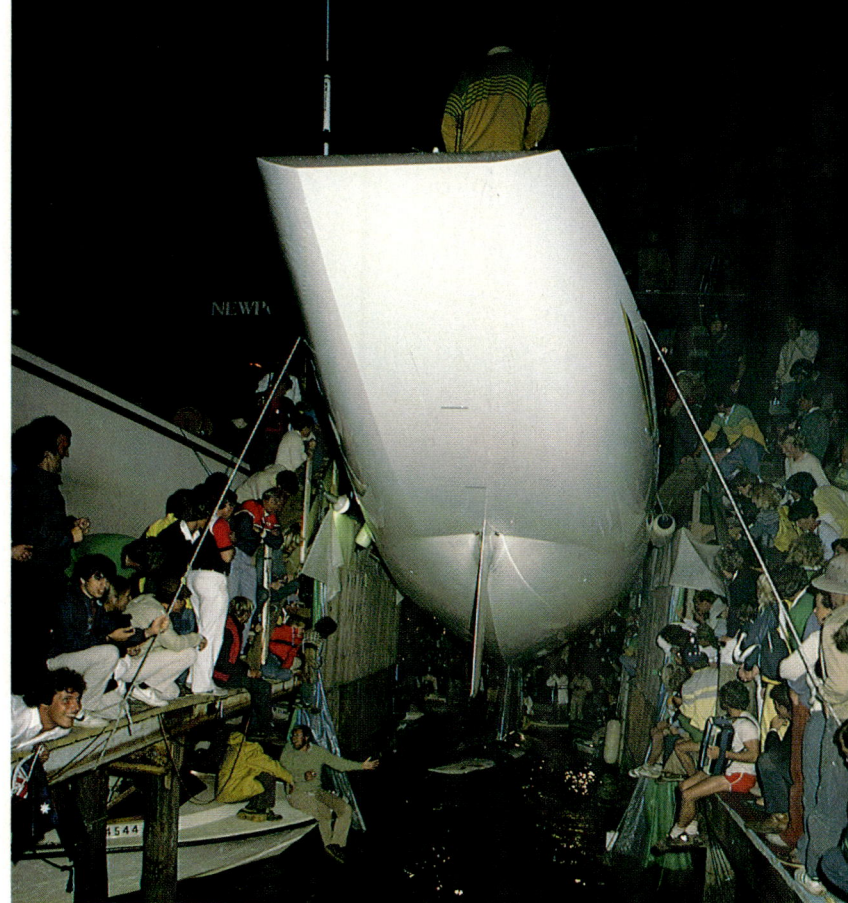

Top left: The long awaited unveiling of Australia II's controversial winged keel in Newport after the Australians had won the Cup. Top right: Victory for Australia II, escorted back to Newport by some happy Aussies. They knew how to celebrate. Right: The trophy they said could never be taken from the New York Yacht Club. Three of the principals, skipper John Bertrand, designer Ben Lexcen and owner Alan Bond.

America's Cup Yachts

SPECIFICATIONS

AMERICA, 1851
MAGIC, 1870
COLUMBIA, 1899-1901
RANGER, 1937
COLUMBIA, 1958
INTREPID, 1967-1970
AUSTRALIA II, 1983

Illustrations by: TERRY WELSBY

AMERICA, 1851

The success of the America helped to revolutionise yachting. She was a two masted clipper, her masts raked back, the mainmast 81 feet and the foremast 79 feet 6 inches. She had a long, fixed keel with a sharp bow and she displaced 170 tons. She also competed in the first America's Cup defence race in 1870, won by Magic.

Sold and re-sold many times, she led a checkered life. The original owners sold her after racing in Britain in 1851 and she was later used in the American civil war where a gun was mounted on her and she was used as a blockade runner for the Confederacy. She was sunk in the St. John's River during the war but later raised and rebuilt. A replica of the America exists to this day.

AMERICA 1851

Designer: George Steers
Length overall: 93ft 6in
Beam: 22ft 6in
Draft: 11ft
Displacement: 170 tons
Sail area: 5,263 sq ft

MAGIC, 1870

Magic goes down in history as the first winner of The America's Cup. She defeated British challenger Cambria and 16 other yachts from the New York Yacht Club fleet on August 8, 1870. She displaced 97.2 tons and was the smallest vessel in the race.

Originally known as Madgie, she was built in 1857 and was rigged as a sloop. She was rigged as a schooner in 1859 and won her first race on June 8, 1865 in a New York Yacht Club regatta. Her racing career was anything but brilliant up to 1870 and she was not among the favourites for The America's Cup race. Owned by Franklin Osgood, who defended the Cup a year later with Columbia, Magic was a centreboarder and suited by the shoals and conditions of New York Harbour.

MAGIC 1870

Designer: R. F. Loper
Length overall: 84ft
Waterline length: 79ft
Beam: 20ft 9in
Draft: 17ft
Displacement: 97.2 tons
Sail area: 1,680 sq ft

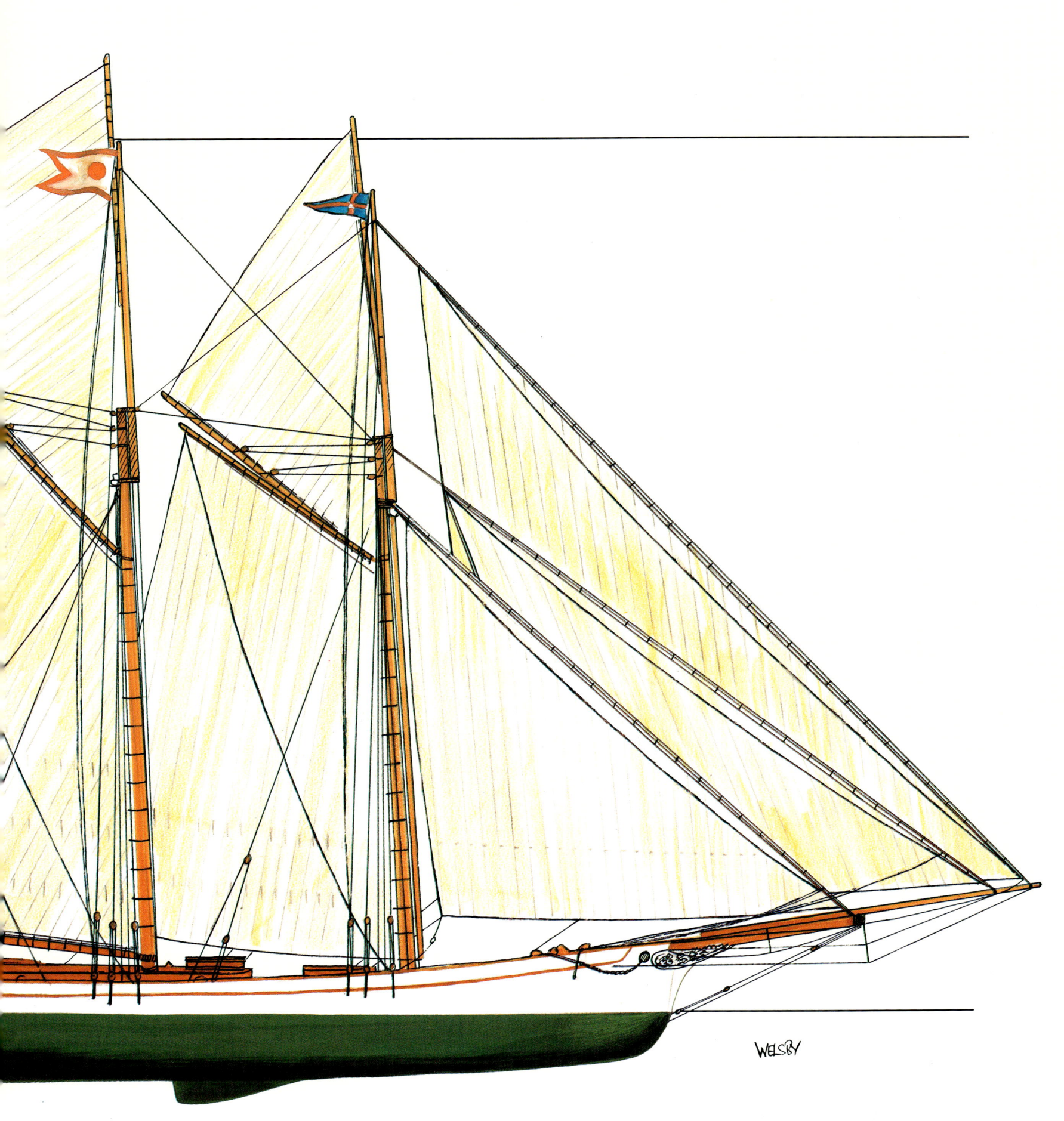

COLUMBIA, 1899-1901

Columbia was the second boat of that name to defend the America's Cup. In fact, three Columbia's won the Cup — the first in 1871, Columbia of 1899 and 1901 and the first 12-metre defender in 1958.

The Columbia of 1899-1901 was built in secrecy and was the first defender to be plated entirely of tobin bronze. She was launched on June 10, 1899 and was considered the most handsome yacht built to that time. Good enough to defend the Cup twice, she defeated Sir Thomas Lipton's Shamrocks I and II respectively. Two American yachts, Constitution and Independence were built for the 1901 defence, but neither was considered as good as the tried Columbia.

COLUMBIA 1899-1901

Designer: N. G. Herreshoff
Length overall: 131ft
Waterline length: 89ft 8in
Beam: 24ft
Draft: 19ft 3in
Displacement: 102 tons
Sail area: 13,135 sq ft

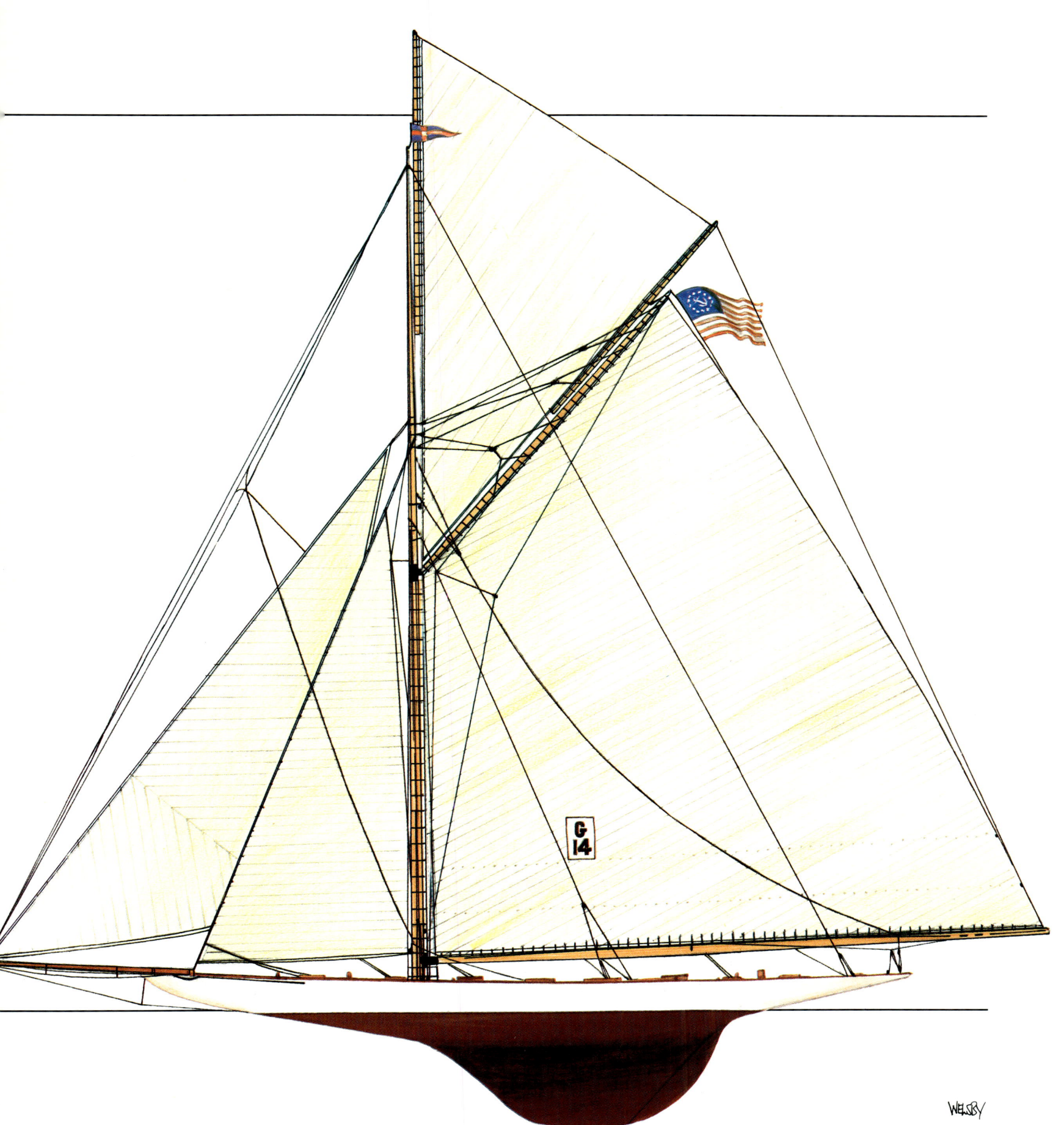

RANGER, 1937

Ranger is still regarded as the greatest of America's Cup yachts. She was a radical design, the combined effort of Olin Stephens and William Starling Burgess, two famous yacht designers who accepted faithfully the results of tank testing in making their final decision.

Though her sail area is given as 7,546 square feet, Ranger's spinnaker measured more than 18,000 square feet. She was of all steel construction, immensely powerful, though unattractive. Her displacement was 166 tons and she carried 112 tons of lead ballast. Ranger was 135 feet 2 inches long and was the last of the great J boats to defend the Cup. She proved to be unbeatable, winning all four America's Cup races against Endeavour II comfortably.

RANGER 1937

Designer: W. Starling Burgess and Olin J. Stephens
Length overall: 135ft 2in
Waterline length: 87ft
Beam: 21ft
Draft: 15ft
Displacement: 166 tons
Sail area: 7,546 sq ft

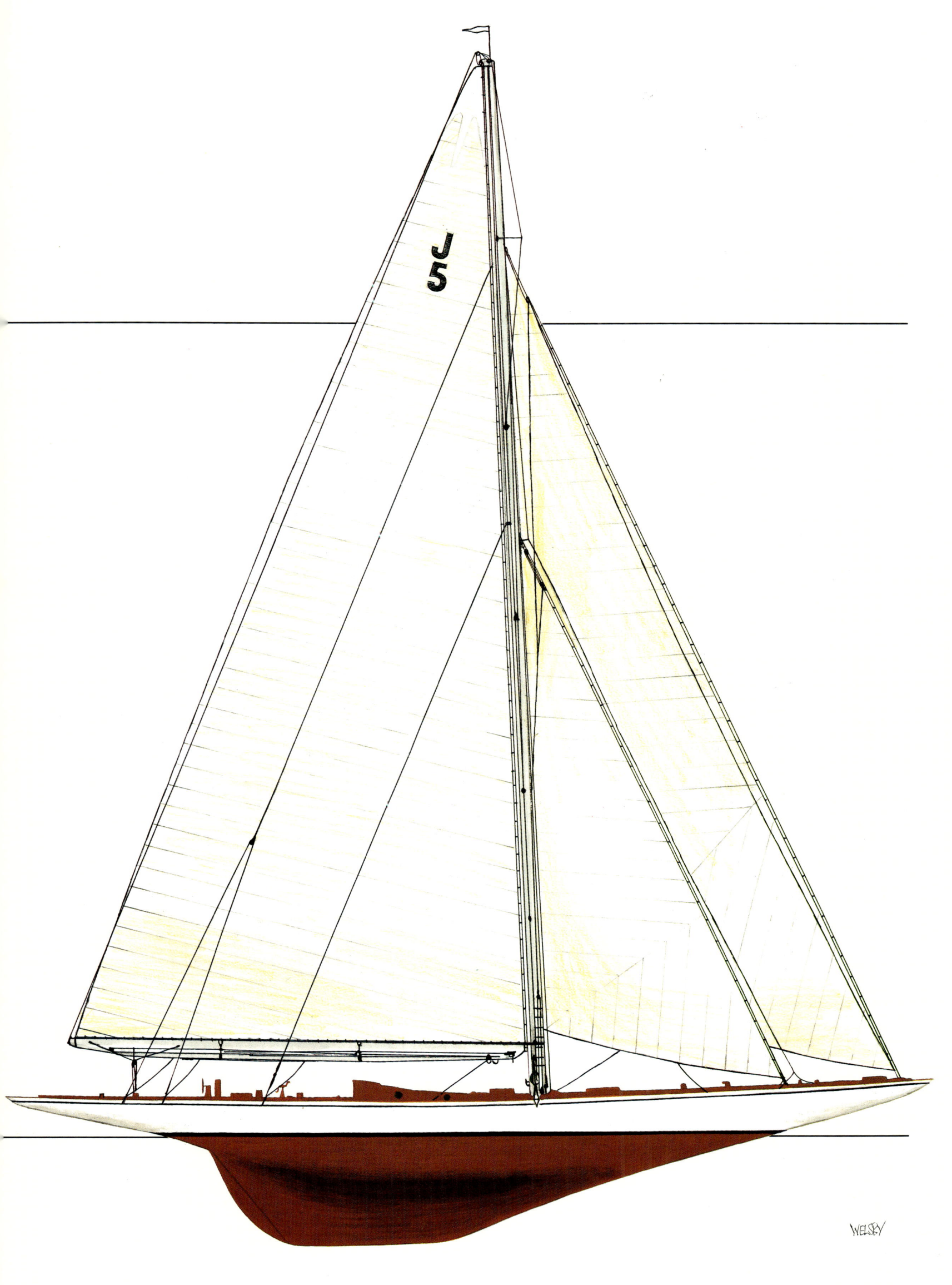

COLUMBIA, 1958

Columbia was the first of the 12-metre defenders, just 69 feet 7 inches in length overall, she was a far cry from the mighty J boats. She was designed by Olin Stephens after extensive tank testing at the Stevens Institute and was rigged by Rod Stephens. She was the first 12-metre designed by Sparkman and Stephens.

Columbia was originally called Swift, but was changed by the syndicate because of the embarrassment they would suffer if she was too slow. Skippered by Briggs Cunningham, Columbia was the fastest of the defence contenders, though only narrowly over Vim. The other two contenders in 1958 were Weatherly and Easterner. While the U.S. elimination trials provided some of the best match races ever sailed, the defence series was a comfortable win for Columbia over British challenger, Sceptre.

COLUMBIA 1958

Designer: Sparkman & Stephens
Length overall: 69ft 7in
Waterline length: 45ft 8in
Beam: 11ft 9in
Draft: 8ft 11in
Displacement: 29 tons
Sail area: 1,825 sq ft

INTREPID, 1967-1970

Intrepid was another radical yacht design, setting standards for the future of 12-metre racing. Yet another America's Cup yacht designed by Olin Stephens, she had two rudders, a main and a smaller trim rudder, less keel than earlier boats and all winches were below deck.

One other innovation was the lowering of her boom to the helmsman's shoulder level. She was regarded as an America's Cup "superboat" and an ugly duckling. Launched at Minneford yard, on City Island, New York in 1967, she was 64 feet long, more than five feet shorter than the first 12-metre defender, Columbia. She became only the second yacht to defend the Cup at successive defences, beating Australia's Dame Pattie 4-0 in 1967 and Gretel II 4-1 in 1970.

INTREPID 1967-1970

Designer: Sparkman & Stephens
Length overall: 64ft
Waterline length: 45ft 6in
Beam: 12ft
Draft: 9ft
Displacement: 29 tons
Sail area: 1,750 sq ft

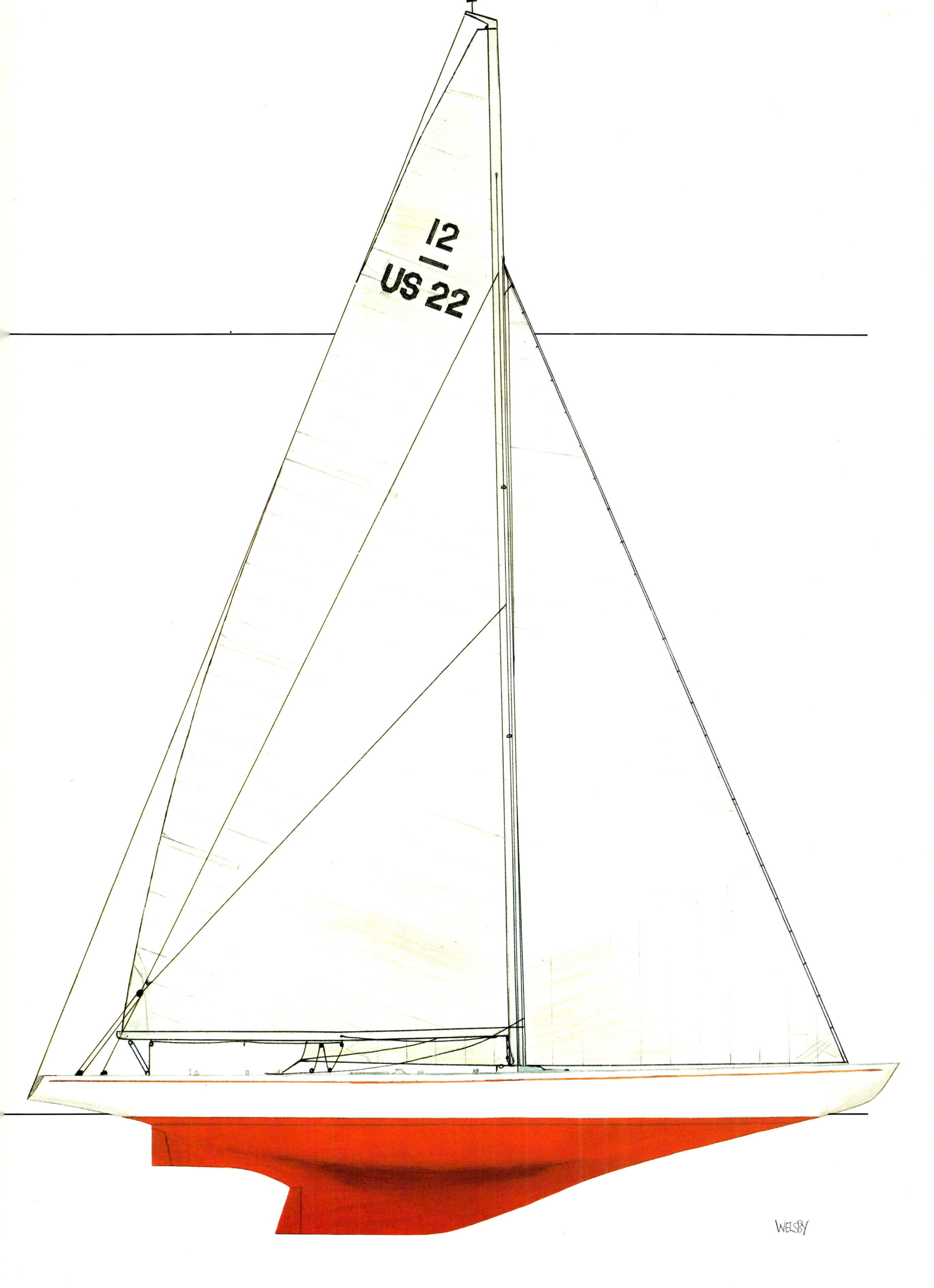

AUSTRALIA II, 1983

Australia II was both radical and controversial. She has a place in sporting history, as the first challenging yacht to win The America's Cup. She came from three races to one down to win the last three and take the Cup from Libery four races to three. Controversy surrounded her winged keel which remained hidden from view until after Cup had been won. Designed by Ben Lexcen, Australia II was 64 feet 7 inches overall, 44 feet 2 inches on the waterline and she displaced 26.5 tons. Her radical design allowed her to turn quickly and her light construction (she displaced 2 tons less than Liberty) was seen as another advantage. Australia II so popularised the winged keel that most 12 metre yachts built today have similar keels.

AUSTRALIA II

Designer: Ben Lexcen
Length Overall: 64ft 7in
Waterline length: 44ft 2in
Beam: 12ft 3in
Draft: 9ft 1in
Displacement: 26.5 tons
Sail area: 1,800 sq ft

the *Australians* took discreet measures to match the black-hulled British challenger. An element of risk-taking was needed if they were to beat the Americans in the finals, and placing all hope in the gamble, Bond authorised the building of a new mast in Newport, possibly in contravention of the Deed of Gift, which states that vessels be constructed in the countries of origin of the challenge.

An old fish-packing shed code-named the Woolshed was leased through intermediaries and a crew of engineers went to work, yards from where Dennis Conner and the crew of *Freedom* were sailing each day. The mast was ready less than a week before the finals and was shipped immediately, its flexible top section painted white to make it difficult for observers to see exactly how much mast bend was being applied. The rig's main problem was that of lateral bend. Various struts and wires were devised to prevent it from sagging to one side or the other but they never were absolutely effective.

Warren Jones, who was closer to the crew than Alan Bond, summed up the decision to use an untried

The America's Cup 1851-1987

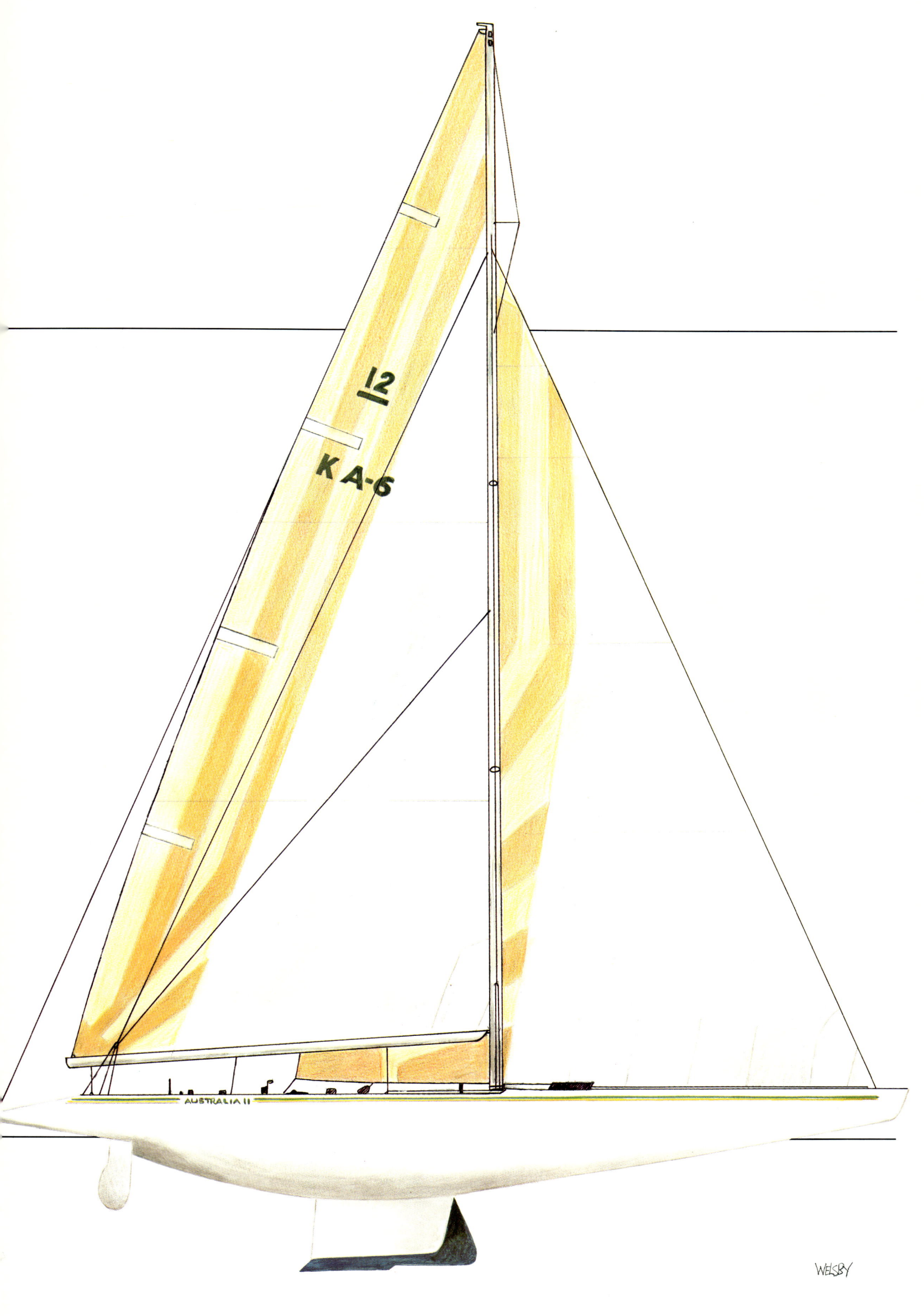

1987

The Latest Challenge

Defender: Royal Perth Yacht Club

BEN Lexcen's prediction that winged keels would become a fixture of 12-metre yacht design was accurate. He was also correct in his forecast that the innovative breakthrough of 1983 would "open a Pandora's box" for America's Cup designers.

After the winged keels were accepted by the International Yacht Racing Union's Keel Boat Committee following the *Australia II* victory, every designer moved to incorporate wings in 12-metre designs.

The problem was that only Alan Bond's syndicate had done the extensive tank testing necessary to refine the modification, and then only for application in the light conditions proven for the course set on the waters of Newport, Rhode Island, where The America's Cup had been sailed solely in 12-metre yachts.

The new course, set off the dazzling white sand beaches of Perth, Western Australia, was an unknown to most designers. Here the winds blew freely from the Antarctic ice cap, westerlies that peeled away from the Roaring Forties, upward over the warming waters of the southern Indian Ocean before reaching the narrow Australian continental shelf.

Dutch, French and English seamen had left their bones bleaching on the sandy islets that fringe the coastline in mute testimony to the unpredictable nature of the forces that lash the largely uninhibited shores of Western Australia.

From October to January, when the elimination trials for the 1987 America's Cup were scheduled, the records indicated that strong, consistent winds of 20 knots or more could be expected, accompanied by heavy swells pitched upward by the shallowing sea floor as they neared the coast.

In February, however, the annual sea breeze cycle which brings the refreshingly cool afternoon wind known to people in Perth as the Fremantle Doctor, goes through its annual period of change.

With the actual date of the 26th America's Cup match set for January 31 1987, the collection of data to assist designers, sailmakers and crews alike, was vital. To this end, the new generation of 12-metre yachts that was developed came with a variety of keels for experimental purposes.

Australia III, which was launched on September 27, 1985, had a new keel fitted within three months, and the other defender contenders replaced the keels on their craft almost as rapidly as they strived to find the edge that would mean a winning margin.

There are four Australian syndicates vying for the right to defend The Cup on behalf of the Royal Perth Yacht Club, and 14 foreign syndicates seeking to wrest it from Australian hands.

Not unnaturally, the foremost of the defence syndicates was the high profile, professional and extremely well-marketed organisation headed by Alan Bond behind *Australia III*.

Warren Jones, who had spearheaded the offence against the New York Yacht Club over the question of the winged keel was the director and the day-to-day activities were in the charge of the veteran 12-metre sailor John Longley.

The new boat was launched with her keel shrouded by a security screen, just as her famous predecessor had been, but she was so perfectly finished that her crew took her sailing on the day of her launch — a tribute to the craftsmanship of boatbuilder Steven Ward, and the syndicate's management. Both Longley and Lexcen, who steered the new yacht during her maiden cruise, said she was exceptionally smooth to helm.

Two days later, the new yacht, which superficially looked like a clone of her victorious sister, was

named by Mrs. Eileen Bond, the syndicate chief's wife, at a spectacular ceremony on the docks of the Royal Perth Yacht Club, the second to ever house The America's Cup.

After being ritually doused with ceremonial champagne, *Australia III* and *Australia II* sailed serenely down the Swan River to the delight of a crowd of thousands.

Understanding the need for tough competition to bring out the best in both boat and crew, the Bond syndicate had entered into an agreement with a syndicate of South Australian businessmen who had the backing of a loan from the South Australian State Government.

The new Lexcen design, *South Australia*, was built in the winter of 1984 at Ward's yards in Cottesloe, a Perth beach suburb, at the same time *Australia II* was being refurbished and brought back to racing form. *Australia III* had not yet been built.

However, trials between *South Australia* and *Australia II* were taken into account before the final design of *Australia III* was completed. The South Australian syndicate had contracted with the Bond team not only for the design and construction of their yacht, but some basic crew training as well.

Four helmsmen were named for *Australia III*, Colin Beashel, Hugh Treharne, Gordon Lucas and Carl Ryves. Both Beashel and Treharne had top 12-metre credentials, while the other two were also well regarded racing skippers.

The former *Australia II* skipper John Bertrand was not actively involved in the syndicate. He had published a controversial biography titled Born to Win, in mid-1985, which did not endear him to many of his former crew members. According to his book, he was almost mystically predestined to helm the yacht that would eventually wrest The America's Cup from the New York Yacht Club, and his motivational skills were largely responsible for the crew's victory.

The South Australian syndicate's yacht was skippered initially by both Fred Neill, a national small boat champion, and Sir James Hardy, the Australian 12-metre veteran. However, in April, Sir James stood down as skipper though he remained with the boat, and Sydney yachtsman Phil Thompson was appointed helmsman.

Perhaps because there was no single individual behind *South Australia* to supply the drive and enthusi-

Above (left): Canada's True North in action off Fremantle. Right: Italy's Azzurra, left, was disappointing during the world championships, but not so French Kiss, a radical design. Inset: French Kiss skipper Marc Pajot.

asm, the yacht did not show exceptional form, though Lexcen also redesigned her keel and Sir James provided invaluable experience. *South Australia*, like *Australia III*, competed in the 12-metre world championships in Perth in February, but all the involvement showed was that the boat stood little chance of qualifying as the defender unless something dramatic took place.

The third syndicate seeking to have its yacht named as defender, the Taskforce '87 group, was backed by another West Australian entrepreneur, Kevin Parry, an electronic and communications millionaire.

Above (left): New Zealand's KZ5 and South Australia take advantage of a freshening breeze off Fremantle. Above (right): Italia was unimpressive during her first stint in Australian waters.

Parry ran a carefully planned program with the assistance of his skipper Iain Murray, who also co-designed the syndicate's yacht *Kookaburra*, with John Swarbrick. The syndicate made provision for two, and possibly three yachts during its campaign.

Murray, who was involved with the *Advance* challenge in 1983, brought a mass of small boat sailing experience to the helm of each of the *Kookaburra's* built for the defence and the yachts performed exceptionally well in early trials. The syndicate declined to race *Kookaburra I* and *Kookaburra II* in the world championships, their confidence buoyed by races against *Australia II* and *Australia III* a week before the championships.

The last Australian syndicate to hit the water was that of Syd Fischer's Eastern Australian team, their Peter Cole-designed boat shown to the public for the first time at the Sydney Opera House in April, 1986. The syndicate had purchased *Australia I* as a trial horse and to train a crew while the new boat was being built

The syndicate was not concerned that they were the last defence contender into the water. They reasoned that their boat had tank-tested in Holland as extremely fast and since the crew had been training together aboard *Australia I*, there was sufficient time before the defence trials to familiarise themselves with the new boat. The Eastern Australia syndicate's confidence was not shared by the other Australian syndicates, although they were not confident of Fischer producing a boat at all. He at least proved them wrong on one count.

The rivalry between defender candidates was intense from the start. In October, 1985, a full year be-

The last Australian defence contender to hit the water, Syd Fischer's oddly named Steak n' Kidney in Sydney Harbour before the official launch.

fore the defender selection series were due to begin, tensions between the Bond and Parry syndicates ran so hot that the Taskforce '87 syndicate lodged a protest with the Royal Perth Yacht Club against their rival's rough house tactics.

According to the protest, Murray, the *Kookaburra* skipper, had raced a high speed runabout close to *Australia III* as she was trialling with *Australia II* shortly after the new 12-metre yacht had been launched.

Murray's small boat was rammed by *Black Swan II*, the Bond syndicate's tender, in an incident which Murray claimed could have endangered his life.

Bond syndicate director Warren Jones accused the Taskforce crew of outrageous behaviour. *Australia III* had been the subject of bomb threats and a building being constructed for the Bond Corporation had in fact been damaged by a bomb months before.

Kookaburra had sailed close against the Italian Costa Smerelda syndicate's yacht *Azzurra* in early 1985 and therefore some of her potential against a known yacht could be gauged.

The Bond syndicate strongly signalled its disapproval of mixing it with the foreign challengers (though *Kookaburra* had no other yacht to sail against), and was not prepared to race against any yacht which might give the challengers an idea of *Australia II* or *Australia III*'s abilities. Feeling had been running high and Murray's action was seen in this light.

Alan Bond bluntly warned, "People who get too close might get sunk."

The challengers were also preparing early for what some saw as the best chance to win The America's Cup. It was reasoned that the Australians might be easily defeated because of their lack of experience in sailing 12-metre yachts in their own waters.

The foreigners were up against one of the greatest problems the *Australia II* team had defeated — isolation, but they attacked it in great style, purchasing blocks of apartments, entire hotels and fleets of small craft to act as tenders to their yachts.

The New York Yacht Club's *America II* syndicate sent its project manager, Arthur Wullschleger, to establish a beachhead at Fremantle in 1984. By the following year, they had a full workshop and dock facility in operation and two 12-metre yachts sailing off Fremantle in a program headed by skipper John Kolius. Kolius' relationship with the syndicate's managers was at one stage extremely strained, and he in fact resigned, but he was back with the crew in less than a month.

Kolius was at the helm when the first two New York Yacht Club boats, US 42 and US 44 trialled in Perth in 1985 and early 1986. US 42, the first of the three new yachts designed by Bill Langan of Sparkman & Stevens, performed well in the world championships, finishing third and losing points because of crewing lapses and equipment failure. She had been the first of the challengers to arrive in Perth.

There was every indication that US 46 would be an improvement on the previous two designs and there was little doubt about the thoroughness of the *America II* syndicate's preparation.

When the world championships ended in February 1986, most syndicates who competed went home, taking their boats with them, either to modify their current models or, as in most cases, to build new ones. Those who didn't go to Perth for the championships, stayed in home bases or looked for similar conditions in other parts of the world to tune their boats.

Plainly, too, some were conserving their dwindling financial resources and just six months before the elimination races were to be held, those clubs with extreme money problems were close to withdrawing from The Cup. The threat of late withdrawals from challenging clubs hung over Fremantle like the storms that blow in from the south.

By April 1986, the other American challengers included the Chicago Yacht Club, Newport Harbour Yacht Club, St Francis Yacht Club, the San Diego Yacht Club and the Yale Corinthian Yacht Club.

The Chicago Yacht Club's Heart of America syndicate was forced to go to the United States Supreme Court to prove that it could meet the conditions of The America's Cup Deed of Gift. Though far from the sea, Chicago won its case to prove that the Great Lakes were an "arm of the sea", sufficient to comply with the Deed.

The Heart of America syndicate used the 1980 defence contender, *Clipper* as a trial horse while a new boat was built. Money was always a problem, but in terms of sailing they carried two men aboard of considerable experience, skipper Buddy Melges and tactician Gary Jobson.

The *Eagle* syndicate from Newport Harbour Yacht Club had Rod Davis as skipper and maintained a low profile. They built one boat, *Eagle*, and observers noted the similarities with *Australia II*, not the least that she had a winged keel.

The yacht was launched with her keel shrouded in a blue tarpaulin, though the shape of her keel was no secret. *Eagle* has a hand painted brown, orange and white American eagle clutching the American flag and stretching almost the length of the yacht's hull.

While the syndicate did not bring *Eagle* to Perth for the world championships, Davis, who advised the *Australia I* challenge on match race tactics in 1977, did go, crewing aboard *Italia*, the Consorzio Italia entry. Early indications were that *Eagle*, a Johan Valentijn design, was a fast boat, and her crew was high class.

High technology went into building both new boats from the St Francis Yacht Club's Golden Gate Challenge syndicate and there appeared little haste in putting the boats, one a radical design, the other more conventional, into the water before 1986. Though the club has had little experience in 12-metre racing, they had Tom Blackaller, skipper of *Defender* in the 1983 defence elimination series.

Blackaller reportedly had laid out an America's Cup course in San Francisco Bay for the 1990 challenge so confident was he of success.

The *Courageous III* syndicate from the Yale Corinthian Yacht Club did not lack money in its attempt. Though syndicate chief Leonard Greene had his crew train through the northern summers in Bermuda and claimed to have made a design breakthrough with *Courageous*, it was difficult to believe that the old boat could make a comeback.

Dennis Conner, determined to win back the Cup and erase the ignominy of being known as the skipper who lost The America's Cup, was preparing a

British boat, Crusader on her first hit out in Perth. This was the conventional design, her radical sister followed. Inset: Crusader's skipper-tactician Harold Cudmore and helmsman Chris Law.

campaign with the backing of the Sail America Syndicate and the San Diego Yacht Club.

Conner's effort entailed two new 12-metre yachts, Stars and Stripes, which he trialled off Hawaii. Conner was also a frequent visitor to Western Australia where his syndicate had experts on hand plotting conditions on the America's Cup course.

The other syndicate which excited interest early on was that mounted by the New Zealanders. True to Lexcen's prophecy, 12-metre designs had become adventurous again and the New Zealand syndicate had a most talented design pool to tap.

After a somewhat shaky financial beginning (the original backer Marcel Fachler struck some financial problems, and funding was then handled by a banker named Michael Fay), the New Zealanders formed a design triumvirate composed of three of the world's leading designers — Ron Holland, Bruce Farr and Laurie Davidson.

Three yachts were planned, each built of fibreglass, a first for 12-metre yachts. The new hulls were constructed on a stiff core understood to contain carbon fibre, to overcome flexing problems which are associated with fibreglass yachts.

The syndicate named Chris Dickson, a young but talented match-racing skipper as helmsman, and in international competition he proved among the best. The two New Zealand boats, christened KZ3 and KZ5, proved to be exceptionally fast during the world championships where KZ5 won the first heat and finished second overall.

If there was a dark horse among the challengers, it was to be New Zealand.

The Yacht Club Italiano, the oldest yacht club in Italy, had a well-funded campaign with plans to build two yachts, and the Costa Smeralda Club (backed by the Aga Khan) built a new *Azzurra*.

When the *Italia* syndicate reached Fremantle for the world championships, they at least had the best dressed crew, hardly surprising since Gucci was one of the syndicate's sponsors. Their boat, *Italia*, a 1985 version, fared no better than fifth in any of the heats. They went home to build to a new yacht and to evaluate conditions off Fremantle.

Canada, with two syndicates, the True North group from the Royal Nova Scotia Yacht Squadron, and the Secret Cove Yacht Club from British Columbia were well advanced by early 1986 with *True North* appearing to have the better chance.

In fact, the hopes of the Royal Nova Scotia syndicate were considerably higher after the world championships where their boat *True North* improved through the series, finishing third twice and sixth overall. They intended to return to Fremantle with a new boat, *Franc Nord* although some syndicate members were keen to modify *True North* and return with her.

In the end, the syndicate decided to take up both options since the new boat was three-quarters finished by February. *True North* would have major surgery and would return to Fremantle with the new boat to determine the syndicate's challenger.

The *Canada* syndicate, which tried unsuccessfully in 1983, returned with a new boat *Canada II*. She was a metre longer than *Canada I* and rumoured to be quite fast. The syndicate trialled her against the Chicago Yacht Club's *Clipper* on the Great Lakes, some of the races sailed in heavy snow storms.

There was little problem with financial backing since the syndicate was backed by automobile parts millionaire Don Green.

The Royal Thames Yacht Club built two new boats, one conventional, *Crusader I*, based on *Australia II* and designed by Ian Howlett, and a revolutionary design, which, as the British admitted, may turn out to be an expensive white elephant.

The second *Crusader*, designed by David Hollam was as revolutionary as any 12-metre built. For a syndicate that looked doomed at one stage because of lack of funds, they had done remarkably well. Their campaign represented three years of planning, research and design. The expenditure was more than $A4 million, a tidy sum for a syndicate which earned some criticism for not having its boats in the water in Fremantle earlier than April 1986.

As many had pointed out, the Australians, the Americans, French, Italians and others had already been and gone with their first boats before the British arrived in Australian waters. But one has to consider that the British only beat the deadline for acceptance as a challenger — April 1, 1984 — by a matter of hours. Admiral Sir Ian Easton persuaded the Royal Thames Yacht Club to challenge, and even had to make out his own personal cheque for $A16,000 as deposit.

Acceptance did not, however, guarantee the *Crusader* syndicate entry to The Cup. Money, or lack of it, seriously hampered early preparations. Designers worked for nothing and it wasn't until it seemed that the syndicate would have to withdraw that the air was cleared of its smell of apathy. Wealthy businessmen and British corporations combined to finance the project.

Finding the right skipper, and afterguard, was not difficult, not when you have such men as Harold Cudmore available. Considered perhaps the most experienced match race yachtsman in the world, Cudmore acted as skipper-tactician, assuming the unusual role of handling the starts and then taking the tactician's position for the rest of the race. Chris Law was selected to steer the boat.

In considering the British challenge, one has to look at *Victory '83's* performance in the 1983 eliminations in Newport. She was fast and many observers believed she failed principally because did not have the time to develop her full potential. It was not surprising that after being sold to an Italian syndicate she was good enough to win the 1984 World 12-metre championships in Sardinia. *Victory '83* was a Howlett design and he had no doubt that *Crusader* was faster. She at least turned and accelerated quicker and she appeared suited to the heavier conditions of Fremantle.

Australia III on the wind in the fresh breezes of Fremantle. She proved to be an improvement on Australia II.

Australia II and Australia III head the charge on a spinnaker run during the world championships. Inset (left): Bond syndicate skippers Colin Beashel and Gordon Lucas. Inset (right): Iain Murray's impressive Kookaburra.

But without doubt the odds makers were experiencing their greatest difficulties rating the Societe Nautique de Marseilles and the Societe des Regates Rochelaise groups, which had named Yves Pajot and his brother Marc as their respective skippers, both fine and fiery sailors.

The Rochelaise group was certainly the best known syndicate at the world championships in Perth. They linked their new boat to a mini photographic laboratories and called her *French Kiss*.

The Royal Perth Yacht Club refused to allow *French Kiss* to start in the first race because her name was linked with a commercial interest. An international jury subsequently cleared her and she won the second race, and the seventh, in the series.

Her syndicate returned to France after the championships and instead of building a new boat decided to modify their current model. *French Kiss* was probably the most radical twelve in the championships and was extremely fast once she picked up speed.

However, there were many who doubted her ability to turn quickly, a failure that the syndicate believed could be righted by crew training. With a modified boat, one assumes for the better, and if the French were accurate in the assumption that at times their boat performed at no more than 60 per cent of her potential during the world 12s, then they may have a serious contender.

The Marseilles syndicate struggled with its financial committments from the start. They sailed in the former Australian boat, *Challenge 12*, bought as a trial boat while their new boat was built. There were even suggestions that they would withdraw before the elimination series began in October 1986.

The New York Yacht Club's America II syndicate left little to chance in their attempts to win back the Cup. Here their second boat US44 tests the strong winds off Fremantle. Inset: America II skipper, John Kolius.

The America's Cup course will comprise eight legs covering a distance of 24 nautical miles. All the seabreeze courses are near the Fairway Buoy about 5 nautical miles off City Beach while the land-breeze courses have windward marks within 1.5 nautical miles of the beach.

Never before had so many syndicates challenged for The America's Cup. Nor had the defence series been conducted in the Southern Hemisphere. While Newport, Rhode Island enjoyed its quiet and solitude in the knowledge that the hype and fanfare of Cup time would by pass them this time, Fremantle was battening down the hatches for the largest challenge of them all.

Fremantle could never be the same. Hardly a tourist resort and certainly not on many world tourist agendas, she has a population of 34,000, a figure that has remained static for some decades.

Her population is mainly working class as one could expect from an old port city and she is virtually a suburb of Perth. Fremantle had little choice other than to accept the role as host since the Royal Perth Yacht Club and its marina are on the Swan River, some 18 kms away. The old town has had to to live with the growing pains and a fresh coat of paint.

While the locals are not so sure she is going in the right direction, they have little choice but to flow along with the tide.

Fremantle, Australia is now on the world map.

The America's Cup 1851-1987

Fremantle and its sheltered harbour with Perth in the background.

THE AMERICA'S CUP RECORD

YEAR	DEFENDER	CHALLENGER	DATE	WINNER	MARGIN (Min. Secs)
1870	Magic N.Y.Y.C. Skipper: *Andrew Comstock*	Cambria Royal Thames YC Skipper: *J. Tannock*	August 8	Magic	37 17
1871	Columbia N.Y.Y.C. Skipper: *Nelson Comstock* Sappho N.Y.Y.C. Skipper: *Sam Greenwood*	Livonia Royal Harwich YC Skipper: *J.R. Woods*	October 16 October 18 October 19 October 21 October 23	Columbia Columbia Livonia Sappho Sappho	27 04 10 33 15 10 30 21 25 27
1876	Madeleine N.Y.Y.C. Skipper: *Josephus Williams*	Countess of Dufferin Royal Canadian YC Skipper: *J.E. Ellsworth*	August 11 August 12	Madeleine Madeleine	10 59 27 14
1881	Mischief N.Y.Y.C. Skipper: *Nathaniel Clock*	Atalanta Bay of Quinte YC Skipper: *Alexander Cuthbert*	November 9 November 10	Mischief Mischief	28 30 38 54
1885	Puritan N.Y.Y.C. Skipper: *Aubrey J. Crocker*	Genesta Royal Yacht Squadron Skipper: *John Carter*	September 14 September 16	Puritan Puritan	16 19 1 38
1886	Mayflower N.Y.Y.C. Skipper: *Martin Stone*	Galatea Royal Yacht Squadron Skipper: *Dan Bradford*	September 7 September 11	Mayflower Mayflower	12 02 29 09
1887	Volunteer N.Y.Y.C. Skipper: *Henry Haff*	Thistle Royal Clyde YC Skipper: *John Barr*	September 27 September 30	Volunteer Volunteer	19 23 11 48
1893	Vigilant N.Y.Y.C. Skipper: *William Hansen*	Valkyrie II Royal Yacht Squadron Skipper: *William Cranfield*	October 7 October 9 October 13	Vigilant Vigilant Vigilant	5 48 10 35 40
1895	Defender N.Y.Y.C. Skipper: *Henry Haff*	Valkyrie III Royal Yacht Squadron Skipper: *William Cranfield*	September 7 September 10 September 12 * Valkyrie III disqualified ** Valkyrie III did not finish	Defender Defender* Defender**	8 49 47
1899	Columbia N.Y.Y.C. Skipper: *Charles Barr*	Shamrock I Royal Ulster YC Skipper: *Archie Hogarth*	October 16 October 17 October 20 *Shamrock did not finish	Columbia Columbia* Columbia	10 08 6 34
1901	Columbia N.Y.Y.C. Skipper: *Charles Barr*	Shamrock II Royal Ulster YC Skipper: *E.A. Sycamore*	September 28 October 3 October 4	Columbia Columbia Columbia	1 20 3 35 41
1903	Reliance N.Y.Y.C. Skipper: *Charles Barr*	Shamrock III Royal Ulster YC Skipper: *Robert Wringe*	August 22 August 25 September 3 *Shamrock III did not finish	Reliance Reliance Reliance*	7 03 1 19
1920	Resolute N.Y.Y.C. Skipper: *Charles Adams*	Shamrock IV Royal Ulster YC Skipper: *William Burton*	July 15 July 20 July 21 July 23 July 27 *Resolute did not finish	Shamrock IV* Shamrock IV Resolute Resolute	 2 26 7 01 9 58 19 45
1930	Enterprise N.Y.Y.C. Skipper: *Harold Vanderbilt*	Shamrock V Royal Ulster YC Skipper: *Ned Heard*	September 13 September 15 September 17 September 18 *Shamrock V did not finish	Enterprise Enterprise Enterprise* Enterprise	2 52 9 34 5 44

The America's Cup 1851-1987

THE AMERICA'S CUP RECORD

YEAR	DEFENDER	CHALLENGER	DATE	WINNER	MARGIN (Min. Secs)
1934	Rainbow N.Y.Y.C. Skipper: *Harold Vanderbilt*	Endeavour Royal Yacht Squadron Skipper: *Thomas Sopwith*	September 17 September 18 September 20 September 22 September 24 September 25	Endeavour Endeavour Rainbow Rainbow Rainbow Rainbow	2 09 51 3 26 1 15 4 01 55
1937	Ranger N.Y.Y.C. Skipper: *Harold Vanderbilt*	Endeavour II Royal Yacht Squadron Skipper: *Thomas Sopwith*	July 31 August 2 August 4 August 5	Ranger Ranger Ranger Ranger	17 05 18 32 4 27 3 37
1958	Columbia N.Y.Y.C. Skipper: *Briggs Cunningham*	Sceptre Royal Yacht Squadron Skipper: *Graham Mann*	September 20 September 24 September 25 September 26	Columbia Columbia Columbia Columbia	7 44 11 42 8 20 7 05
1962	Weatherly N.Y.Y.C. Skipper: *Bus Mosbacher*	Gretel Royal Sydney Yacht Squadron Skipper: *Jock Sturrock*	September 15 September 18 September 20 September 22 September 25	Weatherly Gretel Weatherly Weatherly Weatherly	3 46 47 8 40 26 3 40
1964	Constellation N.Y.Y.C. Skippers: *Bob Bavier and Eric Ridder*	Sovereign Royal Thames YC Skipper: *Peter Scott*	September 15 September 17 September 19 September 21	Constellation Constellation Constellation Constellation	5 34 20 24 6 33 15 40
1967	Intrepid N.Y.Y.C. Skipper: *Bus Mosbacher*	Dame Pattie Royal Sydney Yacht Squadron Skipper: *Jock Sturrock*	September 12 September 13 September 14 September 18	Intrepid Intrepid Intrepid Intrepid	5 58 3 36 4 41 3 35
1970	Intrepid N.Y.Y.C. Skipper: *Bill Ficker*	Gretel II Royal Sydney Yacht Squadron Skipper: *Sir James Hardy*	September 15 September 20 September 22 September 24 September 28 *Gretel II was disqualified	Intrepid Gretell II* Intrepid Gretel II Intrepid	5 52 1 07 1 18 1 02 1 44
1974	Courageous N.Y.Y.C. Skipper: *Bob Bavier*	Southern Cross Royal Perth YC Skipper: *Sir James Hardy*	September 10 September 12 September 16 September 17	Courageous Courageous Courageous Courageous	4 54 1 11 5 27 7 21
1977	Courageous N.Y.Y.C. Skipper: *Ted Turner*	Australia Royal Perth YC Skipper: *Noel Robins*	September 13 September 16 September 17 September 18	Courageous Courageous Courageous Courageous	1 48 1 03 2 32 2 25
1980	Freedom N.Y.Y.C. Skipper: *Dennis Conner*	Australia Royal Perth YC Skipper: *Sir James Hardy*	September 16 September 19 September 21 September 23 September 25	Freedom Australia Freedom Freedom Freedom	1 52 28 53 3 48 3 38
1983	Australia II Royal Perth YC Skipper: *John Bertrand*	Liberty N.Y.Y.C. Skipper: *Dennis Conner*	September 14 September 15 September 18 September 20 September 21 September 22 September 26	Liberty Liberty Australia II Liberty Australia II Australia II Australia II	1 10 1 33 3 14 43 1 47 3 25 41

ACKNOWLEDGEMENTS

This Book is the result of many hours of research and required the help of many people. It is not the first book dealing with the history of The America's Cup, nor will it be the last. But it is a commemorative book, in many ways, and we believe it to be the largest format book on The Cup's history.

It is not possible to acknowledge all those who helped with the book, but I would like to acknowledge the kind assistance of the many libraries around the world, among them the State Library of NSW, the New York City library, the Glasgow Museums and Art Galleries, the Mitchell Library of Glasgow and the National Maritime Museum, London. In particular, my thanks go to the New York Yacht Club and their most cordial librarian, Mr Sohei Hohri.

My thanks also go to the many authors who have previously written about The America's Cup, some of whom have been mentioned in the book. There has probably not been an America's Cup historian who has not been thankful for the large volume, Lawson's History of The America Cup written in collaboration with Winfield Thompson.

Photo Credits;

Baglin, Douglass: p. 144, 145, 146, 162, 164a, 165, 165 (inset), 166-167, 168, 169 (top), 171, 172, 178 (inset).
Beken of Cowes: p. 16, 25, 26-27, 34a, 34b, 35, 42, 47, 48, 53, 56, 60, 61, 64-65, 77a, 80, 81, 92, 97, 106b, 126, 127.
BBC Hulton Picture Library: p 34c, 77c, 120a.
Clarke, Warren: p. 148-149.
Cunningham, Chris: p. 203.
Garwood, Roger: p. 236.
Gurney, Guy: p. 195.
Kaoru-Soehata: p. 223 (bottom).
Knight, John: p. 228.
Le Guay, Lisa: p. 193 (left), 199, 200, 202 (top), 207.
Levick Collection, courtesy of the Mariner's Museum, Newport News, Virginia: p. 38, 46, 58, 63, 68a, 77b, 83, 93, 96a, 100, 106a, 107, 108, 117, 118, 124.
Mitchell Library, Glasgow: p. 89, 90a, 90b, 90c, 94, 96b, 114.
Modern Boating: p. 152, 184, 185 (right), 186-187.
National Maritime Museum, London: p. 11, 22-23, 31, 40, 44, 51, 54-55, 66, 69, 72, 79.
Nerney, Dan: p. 157, 169 (bottom), 175, 176, 178, 180, 182, 184 (inset), 185 (left), 186 (bottom), 190, 192 (left), 192 (right), 193 (right), 194, 196-197, 198, 202 (bottom), 204-205, 206, 207 (inset), 216, 217 (top), 217 (bottom left), 217 (bottom right).
New York Yacht Club: p. 12, 19, 21, 28-29, 32, 36, 61b, 70, 74-74, 86.
Paine Burgess Testimonial, Boston City Council: p. 57a, 57b.
Rosenfeld collection: p. 14, 15, 17, 85, 91, 98, 98 (inset), 102, 112-113, 115, 120b, 121a, 121b, 122, 123, 128 (top/bottom), 129 (top/bottom), 130a, 130b, 131a, 133, 134, 135, 136, 137, 141, 142-143, 150-151, 155, 158, 159, 160, 161, 164b.
Ross, Bob: p. 176 (inset), 177, 177 (insets), 179, 181, 199, 200, 207.
Horizon/Sally Samins: p. 2-3, 5-6, 211, 211 (inset), 213, 214-215, 215 (inset), 218, 219, 219 (inset), 220, 222, 223 (top).
The New York Times: p. 131b.

Australian Picture Library: p. 227 (top right), 229, 229 (inset), 231, 232-233, 233 (inset), 234-235, 236.

DON BROEN
952-686-6063

DON BROEN
952-686-6063